BROADWAY, JEEVES?

Also by Martin Jarvis

Acting Strangely

BROADWAY, JEEVES?

The Diary of a Theatrical Adventure

Martin Jarvis

Martin Jarvis (signature)

Methuen

First published in Great Britain in 2003
by Methuen Publishing Ltd
215 Vauxhall Bridge Road
London SW1V 1EJ

1 3 5 7 9 10 8 6 4 2

ISBN 0 413 77331 0

A CIP catalogue record for this book is available
from the British Library

Methuen Publishing Limited Reg. No. 3543167

Designed by Bryony Newhouse

Printed and bound in Great Britain by
Creative Print and Design, Ebbw Vale

Extract from *Yours, Plum: The Letters of P.G. Wodehouse* by P.G. Wodehouse
and edited by Frances Donaldson, published by Hutchinson.
Used by permission of The Random House Group Limited.

For Ros

I feel that we ought to write a completely new play starring
Jeeves – something a bit risky with a lot of sex in it. What do
you think? American audiences want plays about the relationship
of men and women, while I write about some kind of venture
like finding a diary...

P.G. Wodehouse in a letter to his collaborator Guy Bolton, February 5th 1951

CONTENTS

PROLOGUE

This is a journal of a cliff-hanging year.

There's a precipice or two, the occasional bluff, suspense, a few scars.

Sheer fiction then?

Certainly some of its absurdities might seem improbable. Could I really have been fall guy to the Mafia? Mary Archer's high-rise bed-maker? Alan Ayckbourn's theatrical confidante?

Was it me, dancing (literally) attendance on the stars of *The Producers*, wrenching microphones from the *Mamma Mia* girls? Did I actually lean nonchalantly against the piano as Andrew Lloyd Webber offered me his last diminuendo, and reply 'I don't use them'? Surely *Broadway, Jeeves?* has to be a modern-day remake of an old showbiz scenario: 'Will they make it to the Great White Way?'

Whatever, I've attempted to report the facts every day from the rock-face. It's all here in black and white. And, depending on how you like your characters painted, some shades of grey. It tells how various theatre folk struggled to midwife *By Jeeves*, by Sir Al and the good Lord, onto Broadway. There's a lot of pushing, plus 'hot water, and plenty of it'. Any heroes? Villains? Red herrings? I'll leave the detective work to you.

Such a roller-coaster ride inevitably throws up (if that's the right phrase) observations on how a theatre genius such as Ayckbourn – writer, director, even lyricist – approaches his work and how his actors approach him. The journey also chronicles the rekindling of composer Lloyd Webber's enthusiasm for a shared creation. And it's the story of my own attempts to establish a worthy Jeevesian characterisation – almost singing, virtually dancing, definitely speaking – alongside a cast of Americans who can do all of those things brilliantly.

But – hoping to do it on or around 42nd Street? Moi? Assuredly a work of imagination.

Hang on, though. Perhaps it's only real life that can accommodate such fantasies and, possibly, make them come true.

ACT ONE

Pittsburgh

Wednesday January 3rd 2001

I travelled yesterday from the eighty-degree warmth of Los Angeles to the icy shock of twenties Pittsburgh. I'm here because last summer Alan Ayckbourn asked if I would consider accepting a part in *By Jeeves*, which I had turned down five years before. This is his joyously surreal celebration of P.G. Wodehouse, Bertie Wooster and the urbane valet, Jeeves.

Alan put it succinctly. 'Like you to play Jeeves. Doing it at the O'Reilly in Pittsburgh. Then straight on to Broadway.'

'Really? Which theatre?' I had asked.

'Probably the Helen Hayes, but there's no shortage of houses,' came Alan's reply.

The reason for the cautious note in my voice was that I knew he'd made at least two previous attempts at moving the production to New York, though he had admitted to me he hadn't been completely happy with any of the American actors who had played Jeeves. I'd rejected the part in the original production because I'm no singer and the show has a ravishing score by Andrew Lloyd Webber.

But when I attended the first night in Scarborough (where Malcolm Sinclair was a finely supercilious Jeeves) I wondered if I'd made a bit of a mistake. During the finale, I leaned across to my wife Rosalind Ayres and muttered, 'I reckon I could have done this after all.'

She nodded. 'It's a wonderful part and no proper warbling.'

It's true: Jeeves hardly deigns to sing; it's more a case of speaking in dignified rhythm. So, over the last six months I have juggled other projects, held a few at bay, even rejected a pilot episode of a not-funny

7

American sitcom. No great sacrifice there – they couldn't guarantee that my dressing room wouldn't be next to the lavatories.

Ros has generously volunteered to come with me. She's as excited as I am at the prospect of New York, and is going to help me in Pittsburgh with my lines and generally keep my confidence up. (She knows me well.) At least she won't be idle while we're here, as we also have a load of preparation and programme editing relating to our company's radio productions for the BBC. Broadway, here we come. Hopefully.

We meet up with Alan and Heather Ayckbourn at the airport – they've flown in from Manchester. Heather is as elfin-bright as ever, her Lettuce Leaf specs glinting in the glare of the snow. Alan is beaming and (he says) full of British Airways wine. The great cranium from which, to date, have sprung fifty-seven plays of rare genius, is protected today by a woolly knitted hat. He looks like Benny from *Crossroads*. They'd got up at six a.m. in Scarborough and have now been travelling for about seventeen hours.

With them is a vivacious woman with dark hair in an urchin cut. 'Here she is, the Liza Minnelli of Lancashire,' says Alan. Choreographer Sheila Carter gives me a Judy Garland hug and reminds me we have met before, at the surprise gala performance for Alan's sixtieth birthday. That was the occasion when Alan, who guessed something celebratory was going to happen but didn't know exactly what, had confided to Heather, 'I hope it's not going to be actors doing excerpts from my plays and forgetting their lines.' Which is pretty well what it was.

There's a small greeting committee from the O'Reilly Theatre waiting for us. Ros receives a large bouquet, including a golden sunflower. Heather likewise. Alan and I are already talking about the production. 'Can't remember a lot of it,' he lies, to make me feel better. 'Sheila's very good with people who've only got one leg.' He means me, who can't dance. I tell him I'm hoping the musical director is equally good with people who can't sing.

8

'Oh yes,' says Alan. 'But, ah ha, you can *talk*…!'

This has been exercising me ever since I accepted the part. Having listened to the CD of the original production I'm worrying again that, however little actual singing there is for 'Jeeves', I might still be in trouble. There seems to be a lot of speech carefully integrated with the music. But, I've told myself, Al is not like Peter Hall – master of the catastrophic surprise – who would be more likely to announce, 'Here's a new number I'd like you to *sing*. Oh, and could you accompany yourself on the piano at the same time?' So I'm trusting that all will be well in the *Sprechstimme* department.

The welcoming group consists of the theatre's company manager Kathy Campbell ('Hi hen!'), her student daughter Katie, and Angela, her assistant. They take us in separate cars to (in the Jarvises' case) an apartment building two blocks away from the O'Reilly Theatre. The Ayckbourns are off to the Ramada Hotel.

The third-floor flat on Penn Avenue in downtown Pittsburgh is a large one-room conversion from an old warehouse. It seems fine and certainly a step up from the murky place I occupied recently in Costa Mesa, when I was doing David Hare's *Skylight*. We dump our luggage and gaze out of the wide picture window. It's snowing hard. We can just see the front of the theatre, five minutes' walk along the street. Giant flakes spinning past remind me of the first time we tried the snowstorm scene at the dress rehearsal of *On Approval*, at the Playhouse in London. I have the same thought I had then: not convincing – could the stage management chop the paper into smaller pieces?

Later we venture out. The flakes are suddenly believable as they smack at our faces and freeze our cheeks. We aim to find something to eat, but all the restaurants are closed. We find a sort of *Star Wars* wooky-bar with many furry-coated locals crouching at the counter, where we order Gyro chicken and salad, plus a white Zinfandel for me. At least, that's what I ask for, but when it arrives it's a rosé. A 'blush wine', as the cheery pink-faced girl behind the counter explains.

The theatre folk we met at the airport seemed pleasant, and it looks as though there could be a family atmosphere about the whole thing. That is certainly an Ayckbourn thing too, so it augurs well.

Thursday

Wake to the non-sound of quietness outside – snow-deadened traffic. Ros and I go striding out in our short jackets and bobble hats, all we have against the biting temperature until we can purchase appropriate protection. At present we look like twin tea-cosies. OK for warming the top half, but bum-freezing below.

Later we travel from the apartment by 'People's Cab' to Kaufmann's in search of heavy-duty boots, hat, gloves and coats. On the phone the cab company man is charming but needs guidance on where exactly we are. After I talk him through it like a flight controller, he drawls, 'Sure Mr Jarvis, I guess we could get a cab to you.' I wonder if I have inadvertently called an out of town company? 'No,' he says, 'we just like to be "thoro".'

The assistants at Kaufmann's (a sort of Selfridges) are amiable and raffish. They all have strawberry-coloured noses and complexions that suggest an under-the-counter cache of whisky, which they might periodically whip out and swig as extra buffering against the cold. Mark, in the men's shoe department, takes my credit card (which has my 'gong' imprinted on it), puts it through his machine and hands it back, saying 'Have a nice day, Mr Obe.' I haven't found a full-length coat yet but I select a black Stetson. Judging by the impressive display, it's the right sort of thing for this city.

We walk to the theatre and meet manager Stephen Klein – a stocky ex-actor who grins through his beard and says, 'I worked with orchestras for twenty years before returning to theatre.' He is fulsomely hospitable and takes us on a tour of the building, which is barely two years old. Marble everywhere and close carpeting. It still smells new. There's any amount of space but, like many US theatres funded by rich sponsors and subscription audiences, the place seems slightly dead. In Britain we're used to regional theatres always being open, a performance every night, photos out front, lunchtime events, a sense of something happening all the time. Here it's beautifully quiet, well-heeled, nothing going on. Their Christmas show finished *before Christmas*. It's a no-show situation till ours begins in just under a month's time.

In the rehearsal room a conference is in progress. Stephen says it's a *By Jeeves* production meeting. I refuse his invitation to be led in to say hello. I'll meet everyone tomorrow. I look vaguely for Alan but bet he's still at the Ramada trying to get his computer to work, and recovering from lag.

Back at the apartment, I open the text. I have spent the last ten days in Los Angeles attempting to learn the part. This method of mugging up in advance worked well when I did Peter Nichols' *Passion Play* at the Donmar last year. Ros takes me through the lines which, I think, I nearly know. Don't want to have a repeat of *Skylight* when I spent the whole of three short rehearsal weeks cramming the words every night. I'm hoping that, even if it all feels different when we start, the groundwork of committing it to memory in advance won't be totally in vain.

Ros coaches me on my one major 'song'. It's a cunningly constructed patter number and has to go pretty swiftly. If I can find a way of performing it comfortably I feel the rest of the play might not be such a ghastly task.

★

Friday

I'm beginning to realise that I'll have to build in extra time for getting all the gear on – jersey, hat, boots, gloves, jacket. I must find a
proper overcoat. I set off on the short walk to the theatre and arrive
a minute or so before time. First day at the new school.

We'll be rehearsing in that large room on the second floor. First
the obligatory two minutes to divest. I'm greeted by artistic director
Ted Pappas. He is fortyish, impeccably turned-out with sharply
creased trousers, glossy slip-on shoes and designer cardigan all match-
ing his olive skin. Tortoiseshell specs on his aquiline nose coordinate
the overall presentation. His lips, smiling broadly at the moment,
seem part of the same scheme. There's a dynamic quality about him
as he pumps my hand and hugs me even more fervently than Stephen
did yesterday. They all seem fearfully pleased about something. Meet
various folk, all young men, and mentally cast each of them as characters in the play: Gussie, Bingo or Bertie. Wrong – they're either part
of the administration team or from the wardrobe department.

A short, chubby man holds up a smallish paper parcel and tells me
my costume has arrived. I thank him and say I won't have time to
look at it until later. He winks, and it's not until we're all gathered
round the table that I realise he's playing Sir Watkyn Bassett and that
it was an actorly joke. I've failed my initial test and demonstrated a
temporary irony deficiency. Nerves.

Stage manager Dan Rosokov approaches and says ambiguously,
'Hi Mart'n, heard so much about you.' His oval specs and earnest
demeanour make him look like an adult Harry Potter. He turns, calls
for silence and proceeds to chair a meeting of the cast. We vote for
how long we want the lunch break to last. Very different from the
vagaries of British Equity. We decide on one hour, just as the entire
staff of the O'Reilly Theatre burst through the doors, including the
telephonist, the janitor and cuddly Kathy Campbell, plus Alan and

Heather. There are introductions all round. Kathy is clearly den mother. She twinkles over the top of her specs and announces, 'My time is yours, I never take a day off, hens. My children have left home, and I'm happy to take any of you grocery shopping.'

A slim, youngish man with a wicked smile enquires if her kids' rooms are available. This turns out to be James Kall, who plays Gussie Fink-Nottle. The first Pittsburgh ice is properly broken.

The staff troop out and Alan suggests we might as well read the play. Cleverly, he says we won't sing the songs but 'as I'm so vain, I'd like to hear you read the lyrics.' He adds, 'they do sort of further the plot on occasion.'

Off we go. It's clear at once that copper-headed John Scherer, who plays Bertie Wooster, is a gifted actor. He's freckled, boyish-looking, probably in his late thirties with, as Alan has mentioned to me, a genuine sweetness of personality. He's been Bertie in every version of *By Jeeves* in America. The last production was five years ago. I know it opened at the Goodspeed Opera House in Connecticut and also toured to Washington and Los Angeles. At each venue there was talk of its moving directly to Broadway. Each time it didn't happen. I've been told that Donna Lynne Champlin, Emily Loesser and Ian Knauer have been with it from the beginning too. I haven't sorted out who's who yet.

There are five actors new to the cast including me, and I look around the table, starting to work out which is which. Don Stephenson is Bingo Little. He's married to Emily Loesser who I've heard sings wonderfully as Stiffy Byng. She's the tiny dark girl laughing at her husband's jokes. Don is a rangy guy in his mid-thirties with electric hair, humorous mouth and a querulous voice. When he gets up and crosses the room to fetch a chair he moves like a mobile question mark. Heath Lamberts (Sir Watkyn Bassett) is the one who held up the bag and pretended to be a costume man. He's short and round with a moon face and could perhaps be Richmal Crompton's

Hubert Lane grown into late middle-age. Steve Wilson, who plays the only American character in the piece, Cyrus Budge III (Jnr), is in his twenties, handsome, six foot five with a jutting jaw. Next to him, sweet-faced, fair-haired Becky Watson (Madeline Bassett) leans across to me and whispers, 'I feel I know you Mart'n. I have your *Carry On Jeeves* audio recordings in my purse.' She taps her bag and gurgles conspiratorially 'They're my Bible.' She's a lively conversationalist and maintains a barrage of enthusiastic chatter during the rest of the morning. She tells me her boyfriend is much looking forward to visiting Pittsburgh to see *By Jeeves*, referring to him as 'the gentleman I am seeing'. Later she mentions 'my ex-beau, the gentleman I was with for seven years'.

When we break for lunch I introduce myself properly to Tom Ford, Court Whisman and Molly Renfroe, who are all probably in their thirties. Tom grins shyly as we shake hands and shoves his rimless specs further up his nose. He doesn't say much. Court has a fine domed head with not too much hair left on it. He seems a larky character, now engaged in doing an impression of the Goodspeed producer, Michael Price. Since I have never met the man I have no way of telling if it's any good. I suspect, though, it might be. Molly is glamorous, brown-eyed and chatty, with lustrous chestnut hair down to her shoulders. She's passing round photos of her daughter, born since these three last saw each other. I learn that apart from having been part of the 'ensemble' from the beginning, they also understudy the entire company between them. Molly tells me that the 'ensemble' really means they are the chorus, and also that they'll be dashing on and off stage throughout the performance in the guise of parishioners, organising furniture, setting props, generally keeping the action moving forward. 'Hey, we do the donkey work, Mart'n,' says Court with acted exuberance.

I also meet Ian Knauer, another vastly tall actor who, besides playing the Reverend Harold 'Stinker' Pinker, is our dance captain. His fair hair is carefully parted and as he bends to pick up his briefcase I can see he's just beginning to lose a few strands on top. He smiles as he introduces himself, revealing impossibly white teeth.

At two o'clock Alan informs us that Lloyd Webber has written a new opening number for Jeeves and Bertie, a cassette of which has just arrived from London by Federal Express. He says we won't bother with it until tomorrow. Oh, Lord.

We start blocking. Alan's pretended or real remembering of the play is full of invention. His ideas about the character of Jeeves are bang-on and we both know I need to strive for economy. And stillness. Plus that inimitable murmur-in-the-ear flavour that every Jeeves must have: Dennis Price. Michael Hordern. Stephen Fry. Malcolm Sinclair. Even John Gielgud in *Arthur* was really Jeeves on a Hollywood vacation. Now it's my turn.

John Scherer and I attempt our first shared song, 'Never Fear', round the piano. It's all him really, with spoken interruptions from Jeeves. He's spot on at once. And I surprise myself by being able to keep up. Nearly. All that homework was worth it. Bravely I ask if I can go through my 'big' number. I daren't try it from memory but zip through, reading from the script. 'Neat, that's it!' exclaims Michael O'Flaherty, the musical director. He nods encouragingly over his half glasses, like a science teacher whose pupil has just handed in a good essay on the principles of dissection.

Really? This could be fun.

Saturday

The premise of *By Jeeves* is deceptively simple and wholly delightful. The parish of Little Wittam is to be subjected to a two-hour banjo recital by Bertram Wooster Esq., who is clearly proud of his recent mastery of that instrument's mysteries. His resourceful manservant, the inimitable Jeeves has, in the interests of the audience's sanity, taken matters into his own hands and spirited the banjo away, substituting a frying pan. No tunes can be played on that. It soon becomes apparent that a different sort of entertainment has been secretly prepared by Jeeves. The local players, under his direction, have been rehearsing a histrionic account of a weekend in the life of – yes – Bertie Wooster. This will involve many of Wodehouse's best-loved characters and some (almost) recognisable Wodehouse situations. All it requires is that the central role be spontaneously performed by Wooster himself. Jeeves' stroke of genius (or is it Ayckbourn's?) is that Bertie knows nothing of the plan until it's sprung on him by his faithful valet, in front of the expectant audience. Surely, Jeeves hints, the 'code of the Woosters' must be upheld. Gallantly, despite momentary disappointment at the absence of his beloved banjo, Bertie agrees to improvise the leading part – of himself.

Unrehearsed, he will be perpetually surprised throughout the evening at the exigencies of the plot, even though it's all been taken from the idiocies of his own life. He'll be persuaded to allow his old newt-fancying pal Gussie Fink-Nottle to assume his identity. (Bertie has, after all, in order to escape arrest on boat race night, assumed Gussie's.) This unlikely swap, Gussie believes, will impress the irascible Sir Watkyn Bassett, and assist him in his quest for the hand of Sir Watkyn's daughter, the lovely Madeline. In best Wodehouse tradition, this only leads to further complications when Bertie is blackmailed into travelling to Totleigh Towers, Dorset, to assist Sir Watkyn's ward Stiffy Byng in a scheme to induce her guardian to allow her to marry a hapless vicar. And so it goes on. A third Wodehouse 'drone', Bingo Little, is frantically in love with robust Honoria Glossop. A beefy American, Cyrus Budge, is making moves on air-head Madeline (who's in love with Gussie). There are further mistaken identities, imbecilities, romance and some startling use of costumes, be they from American musicals or British pantomimes, all found lying around backstage. The props — statues, fountains, doorbell, tree trunk, automobile — are engagingly home-spun too.

Jeeves presides like an omniscient puppeteer, masterminding these mistakes of a night and finally conjuring a happy, if eccentric, consummation. *By Jeeves* is both an affectionate parody of an amateur concert and a celebration of Wodehouse's own comic genius. It boasts a beguiling Lloyd Webber score, superb Ayckbourn invention and opportunities for fine acting, singing and dancing.

The play and lyrics aren't a direct adaptation of any of Wodehouse's short stories or novels. But so perfectly has Alan captured the flavour of the genre and the essence of Jeeves and Bertie's relationship, that several people on the theatre staff have already told me they have read the original book. They haven't, it doesn't exist.

Alan has been developing the opening scene. It's now brilliantly staged, with Bertie seated at a low music stand on a lower stool, facing a formidable wodge of music. This makes Jeeves' intervention even more logical. Nobody wants several hours of solo banjo from Bertie Wooster. Bertie will then be encouraged by his dutiful manservant to 'perform spontaneously' for the rest of the evening.

We bash onwards. Occasionally I can't help feeling like an understudy, but if I just hang in there no doubt I'll catch up and think of something reasonable to do — even start inventing a little myself, once the pattern is comfortable and clear. Several bits are sprung on me that I had forgotten from the original production and are not indicated in the text. In particular there are a number of scenes where, in a series of complicated manoeuvres, Jeeves controls a makeshift automobile, apparently constructed out of cardboard boxes. I work on that with dance captain Knauer, who is charming and patient with me. There'll be further choreographed moves to absorb when Emily Loesser and Molly Renfroe dash on to unravel great spools of greenery that, as the car speeds along, are supposed to represent fast disappearing verges on either side of the road.

As the cast chat during one of the short breaks, I become interested in the echelons of who is staying in our apartment building and who is at the Ramada Hotel. Are there class distinctions here? This gives rise to the thought, which is the better place? Surely the Ramada is the superior digs. The Ayckbourns, clearly, are special and therefore at the hotel. But they'll be leaving after we've opened. Steve Wilson is also at the Ramada because, he says, there were no more apartments available. Don and Emily, too, are Ramada people. Well, two for the price of one. The rest are with us at 900 Penn Avenue, except for Heath Lamberts who is a Pittsburgh resident. Actually I'm very happy with our loft-style space.

Donna Lynne Champlin is excellent as Honoria Glossop, Bertie's ex-fiancée, now precariously engaged to limpid Bingo Little. She doesn't present her as a mountainous hockey-playing girl as per the script – more a punchy bundle of backpacking heartiness. Donna Lynne is very pretty but metamorphoses into something distinctly less glamorous as soon as she comes striding on, ready to hitch a lift aboard the cardboard car on her way to Totleigh Towers. Her British accent is based, she tells me, on a study of Barbara Woodhouse dog-training videos. It's pretty good. Her natural speech is twangy New York, from Queens. She and John Scherer are both accomplished singers – their phrasing is effortless and they serve Andrew Lloyd Webber's music with an affecting sensitivity.

Sunday

Alan is on tremendous form, leaping about like a diligent gazelle – a curious loping figure in white T-shirt, leather waistcoat, black jeans and clompy boots. He looks like an old jazzer or rock 'n' roller: different, in my memory, from the larger, more sedate figure who directed me in *Woman in Mind* in 1985. Then (it seemed) he rarely got up from his seat on the edge of the rehearsal space, except once in a while to demonstrate a move or have a brief, diffident word with one of the actors. Now, he's sprightly. Is it that he's grown into his greatness? Or just that he's so on top of this particular project, having worked on it so many times? Maybe there's extra energy all round because half the cast have performed it before. Whatever the reason, it's a remarkably creative force on display. Everything he suggests or demonstrates is intensely revealing as to character and intention. As always, his rehearsals are theatre masterclasses.

There's a music rehearsal at the end of the day, from which I am excused. Jeeves, I am now fully assured, doesn't sing. Not even in the chorus. I'm well relieved. Singing is beneath such a man, clearly. Alan slides up to me and murmurs, 'He might possibly *conduct* though.' Michael O'Flaherty promises to fill me in on this. I change my mind and decide to stay for the rehearsal. It's marvellous to watch and hear how Michael melds the voices together. His direction on how to deal with the quasi-Dixie number is pertinent: 'Don't be tempted to get into an American approach – the fun is an American banjo number being sung in cut-glass English accents.'

I chat to Sheila Carter, whose witty choreography transmutes the whole cast (except Jeeves of course) into the supposedly far less gifted Little Wittam parish players. She's married to a British actor who is currently appearing in panto at Wythenshawe. 'He's playing one of the Chinese policemen,' she giggles. 'He's very good, but I prefer him as a baddie. That's why I married him. I'm always attracted to bastards. I told him, "I'm disappointed – I only married you because I thought you were a bastard, but you've turned out to be very nice!" Only jokin' Martin.'

★

Monday January 8th

Today I'm having a fitting with British costume designer Louise Belson, who has been in charge since the Scarborough opening six years ago.

After trying the various tailcoats on offer, it becomes clear that I'm not the same height as Malcolm Sinclair (the Scarborough Jeeves) or even the previous American Jeeves, who was 'wiry'. John Scherer tells me later that the actor had played the wacky neighbour in a popular US comedy series and brought quite a lot of sitcom breadth to the character of Jeeves. Hmm. Must remember. Be economic.

Back to the rehearsal, and we work through the scenes we have blocked. In fact we hardly stop, so it becomes virtually a run-through. I don't mind because, although I don't yet feel comfortable, it gives me a chance to see what I can remember of what we have briefly prepared so far. I take only about four prompts plus a few near-misses. (Four prompts is the goal I remember Alec Guinness setting himself after two weeks on a new production.) So, not too bad.

Sitting here at the back of the rehearsal room behind Alan and Dan, I take a longer look around at the other new kids on the block: clean-cut Steve Wilson, full of enthusiasm and virtually 'off-book' as young jam magnate Cyrus Budge III. Podgy Heath Lamberts, still very much on the script, but well-cast as Sir Watkyn Bassett and blessed with excellent timing. He may be one of those actors who are intrinsically funny without having to try. Don Stephenson already knows his lines as Bingo Little. I discover that Court Whisman (member of the ensemble and understudy) played Jeeves in Washington when his principal 'left two weeks early'. 'And,' says John, 'Court did a good job.'

I can't help feeling a little gratified when hints are dropped in my direction from several cast members that all was not ideal with the various American Jeeveses, and that they are relieved 'the real thing' has at last arrived. I'm relieved too. But what a responsibility.

I have a conversation with word-perfect Don who says, 'My God, you know most of the act. You must be one of those guys who takes a quick look at the script and has it nailed.' If only he knew.

Michael O'Flaherty records the music for the patter number on my cassette player. When I get home and try to play it back I find it's come out wrong – all I get is Pinky and Perky on speed. So I can't mug it up tonight.

I must try to resist two things: first, the feeling I'm a takeover actor. Even though, I remind myself obsessively, I was offered the role right back at the beginning. And second, that I am somehow expected to glean a great deal of the production by osmosis. Is it my imagination or is more time being spent on old stuff with the 'old' cast? I can't help worrying that my opening two scenes are being glossed over. I can feel myself getting tetchy. Alan says he has yet another idea about the beginning. Well that's good, it's bound to be an excellent one. He seems quite happy to wait until we get to it next Saturday before working on it. I want to work on it now! He's got more confidence in me than I have in myself.

The people waiting near the Penn Avenue bus stop that I pass on my walk to and from the theatre remind me of the crowd that used to gather on the corner of Windmill Street in the 1960s. That was when I proudly swaggered up Shaftesbury Avenue as a member of the National Youth Theatre, making my way to the Queen's Theatre on the corner of Wardour Street. Those Soho lurkers were musicians, waiting for the bookers to come downstairs from the nearby agencies and announce the morning's news: a saxophonist required that night at the Locarno Ballroom, Purley, a drummer needed urgently down at the Hammersmith Palais. Waiting in the cold, these Pittsburgh passengers seem to hang about in the same manner, idle, expectant, forming an eccentric, disparate group. They never stand remotely near the bus stop itself – and certainly don't form a line – almost as if it might be electrified and to get too near could be 'curtains'.

Ros arrives at lunchtime and I introduce her to the company. Some have seen her as Elsa Lanchester in *Gods and Monsters*. Emily Loesser (Stiffy Byng) caught her appearance in the American series *Chicago Hope*.

Tuesday

We're not working today because John Scherer and Donna Lynne have flown to New York to record *Three*, a new musical they have recently performed off-Broadway, directed by Hal Prince. There's talk of it going to Los Angeles for three months – but that would clash with our direct transfer to the Helen Hayes Theatre. John tells me that the *Three* management is prepared to wait for him and Donna Lynne until our Broadway plans are finalised, before recasting. Does that mean someone thinks we might *not* get to New York after all?

I spend the morning doing Jarvis & Ayres work. Radio director Pete Atkin and I talk over future *Just William* ideas for radio and television. Then it's time to walk in the snow to Suite Sound for a voice-over session. It's a couple of television commercials for the Fisher Theatre, Detroit. I have brought with me the tape that was recorded too fast yesterday. After the session is over I ask the engineer if he could have a go at slowing it down. He tries, but there's nothing he can do; the music still sounds like a banjo played by a demented soloist. Bertie Wooster, in fact.

Ros and I walk to Kaufmann's, still looking for coats. Later we hear from Kathy Campbell that Alan went shopping there today, for a pair of bathing trunks 'so he can go swimming in the Ramada pool'. I quash the feeling that we apartment folk are second-class citizens

– we don't have a free pool and gym, plus adjacent restaurant.

I attend my second costume fitting. It's unofficial. As it's a day off for the actors, we're not supposed to arrange anything to do with work. But I wanted to get it done, and so did they, so I hinted I could easily be 'just passing by'. This I do around two o'clock and find that they have rescued one of the Jeeves tailcoats. It might even fit. I'm aiming to get a smooth, svelte line. As I stand there being measured, I am presented with half a fruitcake from pregnant Kelley. Her baby is due on March 17th, the same day my younger son Oliver and his wife Monika expect theirs. The cake is delicious but not good for a slimline Jeeves.

A knot of smokers lurk outside the building in the cold. They're all members of the O'Reilly Theatre team – Tim (PR), John (computers) and Lou (marketing). They're not allowed to smoke inside.

'Nor in the whole of Pittsburgh, pretty well,' Lou tells me with a shrug. 'Except in a few bars.'

'Still,' says Tim, 'it cuts us down to twice a day.'

I leave the smoke-zone and walk the few minutes back to the apartment.

Ros hears me through the play. I know it, though bits of the puzzle keep falling out, predictably in the first act – the one we've blocked. The brain is computing, readjusting to cope with the physical pattern that is now becoming a part of the overall picture in my mind. Act Two goes better, but that's because there are no rehearsal pictures yet to trip me up. They'll come with tomorrow's blocking where, no doubt, more bits of the mental jigsaw will spill out.

Wednesday

We hear on the television news that Republican Linda Chavez has stepped down from a new Bush appointment because she once had an illegal immigrant living in her house. I should think if half of Los Angeles were working for Bush, they'd all be stepping down.

I set out from the apartment feeling optimistic, looking forward to blocking the second half of the play. The sun is actually shining. 'What a lovely day,' is almost on my lips until I remember it's only twenty-nine degrees. Still, lovely for Pittsburgh, I suppose.

Our perfectionist stage manager Dan Rosokov discovers that his assistant, Hillary, has forgotten to call Steve Wilson for rehearsal. So we skip some scenes and go a little out of order, which is confusing. Then we work on my 'song' – without Alan, just with choreographer Sheila. She's full of bounce: 'Now this is what you do, that's where you move.' When she says, 'I'll just show you this bit, then we can go home early,' it reminds me of the actor who had been unemployed for a year. He had almost despaired of ever working again. Finally he gets a job. He's delighted and much relieved. Off he goes to rehearsal on his first day, and comes home brimming with enthusiasm. Tells his wife how great it all was. 'Wonderful director, brilliant play, great cast. It's all fabulous. And best of all, tomorrow, guess what?'

'What?' says his wife.

'Day off!'

I have discovered, with some horror, that there is a little Jeevesian dance I have to perform in the finale. Sheila Carter does her best to teach it to me. It's not as easy as it ought to look; it's going to take me some time. Sheila is very sweet and patient and I like her very much. She must find me heavy going though, as I constantly ask her to 'show me that step again', or 'can you just do the twiddly bit at half-speed?' I think she's more used to singing and dancing actors who can pick this sort of thing up at the drop of a hat. At present, wherever on the ground my hat may be, I can't locate it, let alone pick it up. Musical director Michael O'Flaherty records the music for me. I go home at lunchtime and practise. It's recorded correctly this time.

I make a load of noise on the floor, thumping about, still trying to learn the dance. I must be careful as, this morning, I discovered that ensemble actor Court Whisman has the apartment immediately below. I had asked him if our television was too loud, though I was really keen to know if he could hear me going through my lines and getting tetchy with Ros (and myself) in the process. Instead of replying as I'd hoped with 'Can't hear a thing,' he shrugged, 'Mart'n, my boyfriend and I live in a New York apartment.'

This afternoon I notice how focused Steve Wilson is as Cyrus Budge. He builds beautifully on a couple of pointers from Alan. Steve's an engaging character. He told me yesterday he's trying to live economically as he had to pay for his wedding himself. He's been married for only a month to Roxane, a veteran of eight Broadway musicals. He bites into a frugal baked potato (his entire lunch) and says *By Jeeves* will be his Broadway debut. His wife is already on Broadway in *Chicago* and soon to begin rehearsals for *Follies* with British director Matthew Warchus.

I try my patter number again. It's hard to hear the beats in order to time my entry. No one's fault but mine. 'I can't really hear music,' I hear myself saying to Sheila, and to Wade Russo who plays the Little Wittam pianist Ozzie Nutledge. Can't hear it? What on earth does that mean? Nerves again? Yes, and because I'm breathing too hard. Wade is a fine musician and is gradually going to take over from musical director Michael O'Flaherty at the piano in the next week or two. So I've got some way to go – will need to get up to a few tricks to make sure both my 'song' and 'little dance' work out.

It's a relief that we finish the day with a brief work-through of Alan's new ideas about the opening scene. This involves Jeeves encouraging Bertie to begin the show, then walking out into the auditorium and turning towards the stage to check the sight lines and observe his master's progress. The action is a distinct development from the previous version – and an improvement. It's going to help the audience even more to understand that the performance is meant to be improvised, directed and continually shaped by Jeeves. The comedy now springs totally from the idea that *anything* is preferable to a lengthy solo banjo concert from Bertie Wooster.

Thursday

We block the next part of Act Two. Alan has probably got the message by now that it'll take me a bit of time. On Monday, before we went over what we'd blocked, I had said that if he didn't mind I would try it off the book.

'Mm,' he replied, 'as long as we can get home for tea.'

I interpreted this as 'don't keep us hanging about'. In fact I got through with only a few prompts and the next day he said it had been 'remarkable'. Thank God for Ros and the early learning process. I think, though, that he and others think I am faster and more efficient than I really am.

I had hoped to try my dance again. 'Yes, do it every day,' was a passing comment from Alan yesterday. I mention this to Sheila this morning, like a keen schoolboy rehearsing the school concert: 'Can I do my little dance today?'

She turns from the important job in hand of reworking some moments in the Pig number. 'Oh yes, Martin, we'll do it at some stage today.'

The Pig number, 'It's a Pig', is an extraordinary sequence in which Bertie Wooster, disguised in a grotesque pig mask, breaks into Honoria Glossop's bedroom pretending to be a burglar. It's a mad combination of Ayckbourn's words and Lloyd Webber's music, performed by the entire company. John has told me, 'It's the ideal eleven o'clock number.' When I look blank he explains. 'Just when the audience think the evening is pretty well done and heading for the finale, suddenly out of nowhere comes this fabulous show-stopping extravaganza.'

At a quarter past five, as we're finishing (forty-five minutes early I note) I quietly remind both Sheila and dance captain Ian Knauer about my dance.

'Oh,' he says, in some surprise, 'Do you want to do it?'

'Well, yes,' I say, 'I thought that was the idea.'

Sheila, literally in the act of putting on her woolly hat, says, 'Oh, all right love,' and turns to Wade. 'Wade, could you do us a favour? Martin wants to do his little dance.'

Hatchet-faced, I prance up and down for ten minutes, then we go home.

Just as I'm leaving, a genial-looking guy dressed in black is ushered into the room by wardrobe lady Kelley. She introduces him as Bobby Grayson who in a few days is going to cut my hair. Before I can begin the usual discussion with him he smiles conspiratorially, pushes and pulls at my locks a good deal and says, 'No problem baby, we know what we're going to do.' Oh? Doesn't he want any input from me? Wouldn't he like my views on Jeeves' immaculate pomade?

No, he's quite happy.

After he's gone Kelley tells me he's a 'star stylist' and has won an Emmy Award for his work on *Saturday Night Live*. Well, p'raps he'll get another nomination for knowing how to cut my hair. No one else ever has.

Friday

I have a chat with Sheila Carter to explain I've been getting the feeling I'm expected to know ahead of time what's going on. She is sweetly apologetic. Then I feel guilty that it's not her fault at all. Only mine.

We check the Act Two blocking and I manage to get through with no prompts. Confusingly, I seem to have demonstrated that I do

27

know what I am doing. I don't. Still, I feel better. In fact, during the run of the act I had noticed Don Stephenson (Bingo) and James Kall (Gussie) nudging and exchanging whispers as I shimmered around as Jeeves. I felt distinctly pleased until, after about the fourth scene, I realised I had been shimmering for twenty minutes with my flies open, and their nudges had little to do with my performance.

Saturday

A film script has arrived for Ros. She'll be going to LA on Wednesday to test for the part of Jack Nicholson's wife in a new movie called *About Schmidt*.

This morning we're on stage for the first time. Unusually early of course, but as the set is nearly up and with nothing else in the way, it can only be to our advantage to have reached this point already. The set itself is a triumph for British designer Roger Glossop. He has told me it's based on the well-worn mahogany appearance of a church hall he knows in Sheffield. The scuffed wooden floor and swinging double doors remind me of my teenage membership of the St Mary's Fellowship, South Croydon: we used to meet in a similarly musty venue, the scout hut.

Roger has embellished both our memories by constructing an upper-level balcony walkway, from which Jeeves can periodically view the action and, if so inclined, redirect it. I count a total of eighteen doors, all of which, Alan assures me, have a part to play in the ongoing drama.

We work through the opening scenes. Not too bad. Though timings will be affected when Jeeves' mysterious curtains are fully in place. The idea is that each time Jeeves comes on, the plush red hangings at the upstage right and left entrances are suddenly drawn back, as if by magic. All-powerful, as in the original stories, he seems to have control over just about everything. It's really Alan's theatrical extension of Wodehouse's central point – that Jeeves is almost god-like, certainly as far as Bertram Wooster is concerned. He stands alone. I can see that the effect of even the curtains parting obligingly, apparently of their own volition, will be very funny. Court Whisman calls out, 'Hey Mart'n, the drapes in this show get laughs on their own!'

It's time to rehearse the 'ladder scene'. This is, literally, the high point of Act Two. It's one of Alan's most breathtaking lateral ideas. I remember its astonishing effect on the Scarborough audience. It goes like this: Bertie Wooster has been asked by Stiffy Byng to impersonate a burglar so that her fiancé, the Reverend Harold Pinker, can be the hero of the hour and capture the swag which the masked intruder will be attempting to remove from the house. Such a noble deed will commend itself to Sir Watkyn, Stiffy's guardian, and the couple will be allowed to marry. So far, pure Wodehouse. Bertie reluctantly agrees to climb a ladder in the dead of night and break into one of the bedrooms of Totleigh Towers, via a window. Jeeves, responsible for the whole scenario, has already prepared two remarkable props. At the appropriate moment a gigantic ladder is brought on, balanced at a precarious angle against what looks like a carpenter's trestle. Ahead of this, Tom Ford wheels forward a free-standing complete window and sill. Jeeves directs this to be placed some distance from the ladder. He then encourages the hapless Wooster to don the disguise – a pink pig mask apparently left over from a children's version of the *Three Little Pigs*. Jeeves assists his master onto the lower rungs of the ladder, and then to begin his journey upwards. Bertie is naturally nervous: 'I feel I am about to perform some feat of acrobatics, Jeeves.'

'Only mildly, sir,' comes the non-committal reply.

Jeeves has a plan. Ozzie Nutledge, in the person of Wade Russo, is ready with 'suspenseful music' to enhance the scene. Bertie is travelling upwards and the window unit is puzzlingly earthbound, fifteen feet away. Now it's getting decidedly Ayckbourn. Bertie, high in the air, becomes aware, along with the audience, that the ladder is beginning to sway ominously: it's Wooster's weight cantilevered against the trestle on the ground. The ladder starts to tip forward. Bertie, hanging on for dear life, cries out, the ladder drops gradually to the point of no return, gathers speed and hurtles towards terra firma, smashing onto the top of the window frame which is pushed backwards by the impact, parallel to the ground also. The illusion now presents itself in full: Bertram Wooster at the top of a ladder, balanced against the window sill on the second floor of Totleigh Towers. From the audience's point of view it's as if the camera angle has shifted and they are now looking at the action from above.

> BERTIE: Jeeves, what on earth's happening?
> JEEVES: You're quite safe sir. Just don't look down.
> BERTIE: Why not? Oh yes, I see. That's down, isn't it? Down is sideways?
> JEEVES: Precisely.
> BERTIE: A clearer demonstration of horizontal thinking it is hard to conceive…

The absurd logic of what follows as Bertie, apparently leaning high up against the side of the house, is unable to open the window-catch and Jeeves merely walks across the stage to loosen it, ('Allow me, sir,') is a sublime piece of visual comedy.

This is the first time new members of the cast have witnessed the scene in full. This morning, as John places his foot on the bottom rung, about to ascend, Steve Wilson suddenly springs forward from his seat in the front row of the stalls and leaps onto the stage shouting, 'Stop, stop everybody! Hold it John, stand back!'

John steps sharply aside and we look towards Steve in amazement. He continues urgently, 'There's a crack on the side of the ladder. See. It's not safe guys…'

We all stand still for a second before collapsing into laughter. Alan follows Steve onto the stage, also doubled up. Steve looks confused. Alan explains to him that the crack he has so prudently pointed out is merely painted on, to make the ladder look wooden and rickety. The same with the window. And the trestle. All are highly sophisticated pieces of precision engineering, made of the strongest steel and cunningly prepared to look like hastily commandeered backstage props.

Steve grins ruefully and hits his forehead with his hand. But we know he's a great company member.

We carry on with the rehearsal.

The car is another expertly imagined technological effect. The timing for its numerous twists and turns is crucial. All down to Jeeves. I'm starting to get the hang of it. It's designed to look very simple – an open-topped jalopy supposedly knocked together from old boxes, an upturned table and a decrepit sofa. It's actually an artful construction that spins and pivots as Jeeves stands behind it and hauls on the ropes, transporting Bertie and others from Berkley Mansions, London to Totleigh Towers, Dorset.

Back to reality, I meet Ros for lunch at the theatre bookshop, Curtain Call, a block away. James Kall, already being very funny as a vapid Gussie Fink-Nottle, joins us. When he learns we are still looking for some warmer gear, he says he's an authority on the subject as his partner Randy is vice-president of Eddie Bauer, a popular Toronto men's store. He suggests we try the Burlington Coat Factory a few blocks away. Later we follow his advice and from a vast choice purchase, at last, two generously quilted garments.

We walk back to the apartment, side by side. No one can get past us.

★

Sunday

This morning stage manager Dan bustles over to me, moving like a bespectacled penguin. 'Mart'n, we have a tailcoat for you to wear in rehearsal to put you in a different place.' He adds hurriedly, 'Not that you need it.' He means, I take it, to give me more of a Jeevesian feeling. Good idea. His assistant Hillary holds out a jacket, which in fact has the wiry ex-Jeeves' name inside it. I put it on. It's not such a bad fit after all – am I wirier than I thought? I glance at the long mirror on the wall. No. But now, wearing the 'practice' tailcoat, I do begin to feel more like a gentleman's personal gentleman. It looks a touch eccentric though, above my hefty Kaufmann's boots.

We finish at one thirty. I approach Wade Russo who, besides playing Ozzie, is temporarily in charge of music, Michael O'Flaherty having left to conduct auditions for *Brigadoon* in New York. Wade is nodding and smiling, pleased with the rehearsal's progress and just putting on his fedora hat, ready to go to lunch. He's quite small, with a trim goatee beard, and dresses invariably in black.

I ask, 'Could I quickly try my 'song'?'

Happy to oblige and reseated at the piano, he reminds me of a Russian garden gnome. We run the patter swiftly a couple of times.

Getting better.

I think to myself, as we trek through the snow to a café round the corner, that the words and rhythm seem to have seeped into my head. Well, I suppose they ought to have done, since I constantly repeat the whole thing, like a mantra, especially walking to the theatre. I get some funny looks as I mutter my way past the various bus stops. But I'm getting weird glances anyway, as my Stetson excites a good deal of attention. I had chosen it from Kaufmann's, partly because I rather fancied myself in it, and partly – because of the display – I had assumed everyone in Pittsburgh wore one. I'm now learning my mistake as the otherwise silent bus stop lurkers cry out,

'Yee ha!' and 'Ride 'em cowboy!' as I stalk by.

This evening a cast outing is organised by Sheila Carter and Court Whisman to the Fish Market restaurant. Alan and Heather are the only ones not here. Alan wants his Sunday roast and Heather is cooking. But it may be best, for once, that Alan is not present. It gives the group a chance to gel without being under the benevolent eye of the master. (Many of them of course have already gelled happily over the last three versions of *By Jeeves*.) But it also means we can talk about him. Which is, I think, rather important.

We do exactly that. They all revere Alan. I suddenly notice that Heath Lamberts isn't here. He is the only one who has, on occasion, been resistant to Alan's rehearsal suggestions. Even I, though anxiously at times, have followed his pattern.

Why would I not?

Monday January 15th

Ros spends the morning arranging an airline ticket to Los Angeles for the Jack Nicholson meeting.

We've heard of an area near here called Squirrel Hill, where there are several cinemas. We go up by taxi to see the movie *Traffic*, followed by a meal in the Squirrel Café. I had read that this is one of the best restaurants in Pittsburgh. Don't know where that idea came from. It's a gloomy bar with unfresh pasta dishes, cigarette smoke and obligatory cheese with everything.

Tuesday

Working on stage all day.

Alan suggests some 'colours' in my patter number that might make it easier. He often seems to consider the relevance of the point he's making, even as it emerges from his mouth. 'Mm,' he says tactfully, his voice soft like a cushion of air on which his thoughts ride. 'Don't motor through at one hundred miles an hour.'

I tell him I'm relieved each time just to get through it. I try a more delicate approach. It's getting easier.

I've opened a discussion with John Scherer about areas I need to clarify for myself in the early scenes. These are mainly shared moments between our two characters. I still need to identify the correct rhythm, a combination of pause and acceleration, in some sections of the dialogue. It's tricky, of course, when one actor (Bertie) having played the part many times, is already burning on perform-ance-level cylinders. Especially when the other (Jeeves) is still finding his way. But I exchange a few points regarding the unhurried nature of Jeeves. John is tremendous in the role and tireless in digging down to find new things in the text. He's my sort of actor. And entirely helpful and accommodating. He has asked me about my book, *Acting Strangely*. Today I brought him a copy, purchased from Curtain Call, in a plain brown wrapper. I'm hoping he won't flash it about. In the presence of the most prolific playwright in the world, it might be embarrassing if they're all looking at my autobiography. Luckily many of the cast have gone home by the time John opens the enve-lope. Though I do see him showing it to Wade Russo, who leafs through it, and the book resides for an hour like an unexploded bomb on top of the piano.

This evening Ros and I visit Franco's restaurant. It's just along from the theatre and boasts several stars in the local guide.

The wine's all right but Ros's lobster salad tastes strangely medicinal.

★

Wednesday

Steve Wilson isn't here. He was ill during yesterday's rehearsal and has flu. Court, his understudy, does an excellent job covering for him as Cyrus Budge.

During one of the breaks Alan tells a bizarre story about the murder of a Houston theatre manager. The unfortunate victim had been bumped off a day or so before the Scarborough company arrived in Texas, on tour with *Way Upstream*. Alan had warned the cast that the police suspected it was an inside job. So, naturally, everyone was very jumpy at whichever of the Houston staff were greeting them. Further investigation had suggested it was a gay murder. Which was even more worrying as the theatre seemed full of charming workers, many of whom were a little light in their loafers. Relief all round when the killer turned out to be a sacked security guard. The production, as usual during Alan's various waterlogged productions of *Way Upstream,* purged the theatre soon afterwards with another flooding.

I call Steve. He feels weak, but has been taken to the doctor by den mother Kathy and now has some antibiotics.

Ros has flown to LA today for her meeting. She calls later. Some residuals from television transmissions of the movie *Titanic* (in which we both have cameo roles) have come in. Just as well, as this pre-Broadway salary won't sustain us. Perhaps Jack Nicholson will.

Thursday

Today we're going to run the second half. It starts badly with garrulous Becky Watson missing an entrance as Madeline Bassett and then, after apologising abjectly and expounding a lot about it to Alan, missing it again. She can talk for America.

All goes well until my patter number, when I blow it, pick it up and blow it again. I keep going even when I've lost the words, in a sort of pa-pa pa-pa pa-pum sort of rhythm. I get some ironic applause and Court Whisman pronounces, 'Jeeves as rapper, great!' I have another go later and, after yet another false start, get it back. Each time a bit more falls into place. Hurray. And at least we are really rehearsing the show, as opposed to just running it. So much of it is a technical exercise. As Alan says, 'A subtext show it's not.'

Heath Lamberts has received a local award for his performance as the Marquis de Sade in the play *Quills*. There's an article about him from the *Pittsburgh Post-Gazette* pinned on the noticeboard. As I'm reading it he emerges from one of the dressing rooms and buttonholes me, sniggering like Hubert Lane. He says in a waggish whisper, 'Oh Marty, I went to my Alcoholics Anonymous meeting last night and somebody had brought along the newspaper cutting in case I hadn't seen it. Well, the awful thing was it was passed around, and, oh I blush, it seemed like I'd brought it myself, would you believe, to show off to everybody! Was I embarrassed, Marty!' He cringes like Uriah Heep and moves away down the corridor shaking his head in mock despondency.

I felt like that over my book yesterday. John Scherer tells me he's been reading it – says he's 'loving it'.

Old friend Johnny Wright rang yesterday. He's in New York on advertising business and staying at the Giraffe Hotel. Says it's great, intimate and welcoming. Must remember that when we get to New York.

At lunch John asks me if I have any information about the Broadway plans. He's as keen to know as I am, having other things in the offing. His Hal Prince musical is definitely going to Los Angeles in April and then possibly to Broadway. He'd rather be doing *By Jeeves*, but he doesn't want to lose the other opportunity if we're not going to be on Broadway by April. We finish in Pittsburgh on March 4th.

Ros has had her movie meeting. Seemed to go quite well. She's putting a sizable cheque in the bank. The *Titanic* is keeping us afloat.

Friday

Steve is back, having more or less recovered from his two-day flu. He's lost all the weight he's been trying to put on for the part of the aggressive American. He's still pretty impressive though, at six foot five.

I'm not happy with my number. Mustn't think of it as a 'song'. It's just a 'piece' spoken in rhythm. But once I get off track I can't get back on. Yet. I try it once more with the patient and delightful Wade. He's very supportive and tells me I should play Henry Higgins in *My Fair Lady*. Even offers to coach me in the songs. He says, 'Don't worry Mart'n, if ever you go off beam, I shall stick to you *like white on rice!*'

In the green room Alan talks about the very first version of this show *(called simply Jeeves)* in the mid-seventies. It opened in Bristol. It was disastrous and extremely long. After the performance David Hemmings, who played Bertie, was so depressed he hid in the shower having some sort of temporary breakdown. Alan and director Eric Thompson arrived at the dressing room door to hear David's wife pleading with him: 'Come on David, come out, some of it was quite good, pull yourself together.' Betty Marsden's part, Aunt Dahlia (a leading role) was subsequently cut completely, thus taking an hour off the running time. It didn't help. Alan is quite open about the fact that the show just wasn't ready. It needed many weeks of shaping, but the management, with a theatre suddenly available, forced them into the West End immediately, whereupon it foundered.

Today Alan discusses the pace and refinement required at certain crucial moments of the play. His phrases are interestingly technical in describing, say, Madeline's attitude to Gussie Fink-Nottle or Bertie berating his butler: 'Needs a wing-nut tightened.' 'Try to dowse it down.' 'Give it a bit more turbo thrust.' We know exactly what he means.

He congratulates everyone at the end of the afternoon, especially the 'new people'.

This evening some of us are driven to an area of Pittsburgh called Shadyside, not far from Squirrel Hill. Two founder members of the O'Reilly, Joan and Jerry Epps are giving a buffet dinner for us. They're nice people and obviously love the theatre. The house is 'Fifties modernism' as Ted Pappas puts it. It reminds me of a large Wates Estate show house in East Molesey or Muswell Hill. Conversation is a little awkward, as is often the case when well-meaning theatre patrons entertain the strolling players. I notice an original Matisse drawing on the wall and, to fill a silence, tell my tale of Dina Verny. This was when Ros and I were visiting the Dina Verny Gallery near Saint Germain, Paris. We had wandered around, admiring a selection of Matisse drawings and lithographs. There were several remarkable portraits of Dina, his great model. One in particular was placed directly behind the gallery owner's desk, nude with legs spread wide. We looked back to the desk where sat the owner, and suddenly realised that here was Dina herself, now in her seventies, demurely dressed in black. The contrast between the 'open display' directly behind her, and her current businesslike demeanour, was marked, to say the least.

My colleagues laugh, including set designer Roger Glossop, but our hosts and one or two of their friends – brought in to meet the actors – only smile uneasily. The ice remains unbroken.

Saturday

Our first major run-through.

I'm most nervous, of course, about the patter. To say nothing of the little dance. No one has commented on its progress recently. Not even my kindly captain, Ian. He's probably got enough on his plate, playing the very English Stinker Pinker and doubling as 'The Cow' which, in full bovine costume, leans on its own portable gate to view the roadside action, before hot-footing it round to the opposite entrance to become a second cow doing much the same thing.

The theatre is empty when I arrive so I practise, self-consciously, in a corner of the stage.

It's Ian who comes through the door next. He watches me for a moment from the stalls as he divests himself of overcoat, scarf, head-warmer and boots, then offers a simple piece of advice. 'Try holding your arms higher, you'll balance better.'

I try it. Wow. I float. When I thank him he says, 'Oh sure, it's nothing, my partner Keith is the real choreographer in the family.'

Apart from the patter and the dance, there's the acting itself. Inevitably one has to examine one's character's motives and intentions, but that can add up to over-obsession. I ought to be used to it by now but it never really gets any easier. Perhaps it's an increased sense of responsibility – and it's a fine line we all tread between what is true and good and funny, and what is dull and predictable.

Before we start Sheila conducts a warm-up – The Gay Gordons. (Court remarks that it's singularly appropriate for this company.) The dance is unfamiliar to most of the cast but I can do this, dragged from some schooldays recess of memory. As we leap and spin, it's my partner, Molly Renfroe, one of the ensemble, who apologises to me for being a bad dancer. She exclaims, 'Poor Martin,' as she kicks me in the shin by mistake, meaning 'he has to put up with my ineptitude', but Sheila Carter misunderstands and thinks it's me getting it all wrong. We're back at school.

I'm exhausted after nearly half an hour of cavorting, but the run goes well. I get through my number unscathed.

Alan has almost no notes to give, but 'Miss Carter' asks me to stay behind to do my little dance. Wade Russo has already gone, so we do it without the music and it's unsatisfactory. I'm still not quite sure where my feet have to be on the twiddly bit. I wonder if Sheila is actually a little nervous of me. She keeps mentioning to others that she's told people in England that she's 'working with Martin Jarvis'. Whatever that means. Probably my own unease isn't helping her. But at least, two weeks on, I can get through the play. I'm trying to refine the character. It requires cool, unhurried playing and I'm finding I can now begin to listen more to the others, timing my lines more deftly against witty John Scherer.

On the way back from rehearsal this evening, I call in at Unique Pizza, opposite the apartment, on the corner of Ninth St. The establishment only opened a week ago. A weary-looking Pittsburgher lolls behind the counter. Behind him is their logo, 'Anything but ordinary.' I ask what time they close, thinking I might nip across and get something a little later.

'Eight o'clock,' he replies. As I turn to leave he says, obligingly, 'Wanna menu?' I take it and go across the road and up to the flat.

Soon after seven, having made my choice, I pick up the phone.

The same voice answers, 'Unique, yeah?'

'I'd like to order a Homestead Pizza with extra mushroom,' I begin, but the reply comes back fast, 'No, we're closed.'

'What?'

'Close at seven.'

'But you told me you're open till eight.'

'Not on Saturday.'

That's Pittsburgh. Anything but ordinary.

Unique.

*

Sunday

I'd much rather be working, but we've got two days off. I think Alan has to maintain a balance between those – like me – who want to worry away at the thing and use every minute, and some of the 'old ones' like John, who are ready and don't want to over-rehearse.

I had intended to walk down Penn Avenue to investigate what's known as the Strip District. I've heard there are some interesting grocery stores housed in vast warehouses. (Since when have I been interested in grocery stores? But still…) Instead I mess around, reading the script and trying to sort out the areas where I was woolly yesterday. Also, I'm idly looking at the novel *Ruggles of Red Gap*. Might it make a radio play? It's the adventures of an English butler working for an American family. It had sounded a promising idea when suggested to me, but the book seems pedestrian. I haven't read it thoroughly though. The only text I can study in any depth is – you've guessed it.

I haven't phoned any of the cast as I feel they'll be doing their own thing, and I am the 'oldie' of the company except for Heath Lamberts. He lives here anyway. I decide to go to a movie and at half past five tramp out across the snow to find the bus to Squirrel Hill. I eventually locate the correct stop on 5th Street.

I join the usual wary group. I'm on the bus when John Scherer climbs in at the next stop. He's on his way to see a film as well. We join forces and eventually decide, after getting off at Squirrel Hill, to walk down the slope to the lower cinema. We make an odd couple. He's wearing strange green ear-warmers that clamp around the back of his head like a pair of headphones – a red-headed cold weather disc-jockey. I'm a booted-and-Stetsoned cowboy Brit. Nobody would guess we were Bertie Wooster and his man, Jeeves.

We see *Thirteen Days* starring Kevin Costner. It turns out to be better than either of us expected. More importantly it gives us a chance to chat over a meal afterwards at Gullifty's, an eating empo-rium John used to go to when he was a student here at Carnegie Mellon University nearly twenty years ago.

Naturally we talk about our shared obsession – *By Jeeves*. This encompasses Alan, the cast, and when Andrew Lloyd Webber might arrive. We discuss our concerns about whether there really will be a New York transfer and when we might know something definite.

John fills me in about Michael Price, the show's original American producer. He's artistic director of the Goodspeed Opera House and it was his production of *By Jeeves* that opened there five years ago. The reason it's being tried out again is because John, Ted Pappas and Michael met for lunch last year, during which John cannily suggested that Ted might like to relaunch the show here at the O'Reilly, in a final push towards Broadway.

It's useful to sit and talk, and John provides an unexpected bonus when he tells me the cast all think I'm wonderful in the part. I feel embarrassed because I know I'm not. He says, apropos of a previous Jeeves, 'it was like being on stage with a ghoul!'

When we get back we visit Court Whisman's apartment. The Golden Globe Awards are being shown on television and Court, fellow ensemble member Tom Ford, James Kall, John and I watch for an hour. I fetch a large bottle of Chardonnay from my fridge upstairs. There's some left when the party breaks up. I take it back with me for a nightcap. A good day.

Monday January 22nd

Crunching over the snow I set off to investigate those Strip District shops. It takes about twenty-five minutes to reach what seems like a Greek or Italian area – a strip of large lowish shacks on either side of the road. They are delis, bakeries, butchers, fruit stores and groceries.

I make various purchases including, for some mad reason, four dollars' worth of foul-smelling sausage. I start to walk back but a bus comes along and, since I'm passing a bus stop, I climb aboard and sit down. The man next to me gets up and moves swiftly away. A few minutes later the bus drops me opposite the apartment building. The sausage is stinking me out and goes straight into the trash.

This afternoon I read through the play. Again. Some of the more convoluted speeches now seem to be sifting to a better place in my head.

Ros returns, having got up at four this morning to get a six thirty flight from Los Angeles, via Chicago. She didn't meet Jack Nicholson, but filmed a screen test for the director, Alexander Payne.

Tuesday

Suddenly we're into a full technical rehearsal. It's strange to be, in one sense, so far advanced with the play and yet personally still in a 'work in progress' situation. Even though lighting director Mick Hughes has arrived from London and is adding illuminations, it's useful just to keep testing out one's knowledge of the text and character.

Alan tells a story about the late Simon Cadell, an actor we both admired. Never one to leave stones unturned in pursuing new highs in his career, Simon had invited Alan and Heather to lunch at Le Manoir aux Quat' Saisons. He arranged a car for them and everything. Almost unheard of generosity. What's it all about, thinks Al?

During dessert Simon comes clean: 'I gather you are going to do *Othello* with Mike Gambon?'

'Yes,' admits Alan.

'Well, I'd like to play Iago.'

Alan begins to hedge, as he already has someone in mind. It

becomes increasingly clear that Iago can't be Simon. When the bill arrives Simon says, 'We are going Dutch, aren't we…?'

Alan follows up with a second Cadell story. In Alan's National Theatre production of the lightweight farce *Tons of Money*, Simon had been worrying like a ferret over the play, digging too deep into it. Intellectualising himself out of a good performance, says Alan. One day Alan says to him, 'Simon, when you go on stage, for God's sake leave your brain in the dressing room.'

Simon's camp dresser, who has heard all this, chimes in immediately, 'Ooh, I'll 'ave to lock it up then, it's bound to be nicked.'

I've been observing Heath Lamberts' technique on stage. He's a genuinely gifted character actor who doesn't have to try to be funny as Sir Watkyn. There's just something about him that makes you want to laugh. Offstage he is equally fascinating. He moves almost furtively through the backstage corridors, keeping his back three-quarters to the wall as if afraid of a mugging. When spoken to he invariably answers shyly, his head on one side in an attitude of deference. He reminds me of someone who might work in a gentlemen's outfitters. I can see the tape measure around his neck. At other times he is agreeably revealing. In the green room this afternoon he discloses to me that his hobby is being a drum major.

'Oh, really?'

He touches me lightly on the lapel, 'Marty, you've no idea. It informs my whole life. When, God forgive me, I decided a few years ago this was to be my hobby, I sought out the leading exponent in the United States to coach me. Oh, did I work hard on it! We soared together. And now, oh yes Mart,' he lowers his eyes coyly, 'Now, I win medals for my expertise. It's an invigorating pastime, you betcha. I'll bring in the photographs to show you.'

I meet Bob, a member of the backstage technical crew. He's an ancient, bearded beatnik with shoulder-length grey hair, who looks like screenwriter Joe Esterhaz. He says of *By Jeeves*, 'Heck Mart'n, I watched the run-through on Saturday. You know what, it's pretty comical. But, hey, we gotta concentrate. If we don't pay attention, man, we're lost.'

That goes for the actors as well.

I've been noticing that Alan often speaks to the Americans in a sort of cod Yankee voice as he tells his anecdotes, or converses with them. Today I hear him chatting to Mick Hughes in a decidedly cockney timbre, which echoes Mick's own Londonese. I do it too. I'm reminded of my first landlady in London, Mrs Hogan. For some reason I could only communicate with her in my own version of her strong Dublin brogue. One day I said, 'Now here's the rent for you, Mrs H,' and even I could hear my unspoken 'begorrah' hanging in the air between us. Her eyes flashed dangerously and I was lucky to escape without a wallop as she retorted, 'Are you takin' the Michael by any chance?'

Alan announces that Andrew Lloyd Webber is arriving on Tuesday and will want to hear all the music played and sung through. He mentions that Andrew will probably be keen to insert those 'awful pauses' where, because the audience applauded once, somewhere in the show, he'll want to hold up the action artificially so it can happen again in the same place. Al suggests we put in some pauses, 'and then,' he says airily, 'take 'em out again!'

I receive an email from a friend in England. He's applying for the job of Head of BBC Radio Drama. He still hasn't had his boardroom interview.

He'd be a good man for the job.

Wednesday

Alan has a glint in his eye this morning. He tells me he's 'putting a new line in'. Changing dialogue is unusual for him. A rewrite at this stage is rare. He says, 'I usually sit on it for twenty-four hours before doing anything.' It turns out that the new bit is an extra speech from the Reverend Pinker as he leads away the woozy Cyrus Budge, who has been behaving inappropriately in the grounds of Totleigh Towers. Alan now has Pinker apologising to the audience on Budge's behalf: 'Ladies and gentlemen, I'm so sorry. He's an American.'

John Scherer seems edgy today, but his theatrical tastebuds are absolutely on the button. He asks Alan that a gasp of surprise that he alone is supposed to provide on a cue from Jeeves, should not also be echoed by Don Stephenson as Bingo Little. Don is an excellent actor and John and I have discussed how much we like him and Emily Loesser his wife. But I can see that John is right about this moment. It's sorted out happily.

Later John suggests that our joint positions in a particular scene should be moved downstage. Again he is correct. I had in fact been wondering if he thought I was trying to upstage him. Rather like the actor who, when we did *Twelfth Night* together for Peter Hall's company, always felt he had to be in an upstage position. I have learned from many masters of stage positioning (Alan Badel, Wilfrid Hyde White, director Michael Grandage, Ayckbourn himself) that it's frequently helpful to be downstage, and consequently nearer to the audience. Especially in comedy. Sir Toby did not perhaps wholly understand this and would often comprehensively upstage me (Ague-cheek) and David Cardy (Fabian) by disappearing northwards to the back wall. Unfazed, we would merely move down left or right a little to continue the scene. Belch, realising that instead of pulling focus he'd left it far behind, would come hustling downstage again to be sure of staying in on the act.

We don't complete the play because at five to six Dan announces we have to stop in time to divest ourselves of our microphones. We've been wearing these tiny mikes for the last two days. Most of the cast have them taped to their heads or (in the case of the girls) hidden in their hair. Mine, I'm happy to say, will eventually be clipped onto my tie. I don't fancy the idea of Jeeves with a small black growth protruding from his forehead.

I'm liaising with my friends Gyles and Michèle Brandreth, who are flying from London to New York on business. They are keen to come to Pittsburgh to see the show. There are some good deals on flights, but probably too tricky to coordinate in the short time they'll be in America. They'll just have to wait until we get to Broadway.

I walk back home with talented ensemble player and understudy Tom Ford. He, along with Court Whisman and Molly Renfroe, provides invaluable Ayckbourn/Wodehouse texture to the *By Jeeves* experience – racing on and off as Little Wittam parishioners, shunting furniture, grabbing props and singing and dancing in the group numbers. Between us now, Tom and I carry two extra tables for the apartment, donated by Kathy Campbell. In the elevator we meet a young woman called Christina who apparently lives in the next-door flat to us. They both come in and we encounter Ros spray-painting a huge, metallic, freestanding structure on wheels that has 'Candy Center' written on the front. It's really a rack of about eight shelves set at a slight angle for display purposes. It turns out she found it in the garbage room downstairs. It's probably a throw-out from the news and confectioner's store next door. I explain to the two visitors that Ros is very creative. 'I can see,' grins Tom.

Later it proves to be not only a useful do-it-yourself partition in the one room flat, but perfect for housing our office equipment, papers, scripts, files etc. When we retire to bed we feel we are dossing down in the stationery department of Ryman's.

★

Thursday

There's a photograph on my dressing room table of what appears to be a chubby middle-aged woman in a tartan skirt and beret, holding a giant phallus above her head. I study it carefully. Of course. It's Heath Lamberts, fully kitted and kilted as Drum Major.

Today it's Wade Russo's day. And Sheila Carter's. Music and dance. Although it's good to work on the singing and choreography, I'm loath to leave the 'play proper' for even a day. I manage to do my number efficiently a couple of times, and the opening exchanges with John go smoothly. I'm sent home at four o'clock, having only really worked for an hour or two. Spend the evening reading the script, revisiting lines and speeches, trying not to let it all slip away.

The way memory plays tricks and words drop from the brain can be alarming. Novelist Christopher Matthew told me on the phone today, 'Man goes to doctor. Doctor says, "Bad news, I'm afraid, Mr Hoskins. You've got cancer and you've got Alzheimer's." Man says, "Oh well, at least I haven't got cancer."'

I tell myself that I can actually learn a text in greater depth than I could thirty years ago. And all of us fluffed lines in rehearsal in those days, in a way I don't now.

Friday

In the apartments we meet our neighbour on the other side, Kendra, who works for a radio station. When she finds out that I am 'Mr Jeeves' she smirks, 'I'm always blessed with the leads.' She explains that the star actors are invariably billeted next-door to her. Certainly Lisa Harrow had our apartment when she came here to do *Wit*. I remember Kathy Campbell telling me, with awe, 'Mart'n, you'll be sleeping in Lisa's bed.'

At lunchtime I record a radio interview with Steven Baum, arts presenter for WQED, the local culture station. I think it's the one I've been listening to, because his voice, if not his name, sounds familiar. His initial bearing reminds me of Los Angeles film critic and biographer Richard Schickel, whom I have met several times. Neither man looks at you directly, and each has an air of world-weary superiority, as though he's really the interesting one. (Which, in Richard's case, is true.) Steven's questions are reasonable though and we record for half an hour, closeted in a cloakroom at the front of the theatre. One of his requests, 'Would you indicate how Jeeves speaks?' provokes me foolishly to recite two of Jeeves' speeches. Out of context, I don't get them quite right. He then, unblinkingly, asks if I will be including all the mannerisms in my stage performance. I reply that Jeeves' manner is – ahem – unique, and leave it at that.

Tim, the young PR guy, rescues me from the cupboard. When he called me yesterday afternoon to ask if I would do this interview he pretended to be a telephone-sales person selling theatre subscriptions. I was completely taken in, which I think rather embarrassed him. He probably expected me to be more on the ball. I then described to him my new ploy with the many advertising calls we've been getting recently. You tell the cold-calling sales person, 'I can't talk to you now but give me your home number and I'll call you tonight.'

This usually throws them and they say, 'Oh no, I can't do that.'

You come back with, 'Oh, you mean you don't like being called at home?'

'Yeah, that's right,' they reply.

'Well, nor do I,' you say, and replace the phone.

Tim laughed politely.

My new Jeeves shoes are here, so I wear them for the run-through. Also I ask for the Jeeves tie, which has a little hole in it for the mike.

There are various theatre folk out front. Heather Ayckbourn asks,

'How did your little dance go yesterday?' Which of course makes me wonder if my lack of expertise has been discussed at the Ayckbourn dinner table, or perhaps at one of the many meals they have with 'Miss Carter'.

'Dreadful,' I reply.

Kathy Campbell, sitting near, pipes up, 'You're not *dreadful*, Mart'n.' She possibly thinks we are discussing my entire performance. I'm not wild about her inflection, which suggests, 'You're not *wholly* dreadful.'

Sheila is keen on M&Ms and has offered a handful of them as a jokey sweetmeat reward to John Scherer. While we're waiting to start she dispenses them from a rattly plastic container. She commands John to lie down, then, having hidden the container under her sweater, stands over him and proceeds to eject them, apparently from her crotch, so that they fall into his mouth. She looks up at me and laughs, 'I can't believe I did that, Martin. Don't tell 'em back in England, will ya?'

Michael O'Flaherty has returned, having auditioned about a hundred hopefuls for *Brigadoon*, the Goodspeed's next production.

Molly Renfroe's urologist husband Dan is here with their pretty two-year-old daughter Charlotte. Unfortunately, the child is allowed to sit out front with Daddy and watch. She screams from time to time, particularly when John and I are on. A budding critic. John stops at one point and asks, 'Can we pause a moment?' He then breathes deeply for ten seconds, before saying, 'Let's go back.'

Afterwards Molly is extremely apologetic. During a break I say to Dan, with Jeevesian deadpan, what a beautiful girl his daughter is. He nods. 'Yes, and she's beautiful on the inside, too.' The urologist speaks.

I keep forgetting to bring on the *Times* newspaper in a scene where it's crucial to the action. Irritating for John. Afterwards Alan has hardly any notes, except a couple for me in the car scene. It's too strong vocally, he says. I know. I'm making up for my non-singing with too much speaking.

John closes our dressing room door and explodes: 'I just wish he would learn his lines!' He means Heath, who isn't quite accurate on several of his speeches. I know what John means, but feel in an invidious position since I'm not yet one hundred per cent myself. I'm still making the odd misquote, even though I really do know the lines. It's just the newness of the part. I tell John I understand but accept it takes longer than it used to. He says, 'Yes, but we've known we've been going to do this play for ages!' John is still young enough not to know how much harder it gets to commit lines to memory and retain them, especially when we've only been going for three weeks. I don't think Heath has attempted to learn any of it ahead of time. Three years ago I wouldn't have done either.

Saturday

It says on the call sheet that the 'sitz probe' is at 4.30 p.m. today. So what's that? Harry Potter Dan tells me it's the initial meeting with the band, where we sit down and probe our relationship with the music for the first time.

'It's more relaxing than a 'wandel' probe,' chimes in lugubrious Don Stephenson, 'where you have to walk around.'

Award-winning Bobby Grayson has arrived backstage. I can hear from his voice he's a Texan. He twirls me into a protective gown, sits me in the chair and wields his magic scissors, bumping and grinding around me with the fluidity of a dancer. He tells me that's what he was: 'I always used to cut the girls' hair in the shows I was in, Mart'n. Just for fun. And because I was darn good at it, of course. Oh yeah, babe.'

I nod carefully as the blades swoop in.

'Then one glorious day,' he continues, 'when I was in the national tour of *Oklahoma*, they got the schedule wrong for the Cleveland opening and the wig person didn't show up. Nor did the hair. So – yep, you guessed – the company manager kinda went down on his knees (if you get my drift) and begged me to see if I couldn't do something with some scratch wigs they had in the truck. It was a full-scale emergency, Mart'n, audience out front and the curtain due up in fifteen minutes. Well, I'm happy to tell you I rescued the production that night and my new career was born. Yessir – and I carried on doing the wigs *and* dancing in the show. For one helluva year.'

'Wow,' I manage, as he bends low to snip around my left lobe.

'Oh sure,' he breathes, shimmying behind me towards the other ear, 'they re-choreographed all my exits so I could be first off to attend to the hair. Then my first Broadway show was quite a smash, Mart'n, *Steel Magnolias*. It's all about hair – and Texas. Perfect for me, actually.'

As he thins me out on top I find, somehow, the conversation has moved on to sexuality. Then, as he chips in, American football. He asks me if I've heard of so and so, a famous multi-millionaire super-star quarter-back for the Dallas Cowboys. 'Mart'n, I know *for a fact*,' he gives me a coquettish look in the mirror as he snips, 'yeah, *for a fact* – that he's gay. Oh yeah, baby. Now wouldn't it be incredible Mart'n, just think what it would do for the gay community if he were to come out?'

I tell him I see his point, but wonder what it might do for the football community.

He cocks his head to one side and widens his mouth. 'Ooh, yeah – I hadn't thought of that.' Then he goes up en pointe for a second, whips away the gown, returns to earth and says, 'Voila, baby! You're done.'

A minute or two later Alan nods approvingly at my glistening short back and sides and says, 'Hmm, you're too young for the part now!'

I was surprised when I heard that John was flying to Buffalo after rehearsal yesterday, and coming back in time for the music meeting at four-thirty today. Cutting it fine, isn't it? And suppose his plane is delayed because of snow, like they nearly all seem to be at present. All my 'numbers' are performed with him – I won't get the practice with the orchestra that I clearly need, indeed must have! Suddenly it's all about me.

I'm rather exercised by this, though decide not to make a formal complaint. In fact he arrives just before four-thirty. He slumps down beside me in the second row of the stalls, dressed very neatly in a black sweater and black jeans. I say, 'Interesting gear – you playing Hamlet or what?' He smiles.

Later, in our shared room, I can't seem to leave it alone. I ask him if he'd gone back for anything special. 'Oh, my grandmother died. It was her funeral.'

Of course. I apologise for my inappropriate remarks. He's fine about it. In the green room, the talk turns a little morbid. James Kall is amusing about his own grandmother's funeral and the female cousin who pursued him, throughout the burial, for two seats to *The Lion King*, in which he was appearing at the time. Even at the graveside she popped up to ask, 'You couldn't make it *four* tickets, could you?' James says he felt like saying, 'Put her in with Grandma, will you?'

Donna Lynne then defends the cousin. 'You do things like that when you're young.' She says she once hounded a leading actress about some audiotapes she (Donna Lynne) had made, in hopes of getting work in the star's series. Even as the actress lay sick in her dressing room, Donna Lynne was putting her head round the door and asking, 'Have you had a chance to listen to my tapes yet?'

The band is impressive. It's surprisingly affecting to hear the whole score played on different instruments for the first time. Fascinating, too, to watch Michael O'Flaherty finessing the combination of music and singing. I get through my stuff creditably. I confide to John that I've never done anything like this with an orchestra. 'You're joking!' he says, generously.

53

There's a relaxed atmosphere. Artistic director Ted Pappas has been popping in and out throughout the rehearsals. I tell him he looks slinky in the latest of a series of designer sweaters. This one is a sort of leopardskin, figure-hugging garment. I ask if he got it from Eartha Kitt.

'Oh sure, Mart'n,' he guffaws, 'Actually this *is* Miss Kitt.'

'Ah,' I counter, 'I wondered what happened to her.'

We talk about his upcoming production of *Romeo and Juliet*, which he's still casting. He then suggests that, after we've opened, we sit down and talk about doing a play together, here. 'A part you'd love to do, Mart'n?'

Hmm, another eight weeks in Pittsburgh?

I tell him about Patrick Sandford, artistic director of the Nuffield in Southampton, and how Patrick and he are very similar in what they are trying to achieve in their different theatres. He's enthusiastic and I promise to provide him with all the information.

Sunday

After today's two dress rehearsals Alan actually puts his arm (almost) round my shoulder, congratulates me and says, 'Well done, old thing.' Old thing! And a near-hug! Coming from Alan that's tantamount to a French kiss at least.

Sheila says no one would have noticed that I didn't get the little dance quite right. 'It was great Martin, because you kept going!' Ted jumps up and makes a little speech about how wonderful it all is.

Stephen Klein announces that we can't, after all, have complimentary seats for the first night, though we've already filled in the form requesting them. I ask Dan Rosokov's advice about this change of mind and he tells me he's bought a half-price ticket for his partner, rather than risk getting a poor seat the day before, or no seat at all.

There's an article in the *Pittsburgh Sunday Post-Gazette* about Alan and the production. It even gives information about Heather. I'm in favour of that as her contribution to the 'Ayckbourn experience' usually goes unsung. There are several photos of the rehearsals. None of me. I'm not surprised because when the photographers came ten days ago I was dressed in my rehearsal tailcoat, and they kept well away during the snapping session. I'm sure they thought I was Sir Alan's personal butler – discreet, irrelevant, to be ignored.

Alan tells a good story today about Andrew Lloyd Webber. Alan met Lloyd Webber in the Ivy restaurant one night. Andrew asked if he'd like to come back to the Adelphi where Trevor Nunn was supervising the technical rehearsal for the opening of *Sunset Boulevard*. Alan was delighted, having never seen a huge musical in preparation. They went backstage. Almost immediately Alan bumped into an actress he knew. 'Ah, how are you?' he says.

'Oh God,' she replies, 'wish I was working with you. It's a nightmare here.'

Trevor is in the stalls directing operations, barking into a mike. He sees Alan and Andrew cross the stage. Suddenly he gets up and, grabbing his coat, declares crisply, 'All right everybody, I think that's probably it. Thank you.' And wraps the rehearsal.

It turned out that he and Lloyd Webber had had a huge row about the production earlier that evening, before Andrew had stomped off to the Ivy. Trevor, spotting the merely sightseeing Alan, clearly thought he had just been fired by the mighty composer/producer and that his replacement was being paraded in front of him.

Monday January 29th

Because of the change of mind about comps for February 9th there's now no ticket for Ros. Huh. We'll see. We call in at the office and I hand Ted Pappas details of director Patrick Sandford. I take the opportunity to ask Ted's advice about the ticket, saying we're very happy to buy one if necessary. He says nonsense, of course Ros must come as his guest.

We wander to Market Square where we spy Court Whisman, Tom Ford and another guy (who turns out to be Court's partner Steven) through the window of Primanti's, a famous Pittsburgh sandwich shop. We go in and join them. It's like an Irish pub, despite the Italian name. Tiled floor, plenty of sawdust and a long wooden counter. I order pastrami, Ros has the chicken salad. When it arrives, on grease-proof paper, not plates, I have to burrow to find the pastrami, which is buried beneath cheese, coleslaw and french fries. Ros's salad is also topped with french fries. Delicious.

Later we go with Steve Wilson and John Scherer to see *State and Main* at the Manor cinema in Squirrel Hill. This is David Mamet's film about a Hollywood movie being made in Vermont. It's a satire on both the film industry and small town America. Writer-director Mamet is one of my heroes. This film is enjoyable and highly obser-vant but I wonder if Mamet's theory of 'no acting required' works against the life of the piece. Several of the actors seem to be doing less than nothing. Perhaps some of them feel more hidebound by reigning it all in than others.

Afterwards to Gullifty's. We talk, again, about the question that's exercising everybody more and more. Broadway?

The other day I had a call from my London agent, Jean Diamond, asking what's the news as there's a possibility I could do *What the Butler Saw* with Jane Asher in England, in April. So on Sunday I dis-cussed the situation with Alan. Things are not quite so clear cut as I'd thought. Alan says he has now discovered that nothing is firm. He's obviously frustrated by the lack of information from Michael Price at the Goodspeed Opera House (the theatre that originally premiered the American version of *By Jeeves*). And equally puzzled that there's been no news from Lloyd Webber's Really Useful Group. 'I'm desperate to get it all confirmed,' says Al. 'I'm probably not going to be available again until 2004.'

We agree they've got to pull their fingers out. I tell him of the specious quote I gave to a journalist the other day regarding Broadway: 'I can't say any more than this: if this glorious production finds itself on the Great White Way within a very few months, I shouldn't be at all surprised.'

Alan nods in despairing approval.

Tuesday

A few notes from Alan to the company. Mainly about diction. And from Michael O'Flaherty, who is very pithy and unsentimental in his instructions to the singers and musicians. He tells me he found the way I dealt with the Wooster Code references (reminding Bertie of his family honour) 'rather moving'.

Although just a rehearsal this evening, there's a feeling that it's (almost) a fully fledged performance. In fact in giving instructions, stage manager Dan refers to 'after the show – oops, I mean the *rehearsal*'.

Rumour is rife. Court pokes his head round our dressing room door and says, 'There's a lord out front.' He means Lloyd Webber of course. I can't quite think of Andrew like that. Only as the shy fellow with the fishy handshake to whom I was introduced by Sheridan Morley some years ago. Or the jolly jester who leapt to the piano at Hampton Court Palace during Prince Charles' 50th Birthday celebrations and played Everly Brothers hits, with Ros (and a few bold others) joining in.

We also hear, as the evening progresses, that producer Michael Price himself has been spotted. Dan confirms that Andrew arrived during the performing of 'Love's Maze' and was overheard remarking, 'It's the best ever.' Since he and wife Madeleine had just stepped off the plane from London he may have been referring to the British Airways inflight service, but naturally the consensus is that he's liking what he sees. Word comes back that, in the interval, Price has said that 'things are looking very good'. We are naturally in a mood to interpret this as 'Broadway, here we come.'

Those out front tonight consist mainly of theatre staff and all the ushers – mostly young people – who form the nucleus of what really does feel like our first audience. Maybe thirty or forty altogether. They laugh a great deal.

At the end of the intermission Wade Russo (as Ozzie Nutledge) is just completing the entr'acte music and the audience is, once more, rapt. John and I are ready in the wings to make our entrance when a strapping young woman with a smiling face suddenly presents herself in front of us.

'Hi. I'm Judy, your front of house manager. Welcome to Pittsburgh!' She has a Dame Edith Evans voice that I'm sure carries effortlessly to the back row. We thank and shush her all in one. 'Fab show!' she bellows.

'Ssh,' we plead. 'Whisper, for God's sake.'

Judy explodes with laughter. 'I am whispering. This is just me.' She disappears into the darkness. 'They're all loving it,' we hear her boom, as we stride into the light.

Afterwards Michael Price, dapper, silky-haired with a foxy smile, makes a point of introducing himself to me. 'Marvin, what can I say? You are *won-der-ful!*' (Well, that's a start.) He says the show is sharper than it ever was at the Kennedy Centre in Washington.

Backstage we have a few more thoughts from Alan. He tells me (*now* he tells me!) that all previous Jeeves had terrible trouble with the patter. He reminds me not to over-colour it. It should really seem to be just one long sentence, with a sort of 'fuck off' at the end. He says,

'Be careful, now you're more familiar with it, there's a sense that you're almost singing it.'

Eh? Well, tomorrow I shall attempt a little less 'up and down'.

We talk more about the minimalism of Jeeves' effects. 'There's so much going on around you, that it's always best when Jeeves is not doing too much.'

'Oh God. Am I doing too much?' I ask in horror, since I have been trying from the beginning to keep everything to a minimum.

'Oh no,' Al replies, 'but maybe in a week you might be tempted to. And you'll find more ways to minimise.'

Ah. I wonder what. And where?

Alan's notes about clarity of diction (and attention to detail) remind me of Sybil Thorndike, that great doyenne of speech in the theatre for whom Shaw wrote *Saint Joan*. After she died and the various legalities were taken care of, members of the family went into the house to clear up. As they were cataloguing the contents, they came upon a brown paper bag on which was written, 'pieces of string too small to save'.

I was a student at RADA when Dame Sybil and her husband Lewis Casson presented the end of year prizes. They both made impassioned speeches, and I remember old Sir Lewis emphasising, 'You musht remember, all of you, in your work, the vital importansh of dic-shon.'

In July 1969, after Apollo XI had touched down safely, Dame Sybil was overheard at the Arts Theatre saying to her husband, 'Oh Lewish, how marvelloush. If only we could be the firsht actorsh to play on the moon! How long oh Lord, how long?'

Rather like us waiting to go to Broadway.

★

Wednesday

Alan has to leave rehearsal early to do a press interview.

After Michael O'Flaherty has finished working with the ensemble, it's my turn. My solo is the second half of a musically dramatic exchange between Bertie and his man entitled, 'What have you got to say, Jeeves?' After enduring his master's criticism for apparently landing him in a series of problematic situations, Jeeves suddenly and surprisingly lets fly with this swift and coolly dismissive patter:

> I fear I must confess it, sir,
> Despite my best endeavours
> To ensure a fluid narrative
> Things haven't gone to plan
>
> Events were overtaken, sir,
> By unseen technicalities
> I really can assure you, though,
> I've done the best I can.
>
> There comes the odd occasion, sir,
> When facing up to destiny
> We'd do as well remembering
> A man is but a man.
>
> You have my firm assurances
> That come the grand denouement, sir,
> Events will all resolve themselves,
> In spite of come what may.
>
> I only can apologise
> For any inconvenience,
> Injurious to your dignity
> That happens on the way.
>
> I simply wish to emphasize,
> I have your interests uppermost.
> And that, sir, in conclusion, sir,
> Is all I have to say!

I try keeping everything downsized. Initially it's difficult to adjust to the swifter pace that a less emphasised approach engenders. Dammit, why didn't Alan tell me earlier? Of course I know he waited to see how I got on, in case I found it out for myself. Always better for the actor to make his own discoveries. Eventually I get it. One more go, and as I am pattering away, who should arrive in the auditorium but the composer himself, Andrew Lloyd Webber. He's come all this way and now has to walk in on the only non-singer in the company, who he may think is torturing his stuff. Actually, by this time I'm feeling rather pleased with myself and grateful to Al for the perceptive note. Actors, don't you just love 'em?

I move forward off the stage to greet Andrew, who is standing there with Ted Pappas. The maestro is cordial, his handshake firmer than last time we met. He chats affably to the musicians and members of the cast. It must be great for the band, I think, suddenly to be working not only with the music of arguably the most popular composer in the world, but also, now, to discuss the intricacies of the score with the man himself. Andrew beams all round, waves loosely and leaves us to carry on.

The show (and of course I have to keep reminding myself it *is* only another dress rehearsal) starts at eight. It's completely sold out. This is a cunning move by Ted. He has called it a 'gala' and sold tickets to all the rich founder members, friends of the theatre and others, who are quite prepared to donate up to five hundred dollars for the privilege of sipping free cocktails and seeing (possibly) something go wrong.

There's an air of expectancy backstage. It feels like a first night. As we hover behind the set waiting to start, there are speeches on stage for nearly fifteen minutes from manager Stephen Klein, from Ted, and from several local grandees. Then we start our first public performance of *By Jeeves*.

The play itself kicks off with several 'announcements' from the Reverend Pinker, which does us no favours tonight. We've had all that already. Nevertheless all goes pretty well. I feel apprehensive but settle into it, and there are no major gaffes.

As we wait to begin the second half, John Scherer and Emily Loesser discuss the fact that they both felt very nervous at the start of the show. Emily says her husband Don was jittery too. I tell them I felt the same. Emily stares at me in amazement. 'Mart'n, *you* were *nervous*? I don't believe it.' Clearly it had never occurred to her that the experienced British thespian was as vulnerable as any of them. The thought, not so much of getting the little dance right, but of not messing up the patter, hangs constantly over me. Suddenly it looms and – here it is. And, give or take a little parting of the rhythmic ways in the opening verse, it's fine. Wade, in the character of pianist Ozzie, sticks to me like white on rice and we finish neatly together. The audience applaud. They applaud more, then go overboard at Jeeves' self-deprecation when, having stalked off through the magic curtains, he returns as if by popular demand and bows deferentially, acknowledging this unlooked-for appreciation. Jeeves as old-time actor-manager.

Now – on with the dance. I don't get it wholly right, though who would know? They enjoy the idea of the perfect butler indulging in something so undignified, and then cheer at the unforeseen slice of vaudeville one-legged hopping and pumping that ends it.

The reception afterwards feels like a first night party. Pittsburgh gossip columnists are in attendance, well-heeled patrons, Joan and Jerry Epps, board of governors, the lot. Andrew Lloyd Webber is expansive, perspiring slightly like a bullfrog just out of the pond. Michael Price writhes across to inform me, 'Marvin, you're the best Jeeves we've ever had.'

'Thank you. Er – Martin,' I murmur.

'Michael,' he counters, misunderstanding me. 'Yeah, great stuff.' He pats me uncertainly on the shoulder and slips away through the throng.

We all stand around chatting and, at Ted's request, 'make nice' to those who paid the maximum. I ask Andrew how long he's staying.

'Well, Martin,' he replies, throwing his head back and puffing out his chest as though he were answering questions in the House, 'I'm going to Chicago tomorrow, on to Ireland, then London, but I think I might come back here.' He runs his tongue across his big lips. 'There's a couple of little things at the beginning I can help with. Bring a couple of octaves, if you understand me.' I nod sagely. I like the idea of Andrew travelling back to Pittsburgh with excess octaves in his hand baggage.

Alan chortles when I tell him of the conversation. 'God, he'll have forgotten what he came for by the time he arrives!'

A photographer who ignored me a week or two ago is here again but, now, what a difference. Good heavens, she's focusing her lens in my direction. She's stalking me, simpering, telling me I am '*marvellous*, Mr Jeeves' and shuffling me into various positions for shots with Andrew, with Ros, with Alan and John, and shots on my own. When I attempt to draw Heather Ayckbourn into a group photo she declines. 'Oh no,' explains Alan, 'she'll have to take her glasses off and she doesn't want that.'

The buzz in the large room is tremendous and Stuart Ells, who describes himself as 'Andrew's number two' (curious phrase), says he'll be working hard on the Broadway transfer. Hopes to have news in a week's time. 'But,' he puts his mouth close to my ear and mutters reverentially, 'It'll take a phone call from Andrew to the owner of the Helen Hayes to clinch it.'

He'd better get phoning, then.

Alan is beaming like a cheeky pixie. His voice seems to be disappearing, probably from a combo of apprehension, relief and making nice. He has been receiving plaudits all evening from the Pittsburgh patrons. Someone asks him if he's going to Chicago to see his two linked plays *House and Garden*, already previewing at the Goodman Theatre.

He shakes his head wickedly. 'No. Not a good idea. Heather's going on Saturday, and will report back.' He laughs into his glass of red wine. 'I remember one ghastly occasion when we had to go and see a production of *Bedroom Farce*. Not directed by me. Hated it. Terrible. Afterwards, in the street, I was so angry I punched a lamp-post. Heather said to me, "Now that was very silly, why did you do that?" I said, "Well, because the whole thing is so badly directed. It's so *wrong*, it makes me bloody angry!" Then of course we had to go backstage and there I was saying "Well done, marvellous, terrific," to the actors and director, with a bleeding hand in a blood-soaked handkerchief.'

The decibel level increases. Heather and Ros are having a conversation that I partially overhear: 'Madeleine really looks white. She's got a stomach bug. But she held up really well. She thought it went marvellously.'

I chime in immediately with, 'I'd no idea she was under the weather. Poor Becky. She gave a great performance.'

'No,' they say, 'not Becky Watson,' (who plays Madeline Basset), 'Madeleine Lloyd Webber. She was out front – she's eaten something and isn't at all well. But she thinks the show is at its best ever.'

Ah. Am I getting just a little over-obsessive about *By Jeeves*? Talk about brand identification. And anyway, why would Ros and Heather be concerned that Becky in particular thought it had gone well?

Two sculptured-haired ladies come fluttering across to where John and I are chatting to Alan. They keep up a combined excitable twitter as they present their programmes for John's signature, then mine. They chirp, 'Oh, the evening was so wonderful and, you know what, that Alan Agbern is so incredible, so hilarious – we've never seen a farce like it.' They continue at length, chirruping songs of praise to John and me, only occasionally turning to include the pleasant-looking, bald-headed man they have barely noticed. They notify us with pride that they are 'the only ones in the whole of the Ladies' Club who actually recognised Andrew *Lord* Webber'.

We (and the bald man) nod and smile, and off they scuttle, waving their programmes, oblivious to the fact that they have been in the presence of the master farceur himself. John and I feel embarrassed.

John says to me, 'Wow, you couldn't write characters like that.' Then, catching himself, he turns to Alan and says, laughing, 'Well actually *you could*.'

ACT TWO

Little Wittam

Thursday February 1st 2001

The learning curve of performances, begun yesterday, will continue. Alan gives very few notes this afternoon, though Andrew has had an idea about the opening number, for which Alan has already written a new verse. They feel this will tell the audience that the 'entertainment' Jeeves has apparently cooked up (to prevent the residents of Little Wittam having to endure Bertie on the banjo) will be a specifically musical one, containing all the accoutrements of song and dance.

Andrew listens to the music of 'Love's Maze'. He stands alone on the stage in a rumpled purple shirt, blue tie, grey trousers and dark blazer. He could be the secretary of a Berkshire golf club. Or managing director of a corporate conglomerate, on his day off. Which, of course, he is. Apart from everything else he is. But now he's working – listening, appraising, his moon-calf face thrust forward, mouth moving gently like some great amphibian (sweat-free after last night), a musical Mr Toad. Solemn eyes a-bulge, and watched by the rest of us from the front row of the stalls, he strokes his tummy beneath the purple and checks his flies (always a good idea of course). The number continues. He never smiles, though the rest of us have soppy ones on our faces at the silver purity of Emily's voice. We're all moved by the sweetness of the song, then its unexpected bucolic climax, as the tempo changes into a pastiche of a crazy Morris dance. Andrew's face finally cracks as though he's suddenly caught up with the joke. He turns towards us, nodding with satisfaction.

John, with me in attendance, tries out the new verse and key changes for 'Wooster Will Entertain You'. We gather on the upper level of the set with the band and Michael O'Flaherty. Lloyd Webber and I lean in tandem on the back of Wade's piano. We make further adjustments. It feels like a scene from one of those old backstage Hollywood musicals about Cole Porter or Irving Berlin. Andrew pats John and me on the back. It's decided we'll rehearse the new stuff tomorrow and put it in on Saturday. How very showbiz.

The preview goes wonderfully. The laughs are strong and warm, the music witty and delicate.

Once again, 'Broadway' is on all lips.

Friday

It's snowing outside the apartment. A sharp, bright Pittsburgh day. I attend to BBC work in the morning then ring my parents.

They are both eighty-five. And very comfortable in their new place, Sunrise, an assisted-living community in Sidcup. It's an elegant Queen Anne building set in seven acres of woodland and reminds me of a well-run country hotel. They've been there three months and are much enjoying their own spacious flat. There are still anxieties. Dad is worrying over his faulty hearing-aid. Or is it his hearing? My sister Angela, who lives ten minutes away from them, is at the rock face. Dad suffers from mild diabetes. He's been telling me on the phone that he can hardly walk, that he's 'virtually chair-bound' – then whizzes about the grounds at top speed, with Angela panting to keep up. Mum's collarbone discomfort from a bad fall on Christmas Eve is lessening.

There's no lack of drama around them. One amiable gentleman, an even newer inhabitant than they are, was recently removed from the community to a psychiatric hospital. It looked as though he might be expelled for ever from the Sunrise idyll because of sudden manic outbursts and diatribes to his fellow residents. He had apparently not been taking his medication. Mum tells me today he's now returned, humbled, fully medicated, amiable again.

Gillian Barge has been nominated as best supporting actress for *Passion Play* in the Olivier Awards. Michael Grandage for best director. I have some happy memories of Michael's production last spring and early summer in which I played the salacious 'Jim'. Sadly, when at the eleventh hour a transfer suddenly and unexpectedly became possible, I wasn't able to change my schedule in order to move from the Donmar to a commercial run at the Comedy Theatre. Even sadder, author Peter Nichols became irate with me because I wouldn't at once ditch all other arrangements and continue for thirteen weeks in the West End. Among other engagements, I was already committed to direct Gregory Peck in Los Angeles and I certainly wasn't going to try and wriggle out of that. I have since discovered there is a tradition in the theatre that it's fairly good luck to be the object of the Nichols ire. Many have endured it, including, at one point I'm told, the entire Royal Shakespeare Company.

Our own drama continues. This afternoon John and I rehearse the new lyric and, as I rather suspected, it's ready to be put in at tonight's performance. Michael O'Flaherty congratulates me on my 'song' last night. That's pleasing.

Heath Lamberts (having local knowledge) has predicted that the second preview audience will not be as responsive. He's not wholly correct. They aren't initially quite as vociferous as last night, but build well and the reactions are strong. Again I make a small textual error. Irritating to me and probably to John. I think my inner computer is still adjusting as each performance throws up more experience and knowledge of how the play works. Afterwards, I tell Alan, who is very happy with it tonight, that I'm not intentionally rewriting his dialogue. He comes back with his standard reply: 'Fine, but I'm not giving you any royalties!'

I mention to Heather how annoying it is to me that I'm making these tiny errors. She says, generously, 'But it's allowed, isn't it?' Yes, of course it is. I tell her it usually takes me a month to absorb a major part, and actually, I realise, we started less than a month ago. Ros, too, reminds me that I haven't had anything like as long as I usually have. I secretly think – and of course I know I have been going on about it to myself – that it would have been good to have had a few more rehearsals earlier, rather than some of those short days and loads of time off. Run-through after run-through can have a downside, but that's just my preference. I'm sure that, as I start to really get into the play, I'm adjusting, and discovering in perform-ance, various details that in a different rehearsal process I might have unearthed a little earlier. No complaints though, and I shall bash on, attempting to refine and clean up. I remind myself it was only the second preview tonight.

Saturday

Ros and I go in search of the olde worlde stationery shop discovered by Alan and Heather in which, they have told us, a cat called Inkblot lives much of the time in the window. The shop's closed. No sign of the cat. We walk to Curtain Call, to meet Leanne, the manager, who says she is excited about the *Acting Strangely* book-signing she is arranging. Me too.

One of Alan's simple masterclasses this afternoon. He nods the great cranium, angles it to one side, consults outer-space for a moment, then smiles briefly, almost smirks, before saying, 'Mmm, not new, but always worth repeating – remember the, um, innocence of your expectations when we gave our first performance on Wednes-day. How you gratefully accepted the laughter and reaction, not knowing when, where – even if – it would come. Mmm.' He nods again as though endorsing his own point. 'Laughs – expect nothing. Hope for everything.'

Wade Russo and I go over one or two of my early 'bits' in the first song. He congratulates me on the patter number. 'Mart'n, you're really booking it!' We do a little warm-up with Sheila. The Gay Gordons again. My designated partner is now Heath, cast in the role of the girl. I think of his Drum Major outfit as we leap and twirl outrageously, attempting to outdo each other, calling out comments in camp Scottish accents. Then, under Miss Carter's strict eye we embark on a more sedate Norfolk courting dance with special wool-teasing actions. We change around. I call for assistant stage manager Hillary to come and be my partner. Wade provides improvised country dance music, loosely based on the *By Jeeves* score. Variations on Lloyd Webber.

In the dressing room John tells me that Heath is still 'all over the place' with one of his scenes. Poor old John, who carries so much of the show on his shoulders, has really got quite a thing about what he regards as Heath's lack of consistency. Once again I feel I can't comment as I'm still combing out my own mini-glitches.

Tonight I have a fractional hesitation in the patter, luckily so brief as to be unnoticeable (except I'm sure to John). I pick up immediately and carry on. I've been dreading that happening and I suppose it's heartening, to some extent, to learn that I can rescue myself. Alan reminds me that Malcolm Sinclair had a blank with it on the Scarborough opening night and couldn't, for a moment, continue. Stephen Pacey as Bertie extemporised with, 'Poor old Jeeves, he hasn't eaten enough fish!' Pretty good. I vaguely remember the moment.

I receive emails from both my sons, Oliver and Toby. Toby is arranging to go to Miami. He asks, do I remember when we all went there twenty years ago? Yes, I email back: the air taxi was over the Everglades when the propeller broke and, after a frightening half-hour, we landed on one engine. I certainly remember.

I ring Olly. He and his wife Monika are both barristers. She's fine but had an 'experience' in court two days ago, when she saw lights. The doctor has told her to stop work now. The baby is due on March 17th.

I speak to my father. He's in a bad way, he says. 'Oh Martin,' he almost wails, 'I've virtually no hearing at all.' He hasn't been this despairing for some time. Mum comes on the phone and suggests he's exaggerating. Ten minutes later I ring Angela, who feels he's reverting to his anxiety state of about two years ago. He's told her he's convinced he has a brain tumour, which is causing all this.

Ros and I discuss it. Perhaps we should arrange for him to have a big test – the only way of convincing him he's all right.

Sunday

I'm learning all the backstage crew's names now. George has the deadpan face of a circus clown, and tells me that's exactly what he was. His surname is Valla. I ask him if he's related to the British actor, David Valla. His family, he replies, is a troupe of unicycling jugglers from Czechoslovakia. So, perhaps not.

Playing Jeeves is totally exposing. The problem – and the interest – is that the character knows all, sees all, never makes a mistake, controls all. He's master of his universe. So even a minor error feels, to me, huge. It's been harder than normal, I think, because I haven't had the opportunity to grow together with John in the role from the same starting point. He was at performance level after a few days' re-rehearsal. Inevitably, since he's played it around a hundred and fifty times already, I've had to build, in one sense, alone. Not necessarily a bad thing, I tell myself, since in the first Wodehouse story Jeeves arrives at his new employment and takes on from scratch the task of assessing, then dealing with, the eccentricities and idiocy of Bertie Wooster.

There were other manservants before Jeeves. There were other Jeeveses in this production before me. So, use it. Go figure, as stage manager Dan Rosokov would say. I might even be able to influence John into making one or two adjustments himself. My own performance is nearly there now, if only I can relax over it. I'm keeping it minimal, I hope, and the laughs are coming, without being 'asked for'.

After the matinee we do a quick question-and-answer session with members of the audience. They're from Carnegie Mellon University, where John, Court and Donna Lynne all studied drama. They don't have many questions. Two of them are keen to say they saw me at the Donmar in *Passion Play*. Rather a different part from Jeeves.

As I'm leaving the theatre with Donna Lynne, a well-dressed man in a business suit steps forward with a copy of my book for me to sign. He is courteous and American. He proclaims, like a talk show host, 'Mr Jarvis, it's a different role from acting Alan Ayckbourn's *Henceforward* and *Woman in Mind* in London's West End.' He seems to know all about my Ayckbourn associations. He continues, 'I was honoured to be present in the Scarboro' green room when Sir Alan announced they had got Mart'n Jarvis for Jeeves.'

This is odd. I can see that Donna Lynne is trying to signal me to leave. I sign the book and, as we walk towards the apartments she says, 'I'm pretty sure that was Alan's stalker.'

Ah yes. We've heard about him. The man who follows Alan everywhere and sees every one of his plays. Many times. Even infiltrates the backstage areas. We know he's already seen *By Jeeves*, here, four or so times. I decide he's harmless.

'Weird though,' says Donna Lynne. 'He's a stockbroker and very well off. Yet he behaves like a teenage pop fan following a group.'

Ros comes to the evening performance. In the interval she hears a woman say, 'There was a man in front of me in semi-silent stitches.' A perfect reaction to an Ayckbourn play.

Afterwards a group of us walk over 9th Street Bridge to the Park

Café. It's great to sit around with wine or beer and chat after a long week.

Ros tells us she encountered the strange stockbroker in the audience tonight. She was with Sheila Carter. He approached them and said he'd met 'Mr Jeeves' earlier. Sheila immediately turned to Ros and said, 'This is Martin's wife.' She then announced, 'And Ros, this is Alan's stalker.'

Monday February 5th

We send a letter to the Screen Actors Guild regarding their concerns about a recent proposal that agents should be allowed to become producers. This is now a possibility in the States and, based on our UK experience, we don't think it's a good idea. Monopolies and all that. Some of the very large theatrical agencies who already put their clients together in 'project packages' would like to be able to act as bona fide producers and, more importantly, sell agency shares to manufacturing companies of all kinds. This could open the way for agents to structure advertising deals for their most marketable clients, using their potential value as a sales advantage. If the agent is also a producer, it's likely to be in direct conflict with his job as an actor's representative, which is to obtain the best and fairest deal for his client, both financially and in working conditions.

Ros has talked to Alan and Heather about the possibility of our taking them out to dinner. None of us fancy Franco's again, which relieves Ros after her medicated lobster salad experience there. It's arranged for tomorrow after the show, at the Fish Market restaurant.

Heather reports briefly over the phone about her trip to Chicago, where she has seen *House and Garden*. Not good, she says. We'll no doubt hear more.

★

Tuesday

The usual warm-up with Sheila. I opt out of one particularly strenuous caper but we all finish up doing a Michael Flatley version of the Irish jig.

After it's over I find myself sitting in the stalls chatting to Mick Hughes. Neither of us can quite remember if he designed the lighting for *She Stoops to Conquer* (I was Young Marlowe), which we took to Canada and Hong Kong in 1978. This provokes memories of Peter Dews who directed me at Chichester in *The Circle*, which Mick definitely lit. Dews used to sit in the stalls during rehearsal and, if he was bored by an actor's performance, throw coins onto the stage. We chat about theatre 'bastards'. Alan arrives and joins in. Mick says that Michael Gambon told him he had been authentically scared of the eminent director, John Dexter, feeling he could tell what your darkest insecurities and fears were, and expose them. I certainly endured the effects of that cruel gaze and steel tongue when, aged twenty-one, I auditioned for him at the Royal Court Theatre. As I walked, blinking, onto the stage, he shouted out from the stalls, 'Ooh, a sports jacket! My! Aren't we posh…'

Alan has a story of one young actor, Tim, who could take it no longer. One day at rehearsal he screamed at Dexter for being so callous, shouting hysterically, 'Never, never treat me like that again.'

The director replied, 'There are people I wouldn't allow to speak to me like that who've sucked my cock!'

Dexter completely ignored him for the rest of the rehearsal period. A few days later, when organising the company's curtain call, he said, 'Right, Mike you're there, Derek you're there, then you others come on here – *not you Tim*.' He banned him from taking a call.

Alan then remembers another young actor who asked desperately for a day off from Scarborough (where Alan was directing him) because he had an audition at Chichester with John Dexter. The young man hired a car on the appointed day and drove to Sussex. He arrived half an hour early for his two o'clock audition. He hovered around the stage door and was told Dexter was in a meeting. He waited. And waited. Dexter finally came out at four.

The actor approached him shyly. 'Mr Dexter, I had an audition arranged with you at two o'clock. I've been waiting for you.'

Dexter gave him a glance and said, 'Well, I can't see you now.' He looked at him again, sighed and said, 'Have you got a car?'

'Er, yes.'

'Well, you can drive me to my cottage. We can talk on the way.'

Driving along, Dexter starts to put his hand on the boy's crotch. Then, as they continue the drive, he starts playing with himself. The young man grips the wheel, thinks of England. They arrive at Dexter's cottage where he collects some stuff and asks the actor if he's going up to town. He is, and Dexter cadges a lift.

When they're approaching London he says, 'You can't drive back to Scarborough now. You must come in and spend the night.' It says something for the dominating power of the director's personality that the young man felt it churlish to refuse. There was only one bedroom. 'No, no, you can have the bed, I'll have the sofa,' says Dexter.

The boy, of course, never slept a wink. In the middle of the night, in comes a celebrated writer friend of Dexter. The young man suddenly sees him standing over the bed. Then the great writer and great director have a big row over 'bringing your fancy boys back'. History doesn't relate whether our hero enquired as he left at dawn, 'I suppose a job's out of the question?'

Alan then tells an Anna Carteret story – of her fear of John Dexter when she was a young actress at the National. At the read-through of her first production with him she maintained a low profile. She read carefully and well. She kept quiet, saying nothing to offend the monster or to excite comment. Suddenly and inexplicably, in a silence during a tense scene, she accidentally knocked her script and it fell with an explosive crack onto the floor.

'All right, just a minute,' said Dexter, holding up his hand to halt the reading. He cast a glittering eye on Anna and said, 'I see we're going to have trouble with you.' From then on, he was a bastard to her throughout the production.

In our dressing room John Scherer talks about the American musical star, Betty Buckley, with whom he did *Sunset Boulevard* in New York. He admires her a lot. Once, she forgot the lyrics of her great solo, couldn't continue and finally sat down on the staircase with a desperate, tragic, 'Aaaagh!'

'But, you know what, Mart'n,' says John, 'I don't think anybody in that audience realised. They all thought it was part of the show.'

Comforting, in view of my own anxieties. I often feel like saying 'Aaaagh' and sitting down. But somehow the words keep coming. Though I have stored that excellent Steven Pacey ad lib in my brain, just in case. My version would be, 'I apologise, sir. I clearly consumed an inadequate amount of fish at luncheon.' Hmm.

Backstage tonight, I find that the student dresser has set up the cuffs of my shirt wrongly. I walk up towards the green room calling, 'Cuff-emergency. Cuff-emergency!'

George the deadpan clown immediately remarks, 'Hey Mart'n, I'm really surprised. I thought all British people preferred tea.'

David, a scrawny thirty-year-old crew member, has decided that during the performance tonight he will greet me in a Jeevesian manner as I approach any of the doors backstage. He bows, polishes the wood, kneels, and pretends to buff up my shoes. I smile benignly. This could get very tedious.

During my carefully orchestrated trip into the audience I pass Alan, notebook in hand, at the rear of the auditorium and murmur, 'Good evening, sir. Dinner?' He nods encouragingly. Ros and Heather have arranged our foursome for tonight. I'm not really sure now whether it's a good idea, or a good time. We'll only be able to talk about the play.

After the show I meet Alan backstage and he asks quite tersely (for him), 'Any sign of that taxi?' Ros has arranged to pick up Heather, and they'll be waiting outside to whip us smartly to the Fish Market. I ask him, tentatively, if he's all right.

He jerks his head sharply. 'Well, I'm just idling here.' It's one of his motoring similes. I think he means he's marking time. Waiting. Waiting for the Broadway news. Waiting too, perhaps, for the show to get into a better groove.

The taxi's here. As we're getting into the cab Heather asks me how the performance went. I thought it went fairly well, but out of courtesy to Alan say, 'Well, I'd better keep quiet in case Sir has a different view.'

He shrugs, and mutters, 'Bit Tuesdayish.' He continues to be as jumpy as I've ever seen him. Of course I think, is it me? My fault? Or just the prospect of the upcoming meal?

Things are not helped at the restaurant when, in spite of our booked table, no one comes near us for ten minutes. I feel responsible and go off to the kitchen to find someone. All I encounter are three waitresses salsa-dancing around the ovens. I ask for some service. Nothing happens. We wait, tensely. Alan suggests that he does the wine. OK. Though really it had been our invitation. We do the meal. I ask Heather about *House and Garden*.

'Dreadful – wrongheaded and totally disappointing,' she answers categorically.

This seems to throw Alan into further gloom. I suddenly get a sense of how particularly vulnerable he is – and must be feeling – at the moment. Indifferent reviews in Chicago at the highly respected Goodman will inevitably pull him down. Having never been unassailably established in America, will this not only hurt him but also, crucially, affect the chances of *By Jeeves* in New York?

There's no new Broadway news, except what Ted Pappas told me this afternoon: that Andrew has spoken to the owner of the Helen Hayes, Marty Markinson, demanding a decision. It's apparently a question of Andrew saying, 'If you don't let us have your theatre, you can't have any of mine in the West End.' Alan adds to this that things are 'going on' and we should know by Friday. I tell Alan that John Scherer has said he can hold on for another two weeks before having to say yes to Hal Prince. Alan retorts in mock anguish, 'Don't tell 'em that. They'll only hang it out longer.' We toast Alan and I thank him for his generosity and patience. Don't know what Al makes of that.

We all seem to have a lot on our minds.

Wednesday

After the matinee a woman with mad eyes is waiting for me in the foyer. She says, 'You're the reason I came to see the show. I've seen you in all the British shows on TV.' I sign her programme and ask her, graciously, if she enjoyed the performance. Surprisingly, in view of her opening remarks, she replies, 'Yeah, but the first act needs work.' She goes on, almost feverishly, 'There were people near me almost falling asleep. It's too long.' Then, wrong-footing me again she says, 'But Act Two was the greatest theatrical thing I've ever seen. Bar none.'

Well, there you are. Ros and I have been wondering whether Act One *is* too long, but I haven't considered how it could be trimmed. Interestingly, John said last night he wonders whether the first half needs to be shortened. We're all coming out with our secret thoughts. Though John and I agree that Alan might not be interested in cutting anything now.

I don't, this evening, mention to John the woman's remark about the length. Nothing worse than having to carry one hour and twenty minutes of a first half with comments like that ringing in your ears.

I get home to find an email from newly wed April Gow, our London neighbour, about our television aerial which she has spotted hanging perilously down over our conservatory. Ros immediately calls old friend Johnny Wright. In her panic she seems almost to be ordering him to get the keys from Tricia (our assistant), abseil up the side of the roof, lasso the aerial, lash it to the chimney before shinning down and landing safely, possibly to thunderous applause. All this to a man who's awaiting a hip replacement and has a fear of heights.

She puts the phone down. I suggest we ring back with a more tactful (and safer) version of what we hope Johnny will be able to achieve. She does, and Johnny agrees to deal with it tomorrow.

Thursday

All has gone well with the rooftop drama. Johnny and wife Jan visited the house, Tricia having delivered the keys at seven in the morning. The aerial was dangling perilously, but seventeen-stone Johnny, having squeezed himself through the trapdoor to the roof, hoisted it aloft, lashed it to the chimney and descended safely.

The company meet for afternoon tea at the William Penn Westin Hotel, near Kaufmann's. The Savoy of Pittsburgh. This has been organised by Molly Renfroe. The cast, plus Ros, Heather, Alan, Mick Hughes and Keith (Ian Knauer's partner) sit at a long table. A dinner-jacketed violinist plays a variety of classics: Bizet, Mozart – Lloyd Webber.

Alan, seated next to Ros, tells of Andrew's stay in this hotel last week. Alan visited him here, where he had taken the presidential suite – two reception rooms, two bathrooms, two bedrooms. Palatial carpets and trimmings, cinema-sized television screen, grand piano. As Alan walks in Andrew says, 'Welcome to the hotel from hell!'

When Andrew came to dinner with the Ayckbourns in Scarbor-

ough a year or two ago, his office sent, beforehand, a list of requirements. There were various dietary details and also a note that he
needed a piano in case the muse should strike at any time during the
visit. Alan and Heather had, in fact, just got rid of an old upright so
the theatre had to truck one up the hill. When Andrew arrived, Alan
showed him around, proudly indicating the piano, which Andrew
barely glanced at. He was there for three hours and never went near
it. Alan wonders whether he should himself always request the availability of paper and pencil in case the muse strikes him at any time.

Back at the theatre for a short company meeting. After the fun this
afternoon, Alan looks gloomy again. So it's quite a surprise when he
gets up and announces that it now seems likely that Andrew's company, The Really Useful Group (RUG) is going to finance the whole
production on Broadway. Great. He isn't gloomy at all. It's ninety per
cent certain, he continues, and all that now has to happen is a little
juggling so that we can move into the Helen Hayes and another production can go elsewhere. Also, RUG wants to whisk *By Jeeves* off to
Canada to film the show for television and video, probably between
the end of the run here on March 4th and the beginning of Broadway. Alan says he has made it clear to RUG that he is not free after
mid-May, as he'll have his next production in Scarborough and, 'I
can't leave a new play.' He refers to it as a mother might say, 'I can't
leave my new baby.' So everything has to start before then.

Later Alan confirms to me that it's more like ninety-eight per cent
certain it will now all happen. The atmosphere around the dressing
rooms is buoyant, though there's a slight note of scepticism from
John, Donna Lynne and one or two others. John reminds me, 'We've
been up this road before, Mart'n. We were told we were going to
Broadway direct from Washington four years ago and then nothing
happened.' But I feel Alan wouldn't have made such an announcement unless he was absolutely sure. Or is he so keen to make it happen
that even he is going one step too far, too soon? I don't think so.

This evening's show feels like another first night as there are several critics in, including the most important (in Pittsburgh), Christopher Rawson. Alan says Rawson had better give us a good review after all the calls and conversations he's had with Heather. He's the one who published the big feature on Alan.

Interestingly *House and Garden*, disliked by Heather at the Goodman, has received excellent reviews in Chicago. Alan says, 'Well, if they can give that good notices, then *By Jeeves* should get raves.' Ah, but could it not work in reverse? Perhaps the cultural divide may operate against us: if they can rave about a production that we might consider poorly executed, then this one might get…?

It doesn't bear thinking about.

Friday

Today is our official opening. We always seem to be having first nights. I prepare cards and gifts. I try to write different but equally complimentary things to each of my colleagues, especially bearing in mind those that sit next to each other. It's fine to say something wonderful about them or their performance but not so good if they lean across and see that their neighbour has exactly the same comments on his card, too.

To Al I write that it's been a joy to work with him (it has), thanking him for 'allowing me to be a part of this play / production / musical / adventure, tick appropriate box'. Later I find he's used virtually the same words and sentiments on his card to me. I sneak into the theatre during the afternoon to deliver all the stuff, and bump into Mick Hughes. I present him with a small torch in acknowledgement of his powerful lighting.

He tells me that Andrew apparently has a reputation for getting on badly with the orchestra in most of his productions, and usually ends up sacking at least one band member. One time in New York, the story goes, he asked Alan J. Lerner, 'Why do pit musicians always take an instant dislike to me?'

The reply came back at once. 'It saves time, Andrew.'

Opening nights are an uneasy mix of patrons, theatre folk, nervous friends, wives, lovers, husbands and members of the public. All proceeds well. I'm relieved to have got through the patter number without recourse to any fish references. The famous ladder scene between Jeeves and Bertie, in which Alan turns the world on its side, goes like a dream. Minutes later I'm on the home straight when suddenly, in the speech that begins, 'If I may correct you, sir,' I get a distinct flash of Malcolm Sinclair, the original Jeeves. I feel I have sounded completely like him (no bad thing) and hear myself missing a beat and talking non-Ayckbourn. Impeccable Jeeves becomes waffly and I take the speech on a less than neat detour, before wresting it back onto the rails. Irritating.

Afterwards Ros says, of course, that no one in the audience would have known. The famous old emollient.

Michael Price is backstage and wants to speak to us all. We gather in the green room. He beams around like a silky smiling ferret. He begins by saying that all the funding is in place for Broadway but that Marty Markinson, owner of the Helen Hayes, still has to be persuaded to relinquish the theatre. Andrew has made several calls. So has Alan. The problem seems to be that a one-man show called *Gershwin Alone* has a prior claim. Andrew has offered that production a three-month season at either the Duchess or the Garrick in London, but has been turned down by the writer-performer of the show, Hershey Felder, who is determined to be on Broadway in time to be eligible for the Tony award nominations. Michael continues by saying they'll be pursuing their goal over the weekend and hope to have an answer by Tuesday.

He then makes a final comment that doesn't thrill the assembled company. 'When you go to bed tonight, everyone, you should get on your knees and pray that this all works out.'

John looks across at me and mouths, 'See what I mean?'

It's certainly not quite the ninety to ninety-eight per cent that Alan, in good faith, spoke of yesterday.

As we're breaking up to go out front, Michael calls after us, 'Oh, the television deal from PBS is pretty well in place.'

Court Whisman and Tom Ford cross themselves as they leave.

At the party, Becky Watson's mother buttonholes me. She is an author of books on scuba diving and wants to discuss the literary scene with me as a fellow author. Like her talented daughter she also talks for America. Dance captain Ian Knauer's mother is here too. She turns out to be British, having lived in America for thirty-five years, and informs me that, through my interpretation of Jeeves, she has had a glimpse of my soul. Oh dear. Leaning closer she whispers mysteriously that I should visit a particular part of Montana, somewhere near where she lives: it would be good for my soul.

Does she mean, I ask her, that after going there I'd be a better Jeeves?

'No, but you'd find it there – your soul, Martin.'

Ian explains afterwards that his mum had been trying to say I would appreciate the beauty and spiritual nature of the place. Well, maybe. But not tonight.

I find myself talking to Christopher Rawson, the *Pittsburgh Post-Gazette* critic. He saw the performance yesterday and says he has given us a rave review, which will be out tomorrow. He mentions he'd love to do an interview with me, in the next week or two.

Many of us end up rocking and rolling to the disco music. Sheila's actor husband Mark Stratton has arrived and takes the honours on the dance floor. Not fair, of course, as he gets extra tuition at home.

There are two rave reviews already on the internet when we get back to the apartment at two in the morning. Rawson has been as good as his word.

★

Saturday

All the reviews are raves.

Al and Heather are at the theatre when I arrive. None of us liked the 'get on your knees and pray' comments of last night from Michael Price.

'Well,' shrugs John, 'that's Michael.'

Ted Pappas is encouraging, and mentions other options, including the Booth Theatre. It sounds a better idea anyway, larger than the Helen Hayes. John says it's his favourite theatre.

Alan presents me with a couple of bottles of wine, undrunk from his Ramada wine store. He and Heather will be leaving in the morning and won't see the show tonight. We hug each other goodbye, semi-awkwardly. We are both products of pre-hug theatre. One pre-hug product can hug a current hugger easily, but *two* pre-huggers clasping each other is more difficult. He slaps my back, beams and mutters, 'Jolly Jarvis.'

The show this evening is probably our best so far. Afterwards there are enthusiastic fans jostling at the stage door.

Sunday

Phone call this morning with my father who, incidentally, I think of every time I look in the dressing room mirror as I get ready. Jeeves' flat, sleek hair is a ringer for Dad's. It's good news. His ears have been syringed; lo, he is cured. The visit of the hearing-aid specialist is cancelled. He is calmer, and sounds fairly happy. A relief all round, especially for brunt-bearing Mum.

Everyone here is very excited that the old Pittsburgh baseball stadium is to be blown up early tomorrow morning. There'll be blanket TV coverage and, apparently, many tears.

'Mart'n, it's the end of an era,' PR guy Tim tells me, drawing furiously on his cigarette.

Leaving for the airport, Alan says, 'Time we got out. Some lunatic here has started blowing up places of entertainment at dawn.'

Now we're on our own.

We're really up and running. At the end of this afternoon's matinee the audience stand up and cheer, reluctant to let us go. I'm on top of it at last. John is superb.

We wear our mikes throughout the show. I'm lucky, as I can thread my microphone wire up inside my dark waistcoat and through the hole in my black tie. It looks like a very sober tie-pin. Others are less fortunate, especially those with quick changes. They have to tape the wire up their backs and the little black protrusions peep out from varying places, depending on the actor – from under her wig in the case of Donna Lynne (Honoria), over one ear (James as Gussie) or glinting under his brilliantined hair (John). 'Can you spot it, Mart'n?' John asks me. I can, just a little, but tell him that if any sharp-eyed member of the audience catches a glimpse they'll think it's his sparkling talent.

The sound is cleverly enhanced by engineer Zack, at certain points, especially over the music. This afternoon I find myself in the loo during my one break, and hope I've been faded down.

After the standing ovation of this afternoon, the evening show seems anti-climactic. I feel, though, that the audience is having a good time and I say to Donna Lynne I wouldn't mind betting they'll really come through stronger as the play goes on.

During the scene in which John is perched on the edge of the fountain at Totleigh, I notice he has a long piece of white cotton on his trousers, starting two inches below his inner thigh. As I stand there, I debate with myself whether, as his manservant, I should legitimately lean forward and pluck it off. I decide in the end that Jeeves making a dive between Bertie's legs could be worrying. This is not a John Dexter production.

The audience is hugely appreciative at the curtain call. Donna Lynne approaches me as if I'm some sort of guru. 'Hey Mart'n, wow, you were so right, they were great.'

I shrug modestly.

Monday February 12th

A phone call this morning from Michael Price. He's 'fairly certain' we've lost the Helen Hayes. Marty Markinson and the *Gershwin Alone* guy Hershey Felder have refused all Andrew's blandishments to release the theatre to us. Felder definitely wants to open in April and remain in residence until after the Tony nominations. Who can blame him?

'But Marvin,' says Michael, 'we can have any theatre we want after May sixth – that's the last day of the Tony Awards deadline.'

But what about our availabilities? It has to be sorted, say I, in the next few days. The filming for television still seems to be in place in Toronto. When I quiz Michael about details – exactly where, exactly when, exactly how – he really has no answer. I discuss it with Ros. She thinks we've probably had our chance now and missed it, as regards Broadway. I email Harry Forbes, an American publicity man I know who works for PBS, to see if he can shed light on what might, or might not, be going on.

In the afternoon we go up to the Manor Cinema, driven there by James Kall. Four of us: James, John, Ros and me.

At the box office we buy seats for *Hannibal* from a pair of whey-faced boys. They sit, side by side, bolt upright behind the glass, taking our money and handing over tickets without paying us any attention. Their blond hair is close-cropped, their wide blue eyes gaze above and beyond, minds orbiting perhaps in some far distant galaxy. Are they Venusians?

One of them has heard my voice and clicks his head crisply towards me. 'You British?'

I admit it.

He blinks, then remarks in a monotone, 'I'm studying Scottish.'

'What? You mean Gaelic?'

'No. Accent.'

'Oh. You're an actor?'

'Student.'

'Which part of Scotland?'

'Glasgow.'

'Ah.' I mention Billy Connolly, and attempt an impression.

He's not happy with it. The tow head shifts a little. He does his own version of Billy from within the booth: 'Whey, hey hey, go for it, an' OK Mam, I wanna dance.'

It's poor and misguided. I suggest to him it's not accurate.

'It is,' he counters. He stares at me, unblinking. As I turn to follow the others he rasps after me, 'It's based on the Billy Elliot boy.'

I see. Someone's given him the wrong Billy. I say, 'No, that's New-castle.' Opening my mouth again to elaborate, I reconsider and shut it. I'm not going to try my Geordie.

He clicks his neck, elevating his gaze to encompass the stratosphere once more. Clearly I'm the one from a different planet.

Hannibal is 'gross', pronounces John Scherer as we emerge from the cinema a couple of hours later. We're all in agreement.

We drive to the Brew Works along Liberty Road, beyond the Strip District. It was once a church, now a restaurant. It's really rather magnificent, with vast silver beer vats up at the east end where the high altar must have been. After trying the Monks' Brew ale at the long wooden bar we are shown to one of the booths, whose seats were probably part of the original pews. The food, including giant pizzas, emerges from what looks like the old vestry. Circular stained-glass windows echo the shape and colour of my quattro stagioni.

John and James talk about their touring days across America. Before James arrived in Las Vegas with *Fiddler on the Roof* their manager asked the company what grade of hotel rooms they would prefer; expensive, middle-range or cheap? James requested a 'view of Siegfried and Roy'. When he got to his room at the Aladdin Hotel he opened his window and there, directly outside, was a vast billboard of the famous magic show.

John once toured in *Cats* and each evening had to spend fifteen minutes amongst the audience before the show began. One night as he was crawling about the stalls 'in character' he was approached by a husband and wife, and much stroked and cosseted. Afterwards the couple, great cat lovers, came round to the stage door and invited him home for a feline threesome. He declined.

Tuesday

On the way to the theatre I meet Ian Knauer. He tells me that he and his partner Keith, having got rid of his mother yesterday (in the nicest possible way) were able to have their pre-Valentine's Day tête-à-tête dinner.

These gay members of our company are very sweet with each other. Very romantic and loyal. James Kall said yesterday that he sees his relationship with Randy as being 'for life'. They're funny, too. Ian was in our dressing room the other day discussing shirts. He told us that Keith had asked him recently, 'Which top shall I wear, this top, or that one?'

'And,' says Ian, 'I said to him, "That's not a *top*. It's a *shirt*. Are we really that gay?"'

I speak on the phone to Erin Connor and Jeralyn Badgley. Together they head the Los Angeles agency, Badgley Connor. Ros and I have been happily represented by them in America for some years. It appears they sent a bouquet on the opening night, which was never brought to the dressing room.

After some backstage investigation I find the flowers on a table in a dark corner of the green room, label obscured. I report back to Erin who is mortified and rather angry. I'm embarrassed. Perhaps I should have looked harder for them on the first night. She tells me she's going to ring Stephen Klein, the manager.

John arrives in our room and flings himself down. His attitude to Michael Price is very amusing. He admits he's so angry with Michael for not having a theatre firmly in place by now, that it's affecting his approach to the show. He's cross with nearly everybody about their timing; taking too long over speeches, hanging things out. He cries, 'Oh God, Mart'n, I'd make a terrible director. I'd just want everybody to do it my way! I'm such a control freak!'

He's engagingly honest about himself. And his instincts, especially about pace, are right. I certainly recognise those feelings of exasperation that can occur when you have an unusual amount of responsibility in a production. I think to mention (not now) how that frustration can be corrosive – particularly dangerous when your own performance is affected by it. It can become self-defeating if you are compulsively whipping up the speed, in an attempt to compensate for a lack of it elsewhere. You feel you are, sort of, playing the other person's part too. This is likely to leave the play or scene in a worse state than before. I'm thinking of my problems with *Caught in the Act* twenty years ago at the Garrick, when I had wanted to galvanise everything. It wasn't worth it.

All I decide to say at present is why doesn't he discuss his points with Dan Rosokov, our sympathetic stage manager?

To my relief, John says, 'Mart'n, thank God for you. You're a rock!'

I tell him it's great being on stage with him. Which it is. He says likewise. All very nice and just as well, since we are sharing the 'star' dressing room. Although, having recently enjoyed the communal living of both the Donmar and the Almeida, I really wouldn't have minded sharing with many more. But the rest of the gents are crammed together like sardines next door, so perhaps it's just as well we're on our own.

I don't feel like a rock. But I'm becoming more satisfied with what's happening on stage, and beginning to look forward to playing the house each night.

The fine-drawn canvas so essential to inhabiting the character of Jeeves is certainly having curious side-effects. I'm finding, in pouring everything inside, packing it down, that as I stand behind one of my two magic curtains waiting to come on, I am temporarily a monument of blinks, twitches, coughs and ticks, like a sufferer from Parkinson's disease or St Vitus's dance. Chunky Bob, stringy Dave, and crew members who operate the curtains or doors, watch in fascinated horror as I go through my pre-entrance mantra, trying to achieve maximum motor control. It seems to work though and, as Alan predicted, I'm finding fun and interest in doing the least I can – while thinking the most.

The Broadway question is still on all lips. I have many visitors to the room (members of the cast) asking my opinion, wondering what I know. There really is nothing new beyond yesterday's phone call from Michael Price. I'm starting now to agree with Ros that it probably won't happen, can't happen now.

Wednesday

An article in the *New York Post* today confirms that Hershey Felder has triumphed over Andrew, and bagged the Helen Hayes for an April opening of *Gershwin Alone*. It suggests that Marty Markinson, who owns the Hayes, had a 'handshake' deal with Felder before Lloyd Webber entered the picture.

John tells me that Markinson's theatrical taste is suspect. He is best known for booking a famously short-lived musical, *Band in Berlin*, into his theatre, when he could have had the Pulitzer Prize-winning *Wit*.

So what do we do now? Can we really find another venue? There's surely no time left for anywhere else to become firm enough to prevent John and Donna Lynne having to take up their jobs with the legendary Hal Prince.

A fax arrives from London. Producers from the soap opera *Eastenders* are asking permission to include an excerpt from *Just William*: the Beale family listening to one of my audiotapes. I email back that I have no objection as long as they don't say, "'Ere, turn that crap off or there'll be murder committed!'

It's Valentine's Day. Much more of a festival here than in England. Ros finds hers, in colour, on the computer. Mine, choc hearts. Outside the door is a packet of cookies and candies. Outside everybody's door. The good fairy later turns out to be company Mom, Kathy Campbell.

A call from my old schoolfriend Dave Nordemann. He wants to fly from San Francisco, where he lives, to see the show on March 3rd.

Ted Pappas is waiting backstage when I arrive at the theatre. Dan Rosokov bustles everyone into the green room, the corner of his mouth twitching mysteriously. He says that Ted will be making an announcement. This kind of thing happens in every theatre company I have ever been in, and always reminds me of school assembly; a feeling of excitement, togetherness, apprehension, in roughly equal proportions.

Ted stands coolly in one of his figure-hugging jumpers. This one is maroon and today he has maroon glasses to match. He says he wants to share what little news there is: a 'Really Useful' person is coming to Pittsburgh tomorrow, apparently to work out how the show can be filmed.

Well, that's good.

He asks us not to believe the press, which is reporting that the window is fast closing on Broadway hopes for *By Jeeves*. Things are still happening, and another theatre (he is not at liberty to say which) is under scrutiny. He adds, excellently, that he hopes this uneasy state of things won't affect our approach to the show. It's wonderful, and so on.

School dismissed.

After the debacle of the flowers, I now find my dressing room is like a jungle. A vast bouquet spreads itself across to John's half, plus several small trees, which Kathy Campbell tells me were left over from Friday's reception. Stephen Klein thought I might like them. I tell her it's generous but there's just no room, and remove all forestry to the corridor. Later I notice thankfully, like Birnam Wood in reverse, that all has disappeared. But Erin obviously made her point.

John tells me he has talked through with Dan the points that have been worrying him regarding the pace of the show. It turns out, John says, that Dan has been aware of them too.

There's not a huge audience reaction at the start of tonight's show, but I'm learning that it doesn't matter if initially it's slow. The response can build, and invariably does. For the second night running there are no birdsong sound effects, so I can't say proudly, 'A gramophone record, sir.' (Last night I said, 'Should have been a sound effect there, sir,' and looked darkly into the wings.) Funnily enough, as I stood waiting to go on for that scene this evening I thought, if it happens again, I might clear my throat and murmur, 'I had hoped to play you a gramophone recording at this point, sir. But as there was none available, may I take the liberty of performing a few bird imitations myself. First, sir, the willow warbler…' Luckily for all John came straight in with the next line.

I've been having twinges in my left ankle and heel. To do with the dance, I'm sure. I find I'm limping as I walk home with John and Becky.

I've got the contact proofs of the production photos hidden in my bag. I asked Hillary if I could borrow them overnight. She shook her head. Not allowed. But later she brought them into the room, put the whole folder on a shelf, looked at me hard and said, 'I'm putting them here, Mart'n.'

I didn't get it. 'Oh,' I said, blithely, 'so I can borrow them overnight?'

Again she gave me the look and said, 'I'm leaving them here, Mart'n.'

'Oh,' I replied.

And when I still seemed not to quite follow, she said patiently, 'So I won't know what happens to them, will I?'

Ah.

Thursday

Rumours in the press this morning that Andrew is still hard at work exerting his considerable influence and, says one paper, 'adding his weight' to finding an alternative theatre for *By Jeeves*.

My left heel is getting more painful. Feels bruised. I'm convinced now it's to do with the repetitive hammering it receives every night because of my wretched 'little dance', which ends with that one-legged hopping across the stage. What to do? Ros gives me a plastic bag full of ice and a wet T-shirt, which I wrap around my ankle. I'm sitting there at the computer this morning when the cleaning girls come in. An odd sight; a man at a desk with his foot in a large plastic bag. They vacuum around me. I've also got some arnica, herbal pills for reducing the swelling, and the anti-sprain stuff I was prescribed when I pulled a calf muscle last year leaping off the rostrum in *Passion Play*. Must consider reviving *Le Malade Imaginaire* sometime soon.

News from my radio chum in London that he didn't get the Head of Drama job; a BBC staff-member has been appointed. The lucky winner is a chap I approached a couple of years ago when I was attempting to set up an independent radio production of Shaw's *The Doctor's Dilemma*. He told me then he couldn't help and admitted he rather hoped my production wouldn't be made. I think he was nervous that small companies such as ourselves might start to take away work from salaried members of the BBC. Fortunately we managed to get a commission from Radio 3 and were able to produce the drama successfully, directed by Michael Grandage. Sad though, if there is fear and suspicion at creative ideas offered from outside. I believe our goals should be similar: to provide the listening audience with fine productions of great plays featuring excellent actors.

Ros has been asked to direct *The Cherry Orchard* for LA Theatre Works. Marsha Mason will play Madame. Not, this time, our friend Miriam Margolyes, who played it two years ago in England. She is currently in Los Angeles as the Nurse in Peter Hall's production of *Romeo and Juliet* at the Ahmanson.

Performances here at the O'Reilly are going well – better and better. I've made the shift upwards. It's an interesting feeling, and perhaps why one still does this strange job, acting I mean. To give a good interpretation is fulfilling in itself, no matter where it is. The job, then, for the job's sake? I'm a touch surprised, I suppose, that I think this way after all these years. Interesting how much satisfaction one can still find in developing a character, living more and more inside it, learning how to achieve the best effects via the interior thoughts, the physical approach, economy of behaviour. Well, that's the idea, anyway.

I've reported my ankle situation to Dan. He asks if I want to see a doctor. I'm not sure yet. I've now got a neat black heel support to wear during the show, which seems to help.

At the intermission tonight John isn't impressed with the audience, awarding them only six marks out of ten. I prophesy they'll rise to an eight during the second half. The finale (in which the whole company is dressed in reach-me-down *Wizard of Oz* costumes) is sensational. The audience cheers and stamps and will hardly let us go. John gasps as he staggers back to our room, awash with sweat, 'Mart'n, they were a *ten!*'

After the show we gather for a company meeting with Austin Shaw, who has flown in today from London. He's the film producer from Andrew's Really Useful Group, a tall, frizzy-haired thirty-five-year-old. He tells us he thinks the show is outstanding. He also says that Andrew has spoken of little else than *By Jeeves* since his return from Pittsburgh and that they want to begin filming imminently, probably after a week off at the end of the run. Where, or how, is not established yet. Both Ted Pappas and I make the point that time is of the essence, since many availabilities are hanging in the balance. Windows are closing. Also, Austin says, they are 'positively and actively still seeking to take it to Broadway. Andrew,' he goes on, 'is very angry that he's been thwarted and Andrew when angry is not a pretty sight.'

Court and Tom raise eyebrows at each other and nod sagely.

The mood is ebullient as the meeting breaks up, and James Kall leads a party to a karaoke club on Liberty Avenue.

Donna Lynne, though, is in tears in the corridor. Ted Pappas and I stay behind and ask her, 'What's the matter?' She says she's unable to cope with the pressure. She's referring to her upcoming fortnight's work on a prestigious concert performance of a new musical in New York. She's worried about withdrawing from it – it clashes totally with the proposed filming. She doesn't want to let anybody down, she sobs, especially Brad, the musical's director, who has worked hard to get her the part. Ted urges her not to worry, he'll ring Brad tomorrow. Brad has often pulled people away from Ted's own productions at the last minute, so there'll be no problem. Donna Lynne dries her eyes but I can see she is unconvinced.

I walk her back towards the apartments. She says she doesn't know where to place her loyalty. Rather awkwardly, I suggest that Alan sort of got there first. I also mention that for her not to be part of the cast recording of *By Jeeves* would be a tremendous shame. She's mollified, and apologises for her outburst. 'But,' she says, 'nothing like this has ever happened to me before.' I find that rather touching. She means, I'm sure, that for ten years she has been grafting away, singing, dancing, acting, auditioning, often out of work, and suddenly has three separate projects looming over her, all at once. A great position to be in, of course. I say, rather lamely, that it'll probably sort itself out.

I wonder if it will.

Friday

There's a new notice on the board this evening. It's headed 'A Fax from the Lord Lloyd Webber.' He begins by assuring everyone that 'we are going to take *By Jeeves* to Broadway. It is just a question of when.'

He then says it would be ideal if it could be this season, but realistically he feels that it is likely to be next. He mentions that Alan is prepared to rearrange his schedule to do either time, and so is he.

Michael Price's enlisting help from the Almighty is paralleled here, as Andrew says he *prays* he can keep us all together if we find that we have to go to Broadway in the fall. He concludes, 'Please rest absolutely assured that we are going.' Then adds that he will be back in Pittsburgh again the week after next, and signs off with congratulations on superb reviews.

Andrew's typewritten text is followed, on the same sheet, by a handwritten note from Alan Ayckbourn: 'PS. We're not giving up on this season. Everyone is doing all that can be done.'

Well, the phrase 'we will be going to Broadway' couldn't be more categoric. Interestingly positive. How did they get both their messages on one page? They must have sent the fax back and forth across England. Encouraging though, even if we do have to wait until the autumn.

Award-winning Bobby Grayson has returned to New York, so before the show tonight it's Sherry, the resident wig supervisor, who gives me a Jeevesian trim. I tell her about Skip, the ancient hair stylist at Universal Studios, who took one look at me on the set of *Murder, She Wrote* and quavered, 'Mousse and finger-combing for you, Mart'n.'

John Scherer tells me he had only four hours sleep last night. But he's on good form. During 'Travel Hopefully' in Act One, a man in the third row is talking on his mobile phone. John stalks off at the intermission, incensed. Judy, the stentorian-voiced front of house manager, is summoned and strides away to give the guy a mauling. Her deep vibrato has that same carrying resonance as Edith Evans, who also knew how to deal with audience members who wouldn't shut up. One night on the West End stage, long before mobile phones, Dame Edith and a fellow actor found themselves in competition with a gentleman in the third row who wouldn't stop talking to his neighbour. After a minute or two Edith paused, advanced to the footlights, peered into the auditorium and announced, 'I wonder if you'd mind raising your voice. I can hear you perfectly well, but I'm afraid my colleague is a little hard of hearing.'

Kathy Campbell, ruddy face aglow, is often around backstage, bustling and clucking and organising. Somehow she never looks quite right in the theatre. Despite being company manager she reminds me more of somebody's favourite aunt, or perhaps a visiting parent at school, checking up on whether the kids are OK. Or a wonderfully loyal fan who doesn't quite understand the mysteries of the acting profession but adores being there. In fact this is deceptive, since a great deal of credit for the actors feeling happy about spending so much time away from home in this chilly city must go to her.

Running errands, arranging travel, shopping, finding hotel rooms for friends, ministering to the sick, etc – all part of what she does.

She tells John and me that she loves watching the show, 'especially,' she rattles on, 'as Mart'n is putting in more of those little smirks.' Oh Lord. Am I? Certainly I am gaining control over more and more of the detail of my performance. I'm slightly thrown by Kathy's remark. I thought I was still minimising. But, I tell myself, nothing wrong with tactful developing too. Just don't tell Alan.

The ankle holds up tonight. Now to Curtain Call for a low-key signing of my book, *Acting Strangely*. It's not Cheltenham Literary Festival or Hay-on-Wye, but the customers are pleasant people, genuinely interested in the theatre, and I sell about ten copies.

Saturday

My left heel is still giving trouble, though I'm icing it like mad.

After the matinee Ros attempts to take a picture of me in my Pittsburgh Stetson, posed next to the 'Standing Room Only' sign. Difficult, because members of the audience are still bustling by in the cold. Two teenage girls and their mother ask me to sign their programmes. The girls tell me they are working on *Guys and Dolls* at school. I tell them that Stiffy was played by Emily Loesser, daughter of Frank Loesser, the illustrious composer of that musical. They are bowled over. And when they hear me pronounce the name as 'Lesser' they are amazed, and tell me that at school they always refer to him as Frank Loser.

Back at home we watch a TV biography about Judy Garland. I can trace connections between the singers' techniques mentioned in the documentary and the skills of our own cast. The musical theatre performer's world is subtly different from that of the actor. Surprisingly, it's less sentimental. There is a wonderful, 'glueing' symbiosis between the performer, the music and its composer. We – that is purely the dramatic actor – connect always to the text, the words, to the author in a wider framework. But the music and its notes are pretty specific – hardly any margin of error, no hiding place, no escape.

Sunday

I have been given a copy of Andrew's 'fax of intent', which I have sent on to Erin and Jeralyn. Also to Jean Diamond, my industrious London agent.

Had another of those odd conversations with my father this morning. Now recovered from the hearing anxiety of a week or two ago, he is on a more even keel. He keeps up a reasonable exchange for a couple of minutes before relapsing again into, 'I've got no go in me. I'm virtually chairbound.' As usual I avoid agreeing with him, especially since I know he does a circuit of the Sunrise grounds every day. So then he starts into me: 'You wait till you're eighty-five. You haven't long to go, anyway. What are you, nearly sixty?'

After the matinee we talk to the audience and discover there are now Jeeves groupies. Two couples have travelled from Florida to see us. They've also seen the London production. They affirm, 'We think this is the best version.'

The final show of the week. Maybe my dancing foot is starting to get better.

John's New York agent attends the show tonight. When introduced to me she makes no reference to my performance at all. That's almost an agents' rule. The only person important to the show is their own client. The rest are just necessary ballast.

Still working on minimalisation, I cut out another gesture tonight. Can't help the occasional raised eyebrow, though.

★

Monday 19th February

It's Presidents' Day.

Kathy Campbell tells me that Ros and I have been invited to dinner at Franco's (oh dear) after tomorrow's performance, by Joan and Jerry Epps, the influential theatre patrons who entertained the company at their Shadyside house almost a month ago. Kathy asks tactfully, 'Do you really want to go? You may be very tired, hen.'

I tell her I'll call Joan later, which I do, rather hoping that Ted Pappas has been invited too. He hasn't. Nor has John Scherer. I'm afraid I hedge and say I'll ring her tomorrow, mid-morning, when I know if our friends are coming in from San Francisco. This is a fabrication: I have David Nordemann in mind, who is coming on March 3rd. Only a white lie, I tell myself, so as not to hurt Joan's feelings. Penalty of making extra nice to them at the reception on the first night. I expect we'll go.

Having planned to see a movie – possibly with stage manager Dan – we don't, and slump in front of the telly instead. We sample Alan's donated Montrachet. Excellent.

The film on the local channel is *Gentleman's Agreement*, starring Gregory Peck. It's in black and white, made in 1947. He's in his eighties now, and when I had the pleasure of directing him for a day, just a couple of years ago, I found all that charm and sensitivity intact. His voice too, even fruitier, unimpaired.

I had needed a narrator for our Radio 3 production of Shaw's *The Devil's Disciple* in which we already had Stacy Keach and Shirley Knight booked for two of the leading roles. Mr Peck would be perfect: an American icon speaking Shaw's stage directions, guiding listeners through the story of the American War of Independence. I knew him (from his work with the Los Angeles Library Foundation) to have liberal humanistic views, and to possess a mordant sense of humour that would tally neatly with Shaw's tongue-in-cheek prose.

But how to get him?

I rang him up. After I'd explained the project, dropping the BBC's name several times, there was a silence, then in those leisurely, courteous tones, 'Sure Mr Jarvis, why I'd be happy to do it.'

Ros and I took a small recording unit to his Spanish-style estate hidden behind high gates just off Sunset Boulevard. He greeted us at the door, tall, upright, moving quite slowly, the great mane of hair now white, eyes still humorous under dark brows. As we were setting up in the gracefully furnished living room, surrounded by Mexican artefacts, ceramics and deep pile rugs he said, 'Oh Martin, Ros, I – uh – don't get my breath too well these days. May we record in short bursts?'

His reading of Shaw's epigrammatic scene-setting was spellbinding. After a few minutes he broke off, took a small paper packet from his pocket and announced, 'One moment if you don't mind.' He twinkled at Ros, 'I must take a Voca-Zone.'

As he popped a liquorice throat sweet into his mouth, I told him, 'In England we call that a 'fisherman's friend'.'

He paused in the act of picking up his script again and put it down. He looked at me long and hard. Then at Ros. 'Pardon me?'

'A fisherman's friend.'

He was enormously intrigued. 'Really?' he said. 'A fisherman's friend?' Then, as if unable to believe his own ears, 'You don't say?' Shaking his head in laconic amazement he repeated, 'A fisherman's friend...' And laughed a deep bass laugh.

Every so often throughout the afternoon he would stop, hold up his hand, glance at us enquiringly, and with new-found pleasure, declare, 'I have to take – ahem – a fisherman's friend...!'

When Ros admired the floor-mosaic of huge octagonal-shaped terracotta tiles, he said, 'Oh, Frank Sinatra appreciated those too. He made a painting of them and presented it to me as a gift.' Here he stood up and invited Ros, with me tagging along, to follow him to another room where the Sinatra original was hung. We gazed in admiration, if some bewilderment, at a white canvas on which were painted a number of small orange shapes. The colour was reasonably accurate but the tiles were square.

'Oh yes,' he laughed smokily, 'Frank had a unique way of seeing things.'

Tuesday

The ankle seems improved. I'm still putting arnica stuff on it and taking herbal bombs. Oh what it is to be in a musical.

Our neighbour Kendra has returned from a trip to England and comes in to say what a wonderful time she has had. She stays talking to Ros for twenty minutes. I'm in the bathroom and thus entrapped with no clothes until she goes.

The cliffhanging continues. What will happen to *By Jeeves*? John tells me he has had no option now but to accept the Hal Prince job. This means he (and Donna Lynne) will be in Los Angeles from April to June. Since we can't do the show without him, it seems we're scuppered for Broadway until after then. I don't blame him one bit. His agent checked with producer Michael Price before accepting, but there are no new developments.

Dan Rosokov has spoken today to Austin Shaw and says he's convinced the filming will go ahead for a March shoot. They are budgeting, initially, for nineteen days. Eh? He thinks they'll reduce that.

There's another standing ovation at the end tonight. Nine of John's relations are in front. 'So John, was it all of them on their feet?' I enquire.

Ted Pappas reveals to me that he's concerned John has agreed to do the other job. He says he feels *By Jeeves* is moving forward, not only because of the filming but, interestingly, 'New York directly afterwards.' Well, forget about the Broadway aspect for the moment – no one has made me any offer regarding the television. So what's going on?

I tell Ted that Ros and I have agreed to have dinner with Joan and Jerry. He twinkles at me through his spectacles. Tortoiseshell again today to coordinate with the beige sweater and slacks. He says he had tried to deflect our invite. I get the feeling the conscientious Eppses enjoy their position as co-founder members of the O'Reilly and take it extremely seriously.

Dinner at Franco's is all right and no sign of the medicinal season-ing that worried Ros last time. The evening is made even better because Ted passes by the window and we beckon him in. Joan is clearly a political force behind the scenes, a wealthy patron who can, to some extent, control the theatre's policy. She is anxious to learn about the credit the O'Reilly will receive on the Broadway marquee. Ted has gone home by this time so I assure her, crossing my fingers, that the theatre will definitely have one.

I'd like to be sure of mine, too.

Wednesday

This afternoon Ros and I judge the annual Student Shakespeare Competition run by the theatre. Children from about seven to eight-een take part, either as soloists or in shared scenes. It's rather moving, especially a pint-sized boy of twelve doing Romeo, a thirteen-year-old girl who is a mesmerising Richard II and a wonderfully flamboy-ant Cassius from a sixteen-year-old girl. A big African American girl of seventeen makes a feisty attempt at Hamlet. We both find it almost impossible to sort out the top ten who will go on to the final.

Indefatigable Ted is in the theatre this evening, touring the rooms with a calendar, obtaining everybody's 'conflicts' regarding the apparently now definite filming dates for *By Jeeves* in Toronto during March. I mention that I hope RUG will be contacting agents soon, and tell him about my two days, March 23rd and 24th, when I've been invited to Buckingham Palace to a book reception. It seems the Queen wants to chat informally about audiobooks to some of us in the industry. Is she thinking of going into the business herself? Look out Miriam Margolyes.

I overhear Donna Lynne telling Ted, firmly, that she will still not be available across the vital two weeks because of her concert performance in New York. Ted is beside himself at this and minutes later marches into our dressing room, eyes popping with anger, slams the door and explodes: 'John! You've got to talk to her! As a friend! We're only fixing it like this so she can do the Hal Prince show in LA starting April 3rd. What's the matter with her?' He self-combusts and leaves the room.

John and I discuss that there's not much he can do if Donna Lynne has made up her mind that the concert is more important to her. Ted returns in five minutes and apologises for his outburst. I make the point that perhaps a note to Donna Lynne from Alan himself, possibly via Ted's email, might help.

The show goes up ten minutes late. Which makes it hard for us and harder, too, for the audience. John is especially angry about this. James Kall is not appearing tonight, struck down with the flu bug that felled Steve Wilson for a couple of days. Understudy Tom Ford goes on for him and is a really excellent Gussie Fink-Nottle. Bulging a little from his tightly buttoned grey jacket and squinting behind period spectacles, he looks like a Wodehouse woodlouse.

Dave the stage carpenter, normally garbed in black leather, suddenly appears in the wings unrecognisable in a Fair Isle pullover and bow tie. He's covering some of Tom's usual stuff, racing on and off madly and shifting furniture about. Two hours later I notice that Dave has even dressed as a *Wizard of Oz* munchkin, which is Tom's usual dancing and singing role in the finale. I ask him why he's done that, since he's not going to appear at the end. He replies, with a stage-struck smile, 'Just wanted to see what it feels like to wear the costume, Mart'n. I love showbiz.'

Afterwards John spends time with Dan in the office airing various concerns. My gripe is the late start. I wait to talk to Dan but, as John is still in there, I give up and go home.

Thursday

I manage to speak to foghorn Judy myself, and at least we go up at a better time tonight, four minutes past eight.

Dan has told me that things are being worked out so Donna Lynne can do her performances in New York *and* film the show in Toronto. It now looks like we'll shoot in later March. But I need something concrete. Apparently a general manager has been appointed by RUG, who will start calling agents with some offers.

Friday

A fax is on my dressing room table.

Basically it indicates that Austin Shaw and the Really Useful Company have now set the dates for the recording and filming of *By Jeeves* in Toronto, from Monday March 19th for two weeks. Agents are being contacted forthwith.

James Kall is back as Gussie and it's a very good show all round. John is beaming again.

★

Saturday

There's a notice on the board from Michael Price, saying he won't, after all, be coming to the final performance in Pittsburgh – he and his wife have had an invitation to go skiing. He's thrilled that we will be going to Broadway. (Are we going?) He writes: 'Of all four of our productions of *By Jeeves* this is by far the best.'

Ted Pappas is reading the letter alongside me. 'How dare he,' he breathes. 'It's not his. He hasn't put a penny into this one. *We've* done it.' He is wearing his Eartha Kitt sweater, which adds conviction to his throaty growl.

In the evening John tells us that his parents are out front. He's clearly anxious that it will be good. Mysteriously, Saturday nights are notoriously difficult houses. In England, too.

It's a good performance, though the house is not as accessible as this afternoon's. Suddenly, from a few rows back, a mobile phone rings. Quick as a flash John says, 'Was that a cell phone ringing, Jeeves?' This gets a round of applause.

I hear myself replying, 'Can't have been sir, they haven't been invented yet.' More applause.

The show goes wonderfully from that point on.

Perhaps we should arrange for a phone to ring every Saturday night.

Sunday

There are two performances today. Between shows I do an *Acting Strangely* signing in the foyer – in costume. Various Jeeves fans attend, including an elderly gent who tells me he has read most of Wodehouse and quotes, in a strong American Texan accent, '"Lord Emsworth strode pigward." Yeah, ah'm from Dallas an' ah jus' love that!'

Later we watch the second half of the Judy Garland mini-series in which James Kall appears. James has recorded the whole thing so we ask him to call us when he re-runs the bit we missed while we were doing the second show. Ros and I go into his flat across the hall and watch with him, Donna Lynne, John and Wade Russo. The series is well-shot. James is witty as the tin man (Jack Haley). He's proud that his ad libs helped to improve the part from a semi walk-on to a principal role.

John is in expansive mood. 'God, I was funny tonight,' he announces. There are some people who are able to enjoy – and share – the richness of their own talent. John is such a one. And how much more refreshing than false modesty. He *was* very funny tonight.

Monday February 26th

We are supposed to hear today about the filming deal. I've forwarded Erin Connor all the information I have, plus my own thoughts as to what I might require.

At two, Ros and I go up to Squirrel Hill on the bus, with John. I keep them waiting, answering an email from Heather Ayckbourn. She had sent a message from Alan about 'the gloves'. I had suggested the other day that I could wear white gloves while operating the car. Not only, I felt, would they be appropriate for Jeeves when 'on duty' but might also prevent more of the burns I've been suffering as I haul on the rope. Such is the life of the theatre that it's not especially unusual for a major playwright and director to send an endorsement by satellite to an actor, stating that 'gloves seems a good notion.'

At six o'clock I am a judge at the final of the Shakespeare Competition. Fellow judges are Becky Watson, Stephen Klein, Ted Pappas and the Pittsburgh critic, Chris Rawson. He's late. He's the one who said he would love to do an interview with me. I've never heard a word since.

We sit in judgement. I'm surprised not to see one or two of the children we marked highly last Wednesday. Has there been some political chicanery? Ted tells me there are various schools that nearly always win, and that the organisers try to share it out. It's a full house and for two hours they do their stuff.

The judges retire to confer. Rawson appoints himself our chairperson. He is intransigent. He doesn't really want to discuss the relative merits of the students. I make the point that it's a Shakespeare competition and we ought to consider the way they have dealt with the verse: not breaking it up too much, obscuring the sense. Ted and others agree it's a reasonable point. Nevertheless Chris asks for our decisions immediately. He doesn't seem to write much down. Is it his choice that he declares as winner in each category? A minuscule Demetrius and Helena win the under-eights. I'm delighted the female Cassius wins the 'upper'. Two little lads win for a mini-Mark Antony and Boy from *Henry V*. Nothing for pint-sized Romeo.

Rawson dashes away looking pleased with himself, calling back that he has a deadline for tomorrow's paper. I wonder if he'd already written his piece about the competition, including who the winners were, before the evening began.

Tuesday

Erin Connor in LA tells me she has received a fax from RUG saying someone will be in touch on Friday.

Ted rings to say that Austin Shaw, the hands-on film producer, is now in Toronto, setting up a studio. He and Andrew will be back in Pittsburgh on Thursday.

The loudest laughter in the audience tonight comes from Jo Sullivan, mother of Emily Loesser and widow of composer Frank Loesser. She was the original star of his *The Most Happy Fella*. Now, apparently, she spends most of her time on Broadway committees and administering the multi-million-dollar Frank Loesser estate. She laughs particularly heartily at the antics of her son-in-law Don Stephenson.

Wednesday

There's an article in the *Pittsburgh Post-Gazette* this morning reporting that *By Jeeves* is definitely going to Broadway 'this summer'.

Interesting.

I'm now dashing off to the local PBS Studio. I've been informed by Tim, the theatre PR, that it's to be an in-depth interview with the local TV anchor. Not about *By Jeeves*, not about Ayckbourn or Lloyd Webber. Not about the wonderful reviews (even the bad one, in *Variety*, was quite good). Nor even about Broadway. No. They want to do a short head-to-head on my current appearances on the network as a giant butterfly (Prince Hilio of the Menopteras) in some ancient episodes of *Dr Who*.

Ros has generously agreed to act as my manager. A car arrives early, at half past one. Twenty minutes later we are waiting in the dilapidated hallway of an old building that might once have been an elegant mansion. We sit near a clapped-out elevator which, every ten seconds, sounds a high-pitched siren as if something alarming is happening within. An assistant eventually appears and escorts us (via the worrying elevator) to the third floor studio. I check with her about the interview, asking, 'How much time are you looking for?'

She thinks I mean how long before I leave, and says, 'Oh, you'll be home by three.'

Good.

We hover about in the studio, which is really a spacious drawing room with what looks like the detritus of a cooking programme set up at one end. There are two cameras standing off to one side and a sort of desk and a pair of stools where, I imagine, I'll do my chat. We wait. It's quite dark in the room, and no one's around. I wonder about make-up. It's now twenty past two.

Finally the interviewer arrives. He is a chubby, dark-haired man-child of about thirty-five. His face is glowing with an orange tan which, as he comes closer to shake my hand, I can see is a pretty comprehensive television make-up. His name, he says, is TJ and he is the local anchor. He tells me he's a lifelong *Dr Who* fan and has enjoyed my three different appearances in the series. Well, that's good. I don't know it well but I've always enjoyed the programme on the occasions I've caught it.

We sit on our stools. Ros observes from a chair a few feet away. Then follows an unconscionable delay, since there is only one camera-operator present, a homely-looking woman who arrived a minute or two ago and is now quietly knitting. A search party is sent to find the other.

TJ, Ros and I chat desultorily. For nearly an hour. This is all good stuff and could actually have been the interview itself, several times over. Still no sign of the operator. TJ tells me how young and dashing I look in *Dr Who and the Dinosaurs* and how astonished he is to find I am an 'older gentleman'. I'm equally surprised that, as a *Dr Who* fan, he has forgotten that that particular story was shot twenty-eight years ago.

Finally our other cameraman arrives. There's a further hiatus while they try to link up electronically with the room next door in order to be able to record. After ten minutes they're just about ready. Several arc lights hidden in the ceiling suddenly blaze on. Then they go out again, with a spooky sizzle. It's a power blackout. Yet another ten minutes, and finally with nothing left to say to each other on any *Dr Who*-related subject, we are about to begin.

TJ now tells me he wants to record four segments of fifteen minutes each. (Whatever happened to the swift chat and home?) He announces, 'Three, two, one,' and we're off.

Immediately his personality changes. Gone is the mild, nerdy *Dr Who* fan. He has transmogrified into a word-eating, large-scale television presenter who doesn't (or can't) draw breath. Occasionally I get a word in. He begins with a long piece to camera telling viewers that 'although you won't know who the hell my guest is, he's very important to the history of *Dr Who*.' I sit there with a talk-show grin on my face.

The conversation is all *Dr Who*-based and although I do manage a word or two about *By Jeeves* in one of the segments, I stupidly forget to mention where we're playing. I suppose it doesn't matter, since we're sold out. But still. This whole programme, wrapped around the screening of *The Web Planet* episodes in which I was the aforesaid insect, will be transmitted throughout Saturday night and the early hours of Sunday morning.

In the third segment of our interview TJ shows off by reciting the names of all *Dr Who* story titles from the beginning of creation. I can't resist correcting him a couple of times. He's not best pleased, and decidedly miffed when, after his second mention of Carol Ann Ford as the girl in *The Web Planet*, I remind him that it was Maureen O'Brien. (God, I'm a nerd myself.) He at first thinks I've got it wrong, then slaps his head as he realises that he's made a boo-boo. And since the budget doesn't run to any retakes, he will make this disgraceful error again and again when the interview is aired numerous times across the weekend.

We've finished. He's forgotten to 'cut in' the still photographs of *By Jeeves* we have brought. It seems he can't stay any longer and bustles off, leaving us to film the inserts ourselves with one cameraman, who has to be re-found as both operators have now disappeared. Ros directs the re-shoot. Then we're in the car and arrive back at the flat around five, two hours later than advertised.

Tonight a single camera is recording the performance from the back of the auditorium, which will be helpful to Austin Shaw's team in working out a shooting script when we film in Toronto.

If we do.

Thursday

Average age at the matinee is about seventy-three, I should think. A tottering ovation at the end.

We have a company meeting with Austin Shaw and other RUG officials, after the show. There are also two women here from Tapestry Pictures, a Canadian production company working in conjunction with Austin. Wasn't Andrew Lloyd Webber meant to be coming back to Pittsburgh today, somebody asks? Austin pauses for a moment, gives a half-grin and announces that all is in place for the recording at CBC Studios, Toronto. (I wonder what happened to those travelling octaves?)

I keep a low profile.

Another producer, Kevin Wallace, then speaks about Broadway. He says they are talking every day to theatres and it 'will happen'. June 15th is a possibility.

Steve Wilson puts his hand up and enquires how soon payments will be made for the filming. 'Each week?' he wonders.

'No, within ten days of the completion of shooting,' says Heather Goldin, briskly. She's one of the Canadians, a short, tough-looking redhead with a mannish native-American combo hairstyle of ponytail and short-back-and-sides.

Steve explains he meant no offence. He'd just like to know how to budget until the money comes in. He's still paying for his wedding.

They won't have any problem negotiating with him.

Afterwards, Austin takes me aside and murmurs, 'Your agents have not been contacted yet as, obviously, you are on a different scale. They'll be contacted tomorrow.'

I've noticed he limps, as if he might have something wrong with one of his legs. Do I detect a slight East Anglian accent? The Ham Peggotty of the Lloyd Webber group.

John Scherer asks if it will matter that his passport has expired. Apparently it won't, in his case.

Just as well; there's no show without him.

Friday

This afternoon Ros and I bump into the RUG gang in the street. They tell us they're very pleased with the way it's all going. Irishman Kevin is positive about the Roundabout Theatre Company, which is housed in the newly refurbished American Airlines Theatre on 42nd Street.

'It's not technically a Broadway theatre,' he says, 'though highly prestigious. And a great stepping stone to a full Broadway house – which would make *By Jeeves* eligible for Tony award nominations.' He concludes enthusiastically, 'It's pretty certain we'll go there in June. Firm news by Monday probably.'

As we part he calls after us, 'Keep your fingers crossed!'

I wish he hadn't said that.

John is jumpy tonight. He's heard that a New York promotional man, already working on the Broadway pre-publicity, is in front. Amazingly John makes a tiny semi-textual glitch near the end of a particularly good performance, for which I automatically apologise, though it's not, this time, my error. John, always on such a high as the show reaches its climax, afterwards says generously, 'I think it was me.'

We laugh a lot in the room about our shared obsession with perfection and the endless fascination of the craft of acting. I tell him I was always going on about it when my sons were young. Forever pointing out good (and bad) examples while we were watching television. And how, when I proudly showed Olly the final manuscript of my first book, he picked it up, riffled through, stopped at random to glance at a page and cried, 'Oh God, Dad, the first word I see is 'craft'!'

I encounter Heath Lamberts' agent afterwards in the dark street outside the theatre. He's dressed in a long black overcoat and velour hat, for all the world a Mafia don.

'Hey.'

He detains me with a gloved hand, bends close to my ear and emits a hoarse whisper. 'I look after Heath.' Without moving his mouth more than an inch or two away from me he half-turns to his client, who is smiling silently by his side, and clarifies, 'Exclusively. Yeah.' He winks, then turns back to me. 'Not a bad little show you got here. I was quite entertained watching you tonight. Liked how you controlled the action.'

I thank him. He stays close to me, nodding. I can smell garlic.

I make conversation. 'Are you working out of New York?'

'No way. I'm workin' outta right here in Pittsboig. I have – uh – fam'ly here. There's a lot goin' on. I'm gettin' a lotta contracts. I'm makin' deals in Hollywood and I hope to make deals in New Yoik.'

'Great,' I murmur.

'Yeah. If you've got the talent on your side,' he breathes, turning to Heath and clasping him in a tight, one-armed embrace, 'then you're a made man.'

Saturday

In the dressing room John and I discuss the fact that Steve Wilson, who we both agree is excellent as Cyrus Budge, and an extremely nice guy, has been (with the best will in the world) 'improving' bits and pieces of his performance. In an attempt to wring even more meaning from a particular exchange, he has been placing extra emphasis on several lines delivered to Bertie Wooster concerning the lovely Madeline. The confusions of the night at Totleigh Towers lead Steve, as the jealous jelly manufacturer, to accuse Bertie of 'procuring her for immoral purposes'. This has all got rather drawn out. And he's been backing it up with an over-signalled physical attitude. Ten out of ten for passion and panache but it's now too much. John isn't happy about the consequent slowing down of the pace. He feels, quite reasonably, that instead of the interchange being light and swift, the point has begun to get obscured. Alan once told me that so much of the humour in his plays occurs in the 'niches' between lines, almost more than from the lines themselves. If the niches become stretched or enlarged the laughs can start to disappear. Certainly the last few audiences haven't found the scene so spontaneously funny. John has now discussed this with Dan, whose responsibility it is, if he agrees, to pass on such thoughts to Steve. This he has obviously done; this after-noon Steve is clear and clean on every line and, what do you know, the laughs are back.

Despite all reassurances, neither my agent Erin nor I have heard anything about a deal for the Toronto filming. Suppose I had a major conflicting offer, another film or play, what would I do? Do they just assume I'm on board whatever the deal? What's going on?

Dave Nordemann (Nordy) has arrived in Pittsburgh from San Francisco. He's staying at the Ramada. Ros is going to pick him up by taxi at seven and bring him to the show. Nordy is a great worrier and on this occasion he's debating whether or not to bring his raincoat to the theatre – he hates 'having a raincoat'. I advise in favour of it.

It's always an odd feeling when friends are in. You want to be at your best, of course, but when you're up there on stage it's hard to get them out of your head. I tend to see the performance through their eyes, and wonder about their reaction to particular lines or scenes. It's even harder if you know your guests really well.

He seems to enjoy it. Afterwards I find myself telling him the audience was much better this afternoon. Oh yeah? On this occasion it's true. Ros, who hasn't seen a performance for some time, says that John and I are still doing well because we are clear in our intention and don't hang about trying to glean extra laughs. That's a relief. But she would say that, wouldn't she? I believe her of course because, hang on, I respect her judgement.

John and others have been worried about the big storm that is said to be approaching New York on Monday. This may close down JFK airport and make it difficult for those flying north to leave Pittsburgh on Monday.

We turn on PBS at midnight to find that *The Web Planet* is in full swing. It's surprisingly compelling. William Hartnell as Dr Who is more fluid and has a lighter touch than I had remembered from those long-ago episodes. They play chunks of my interview, twice or thrice, constantly cutting back to the programme. But where is Prince Hilio? Have I remembered my giant butterfly appearances wrongly? Was I after all not the leading insect? The Hamlet of his galaxy? There are other Menoptera whizzing about, but not me. Eventually a furry creature zooms in on a wire and lands clumsily on a lump of studio rock. It's me. It speaks. Not bad, though the dogged delivery reminds me of that Venusian boy at the Squirrel Hill cinema.

Ros kindly says it 'it cuts through the costume'.

Sunday

The final matinee – the last show in Pittsburgh. Or anywhere?

As always with last shows, I discover one or two new ways of delivering a line. I make notes in my script, in case I forget. Could be useful for the filming. And for later, when we reopen (if Kevin Wallace's optimism is to be believed) on Broadway. We're told some-body called Jim, a 'powerful guy from the Roundabout Theatre Company' was in front this afternoon. Good, he witnessed one of our best performances, and it was a responsive house. At the farewell party afterwards Ted Pappas reports that 'Jim loved it'. Perhaps we really will be opening there on June 15th after all.

All the weather channels say a storm is still brewing. There's further speculation as to whether we'll get away tomorrow. 'You guys should be all right, hen,' says Kathy Campbell soothingly, 'you're going the other way.' (We're flying to our house in Los Angeles.) She turns to Donna Lynne and John. 'But you New York folk may not have planes.'

We peer out onto Penn Avenue. It's starting to snow. Heavily.

Monday March 5th

Leaving town.

It's raining outside the apartment windows, but there's no more snow. Nordy has already left for the airport, grateful no doubt for his raincoat.

At the terminal, a television news crew lurks near the check-in asking for comments on the weather. I obsessively plug *By Jeeves* and the O'Reilly, even though we've closed.

The runways have been cleared and everyone gets away on time. Ours is a five-hour flight.

When we get to Los Angeles there's a message from Jean Diamond who says I've been offered the new Peter Nichols play. Can it be that cranky Peter, so cross with me because I wasn't free to transfer from the Donmar with *Passion Play*, now hopes I will do this one? Doesn't sound like him.

But no news from Erin Connor about Toronto.

That's strange.

We're supposed to start filming in less than two weeks.

ENTR'ACTE I

Los Angeles

Tuesday March 6th 2001

Jean Diamond is going to send me the Peter Nichols play. I already know I won't take it. I'm pretty sure it's the one about an old mother and her middle-aged son and daughter, which was tried out a year or so ago in Bristol. This production starts in July, tours and 'comes in'. Anyway, I'll read it.

Meanwhile I've changed a proposed recording date of a Clare Francis novel to April 10th, ie, after Toronto. If Toronto ever happens. Erin Connor tells me she has actually had a conversation with Austin Shaw, and he's going to fax an offer. Odd that RUG should be so far behind, since I would have to fly to Canada by the end of next week.

Spend the afternoon reading through the *Colonel Clay* material. This is our third series of *Colonel Clay – Master of Disguise*, commissioned by Radio 4. I've somehow got to concoct five episodes out of only three stories. I'll probably do that in the next week and postpone the *101 Dalmatians* audio recording I've been asked to produce in England, since it doesn't have to be ready until September.

Could even record it in New York during the time we're on Broadway.

Well.

★

Wednesday

At the end of the day Erin calls to say they now have an offer from
Austin Shaw in London, which she then faxes on to me. Jeralyn
Badgley (Erin's business partner who often advises on the finances)
also rings and says 'it's surprising'. It is. It's the same minimum proposal that was made to the other actors plus a ten per cent uplift.
This really is quite comic. I ring John Scherer in New York. He has
received the same offer. He says he doesn't know what to do and that
his agent is not being particularly helpful. 'One thing Mart'n,' he says,
'they can't do it without us.'

Thursday

I convey my reaction to Erin and Jeralyn. The offer is not acceptable.

I'm quite surprised by all this. While it might be agreeable to
young actors, for whom this represents the first time in a film studio,
it's really a million miles from fees I have established over the years.

Time is getting short.

The film transportation person rings me this morning. She says
they will require me to fly to Toronto earlier, in a week's time. I tell
her I don't have a deal yet. She says, quite rightly, 'We'd better leave
that to the powers.'

Hard-working Jean Diamond rings from her car – she's driving
back from seeing a show in Basingstoke, having previously been to
a Chichester matinee. She tells me she has had an embarrassed call
from the producer of the Nichols play: he had failed to check with
Peter about having offered the play to me, and Peter has said I'm 'not
right'. Well, that makes sense. I tell Jean I have no problem with that
at all; I was unlikely to take the part anyway.

I talk to Mum and Dad on the phone. Dad says the state of his brain is 'not good'. Then mentions he has just completed *The Times* crossword puzzle.

Friday

Erin and Jeralyn ring me on a conference call with the latest developments. Erin says, 'Honey, we are staggered but nevertheless we have to tell you.'

What's coming, I wonder?

She then says that Really Useful won't give me first billing.

Oh, is that all? I am very touched by such unremitting care and loyalty to me as a client. I explain that I wouldn't expect top billing, and that it would be wrong in the context of the production. I tell Erin that however great a part Jeeves is for me, Bertie is indisputably the leading man, with mine a marvellous second star part. I tell them I wouldn't want for a moment to take that away from John.

'But dear,' says Erin, 'yours is the title role!' It's wonderful to have such supportive agents.

We then discuss what money we should ask for, given that what is on the table is absurd. After talking it over with Ros, I ring them back. It's infuriating that we are only doing all this now, when we should have received a firm proposal more than two weeks ago.

Irish actor Jim Norton rings and we talk about Broadway. He's recently done an O'Neill play at the Roundabout Theatre and warns that even small apartments are very expensive in New York. Also, he says, the Roundabout is mostly made up of a subscription audience, which means playing to loads of empty seats or mainly pensioners – not ideal.

★

Saturday

We drive downtown to the Ahmanson for a matinee of *Romeo and Juliet*, in which Miriam Margolyes is the Nurse. Fascinating to see it in performance again, directed with great intensity by Peter Hall. My strongest memories of the play are Zeffirelli's Old Vic production in the early Sixties with Judi Dench as Juliet. And before that our school effort in the Fifties when, as Lady Capulet, I teetered about like a Tommy Trinder version of Widow Twankey.

Round to Miriam's dressing room afterwards, where she is busy making arrangements for a party she is giving for the cast tomorrow. It's great to see her and we tell her that she, Dakin Matthews as Capulet, and Michael Gross as Friar Laurence were excellent. Which they were. Also that the girl playing Juliet was very good, which Miriam doesn't particularly want to hear. She disapproves of this actress and thinks her performance is 'rather coarse, darling'. I felt it was effective and that she conveyed the teenage vigour of a bubbling fourteen-year-old.

Later I email Peter with congratulations. It really is a great 'young man's' play. Shakespeare I mean, not Peter.

Sunday

We meet up with our friends Ken Danziger and Tina Scott at Café Montana. Miriam had rung them to say she was upset because they hadn't asked her too.

'But,' they said, 'we know you are giving a cast party.'

'Oh well,' she then replied, 'I may not go, I may try to wriggle out of it.' She explains this by saying she doesn't like to feel even the slightest bit 'rejected', even though she's patently not available. She's obviously quite stressed, not having an especially happy time with the production.

It's good to catch up with old chums. I tell them about the insulting Toronto offer. Tonight the two-part film of *Lorna Doone* I shot last year has been airing on American television. Since I have featured in the trailers and there were a couple of good reviews, one in *Variety*, my performance seems to be coming out of it quite well. We zip through the tape when we get back. I've never seen it before. It's well directed by Mike Barker. I'm more convincing as Baron de Whichehalse than I had thought, despite some (possibly American) cuts. It's being transmitted against the SAG Awards so many will miss it, or maybe flip back and forth. That can sometimes work in your favour: 'I caught a couple of your scenes in *Lorna Doone* yesterday, Martin. Didn't see it all though. Looked like a great part.'

Monday March 12th

Erin's counter-letter seems to have worked. We can have 'as Jeeves' billed on screen and in advertising, if we accept second billing. I have no problem with that. We will accept business class air fares. Austin Shaw, even though expressing himself surprised at the amount of money I am asking (cheeky bugger) has doubled their initial offer, so he can't have been that surprised. It's still less than we want, considerably short of what we think is fair.

Having previously been anxious about what's going on with these negotiations, I'm now feeling buoyant and decide to come down a little in price. Jeralyn and Erin agree that this would be right. We'll maybe settle in the morning when Austin calls.

★

Tuesday

Nothing from Austin Shaw.

The paranoia that all actors understand starts to set in. Those taunting little thoughts start to buzz around. Have they, I ask myself, in order to save themselves money, communicated with Alan Ayckbourn, and then, on his say-so, got in touch with Malcolm Sinclair (the original Jeeves)? Is he even now mugging it up and practising his little dance? Could this multi-million-pound company really want to save themselves such a small sum? Perhaps they don't mind jeopardising the whole project by losing a leading actor. Or, it suddenly strikes me, do they want the whole thing to stop right here? Now there's a thought. And what would I do if tomorrow I was offered a theatre or television engagement whose dates conflicted?

Coincidentally, Jean Diamond rings. I *may* have been offered Sir Robert in *The Winslow Boy* at Chichester, directed by Christopher Morahan. No thanks. I tell Jean the current status of the Jeeves situation. She says that RUG always expect that everyone will kowtow and cave in.

At three o'clock I'm pacing anxiously around. At last I can bear it no more and ring Erin. She's not available but, talk of the devil, says her assistant, she has just had an approach from *Stargate,* a series shot in Vancouver starting on March 28th. Erin will ring me in ten minutes. She does and it turns out that Austin Shaw has just called from England, to say that he is going to bed now and will email tomorrow.

So, another uneasy evening.

To Chez Mimi for dinner. It's producer Susan Loewenberg's birthday and Sherry and Doug Jeffe, Ros and I are taking her. She won't drink anything as, she says, 'I'm on a very special diet.' She moves her wraith-like body and stretches a scrawny arm across to pick up her glass of water. 'I'm so fat,' she moans.

Wednesday

At 10.30 a.m. a fax inches its way out of our machine. It is from Erin, forwarding Austin Shaw's latest offer. He's now come up with some more, and is offering a business class flight to London after filming in Canada is complete. At last we have a reasonable deal. Now of course my anxiety has dissipated, and I say to Ros, I wonder if I should still hold out for what we are requesting. Ros says don't be silly, and reminds me of the 'Dennis' tale. Dennis Doty, husband of Jeralyn, once told us how he, as a producer, can never get it out of his mind that however nice and good the actor is, he (Dennis) is on the set every day with a performer he believes is being overpaid, whose agent screwed them when they were over a barrel. 'Not good for the future,' Dennis declared. 'I'll do my best not to work with that actor again.'

I call Erin and say that it all looks OK now. I remind her of the Dennis story, too. She says she hasn't passed the increased offer in front of Jeralyn yet; she'll ring before she 'sets me'. She calls back and says, 'You know what, Mart'n, Jeralyn said immediately, "Why don't you ask for more!" And Mart'n, I reminded her of her own husband's story, and she laughed!'

Erin calls again later and says she has now spoken to Austin at the airport – he's just arrived in Toronto – and they've closed the deal satisfactorily. I'm now to fly on Saturday. I'm pleased that it's worked out and think it's fair – certainly not extortionate.

But there's been something else in my mind. I have been thinking about John Scherer's deal and discuss with Ros, then Erin, that I believe it's likely his agent has an agreement with Really Useful that he won't be paid less than me. Ros disapproves of agents doing this as it means we have done the work, and the actor just comes in on the coat-tails of all our hard won experience, nail-biting and brinkman-ship. Well, if that is the case, John will now have a deal he could never normally have hoped for, with little involvement in television or film. I don't begrudge it him for an instant; his talent deserves proper recognition. He mentioned to me on the phone the other day he didn't think his deal had been fixed yet.

Bet it will be now.

The Peter Nichols play has just arrived from England. Out of date, as it's a letter from the producer saying how much they'd like me to do it. I toy with the idea of emailing Peter directly and turning it down. Or even accepting it.

For the second time today, Ros tells me not to be silly.

Thursday

A message from Miriam Margolyes. *Romeo and Juliet* is in trouble. The star-crossed lovers are now having an affair offstage. Two nights ago, neither of them turned up for the performance. They had decided instead to have a night of bliss out of town and phoned the theatre with the excuse that their shared car had broken down miles away. It later transpired they had already secretly warned their respective understudies that their own big chance onstage had come at last. So the understudies appeared in the leading roles that evening. Next day when the lovers returned Miriam discovered the truth. She was apoplectic with fury at such unprofessionalism. Still is. So are the most of the rest of the cast. She is equally outraged that the understudies went along with the plan, though she says they did acquit themselves nobly in the roles. 'But,' she continues, 'for the principals to leave the rest of the company – and the audience – in the lurch like that, well it's just not on.' She asks, is she wrong to be so outraged? Of course not. Unfortunately the director, Peter Hall, is in New York working on his next production, so nothing much can be done except to rap knuckles from afar. 'But I've given all four of them a bollocking, darling,' says Miriam crisply.

I'm glad I wasn't there.

Friday

My final contract was faxed from Toronto today. Erin tells me there are holes in it. She will study it closely over the weekend.

Tricia, our London assistant, has told Buckingham Palace I won't be able to attend Her Majesty's chinwag about audiobooks.

Susan Loewenberg has offered me the part of C.S. Lewis in the LA Theatre Works production of *Shadowlands*. It's in May. I might, or might not, be available.

I speak to Olly. He and Monika are still waiting. Their baby is due tomorrow.

ENTR'ACTE 2

Toronto

Saturday March 17th 2001

A lovely morning in the Los Angeles hills above West Hollywood.

Ros and I sit on our deck for ten minutes in the sunshine.

A tiny green hummingbird is zipping madly across the garden, pausing for seconds at a time, wondrously suspended in front of the jacaranda, then the roses, before flicking itself, against all the rules of aerodynamics, away over the hedge and into the canyon beyond. A dove with beige and cream undersides to its wings calls desperately to defend its territory as a marauding crow cruises above us. He's been considering for more than a week the possibility of nest-building in one of the great beech trees beyond our gates. The little dove will have none of it. She prepares for aerial battle. Taking off from the lemon tree, she makes a couple of circuits of the area, climbing higher all the time, then suddenly dive-bombs into attack, swooping, harrying, nagging, pecking the interloper who is more than three times her size. The crow doesn't fight back, merely ducks and weaves then lazily gains height and settles heavily on a branch at the top of the tallest tree. The dove returns to base and continues to sing, making her claim to jacaranda, beech and lemon. To say nothing of our surrounding Eugenia hedge where she successfully nurtured a family of four last year.

Ros will be here another week to supervise the roof being repaired, the deck repainted and possibly observe the beginnings of home-making for both dove and crow. And to have a second meeting about the Jack Nicholson film, which they haven't offered her yet. Small part, big movie.

At the airport the Air Canada flight to Toronto is over-booked and they're asking for volunteers to take the next one. I volunteer, not to stand down, but to be upgraded from executive class to first. The guy at the desk laughs and says, 'There is no first class on the flight. You got the best there is!' Nice try.

A young man called Marcello Onewa is sitting next to me on the plane. He tells me he works in internet marketing. He's had a weird overnight experience – his leather jacket was stolen from Miyagi's Japanese restaurant on Sunset Boulevard last night. Lost his wallet, money, keys, everything except his briefcase. Slept on a bench. He was about to call the Canadian Embassy when he decided to kneel for a moment in divine entreaty, while the early morning Hollywood traffic blared past. Next minute he opened his case and found his wallet nestling there.

Perhaps Michael Price has a point about the power of prayer after all.

In the flight magazine is a picture of me as Henry V from years ago, being used now to advertise a travel organisation. I can't resist showing it to Onewa, who probably doesn't believe that this young man is me anyway.

One of the forms I have already filled in, in order to be able to enter Canada, indicates I may be asked to demonstrate the kind of work I do. Fortunately the woman behind the immigration desk at Toronto airport does not invite me to give an indication of how I will be playing the role of Jeeves. Or ask to see my little dance.

There's no one waiting for me as arranged. I ring Tapestry Pictures. They're apologetic and suggest I take a taxi to the hotel. As we drive along the freeway into town I notice a large traffic sign: 'Jarvis Exit'. Is somebody trying to tell me something?

The unit driver is already at the hotel with my per diem, schedule etc. He'd been waiting at another airport entrance.

I ring John Scherer. We meet downstairs in the lobby. Austin

Shaw is there, plus Dan Rosokov and two new faces: Nigel Wright, a burly, husky-voiced Englishman who is music producer for the soundtrack (and CD) we shall be recording, and his engineer, Robin Sellars. Familiar names. Designer Roger Glossop has arrived from England with Nick Morris, who will direct the cameras. Alan of course is directing the whole thing and will be here next Thursday. Nick is a beaming, balding Brit, very relaxed. He's made a number of these productions for Lloyd Webber and is a doyen of the pop video world.

We decide we'll eat at an Indian restaurant five minutes away. As we set off, John steps alongside me, does a quick tap dance and twinkles, 'Well, thanks Mart'n. And thank your agent too!'

Aha.

Around the table we all chat about tomorrow's sound recording. Neither Austin nor I mention the negotiations that have been going on for the last few days, which still aren't completed. It emerges that he's thirty-four, father of two girls and lives near Ipswich. He's been working for Lloyd Webber for several years. He can testify to the one-off character of his boss. And if Andrew doesn't want to speak to anyone, nobody is going to alter that. Austin tells a story of once being in a restaurant with Lloyd Webber. A call comes straight through from Andrew's PA who tells him that Michael Jackson is on the line. 'No, no,' says Andrew, 'I can't take it.' But the PA suddenly puts Jackson through. Austin sees Andrew start to say 'Hello Michael,' and then deliberately press the 'off' button.

Nigel then chimes in with a throaty, 'Oh yes, Jackson: "I'm going to Tampa with the kids,"' and chuckles inordinately.

★

Sunday

The huge Canadian Broadcasting Company building is almost opposite the hotel. It resembles a great liner, sailing its way down the street. Rather like its junior sister ship across the ocean, Broadcasting House, which has been steaming up Regent Street, north of Oxford Circus, for nearly eighty years.

We spend the day working in one of the sound studios. We'll be pre-recording all the songs and music here over the next few days. When we film next week, we'll be singing to playback in front of the live audience. Well, not me, I'll do most of my stuff live. I spend a lot of today listening and watching John and others slipping right back into the groove. Donna Lynne Champlin is here, but flies straight back to New York where she has already opened in her concert performance, directed by the fearsome Brad. She'll be back next week.

In the evening I have a drink with Nigel, whom I have already placed, Henry Higgins-style, as from somewhere south of the Thames, probably brought up in the Fifties, not far from me in Norwood. I'm right; he's from Penge, Purley and Streatham. Former keyboards player with a group called Shakatak. Clearly reveres Andrew Lloyd Webber – he was specially chosen twelve years ago to produce a new *Joseph* CD and now works with him for approximately five months of the year. He tells us he spent fifteen months on the film of *Evita*. Nigel is laconic. Cool. Dresses in black. He's very good at his job. I watched him today, impressed at his 'ear' – how, with one casual comment he is able to improve the performance of one of the singers, or sweeten the sound of the flute or keyboards.

Our good-natured dance captain Ian Knauer has arrived, flying in like most of the others from New York. He too spotted the Henry V photo in the flight magazine, although he wondered if it was the young Laurence Olivier! 'I wasn't sure, Martin,' he says, 'because I don't really know what Olivier looked like.'

Erin rings and says she'll be sorting out the errors in my contract tomorrow. I suggest we'll still be working on it when the filming is finished and we're all leaving town. She laughs hollowly and says, 'Tell me about it.'

There's no Olly and Monika news yet.

Monday March 19th

I record my patter song today – just in case I need to perform it to playback, rather than live.

There is a film crew here, filming us making the film. *The Making of By Jeeves*. It's the usual adjunct to such a production and will act as a publicity tool for the project. While Emily Loesser and John Scherer are recording 'Love's Maze', the documentary director, Martin Harbury, corrals me into giving an interview about my involvement in the project, what it's like working with Ayckbourn and Lloyd Webber, my attitude to the character of Jeeves etc. As I speak I can hear the appropriate soundbites falling out of my mouth along with a load of guff, and can guess which bits are most likely to serve the promotional requirements of the project.

Dinner at a local Italian restaurant, with Dan Rosokov, Ian Knauer, Steve Wilson and John. Afterwards, in the brisk night air I walk with John (whose headphone ear-warmers have reappeared) to revisit the O'Keefe Centre for Performing Arts, now known as The Hummingbird, where we have both played in the past. I was here with *She Stoops to Conquer* in the late Seventies, bawling out Goldsmith's intimacies to the distant recesses of that three thousand-seater mausoleum. Toronto itself seems bigger now, more new buildings, wider streets.

As we stroll we catch up on any Broadway whispers. John surprises me by saying that the Roundabout Theatre is no longer a possibility.

Ted Pappas told him two or three days ago, 'That's over.' Apparently, says John, Jim of the Roundabout hadn't liked our production as much as Ted Pappas had indicated. They'll be doing *Major Barbara* instead.

Leaving John to continue walking, I go back to the hotel and join Court Whisman, Tom Ford and Molly Renfroe in the bar. Austin Shaw wanders in. Nigel is already ensconced. His tipple is gin and plenty of it, with a small amount of tonic. Chris the barman is pouring out a double and setting it before him. Even after a night out Nigel is raring to go. His jet-black hair (possibly dyed) is still razor-sharply combed and greased, and his heavy-duty growl is as sonorous as at any time during the working day. While he moves systematically through the several gins now lined up in front of him, I note how well he would be cast as the love child of, say, Ray Winstone and Bob Hoskins.

We find that our worlds, apart from Fifties Norwood, cross over at one other point. We both worked with the Canadian voice-over king, the late Bill Mitchell, whose Guinness and Gauloise tones dominated the recording studios of Soho in the Seventies and Eighties. Like Nigel he always dressed in black, but with the addition of a Stetson and shades.

'Marty,' Bill once said to me in the fragmented gravel that launched a thousand products, 'you, you're a classical actor – me, I'm just a noise...'

Tuesday

To the vast chunk of concrete and glass that is CBC. Today it's into costume and make-up for some publicity photographs. These will form part of the promotion that accompanies the TV transmissions, the video and no doubt *The Making of By Jeeves*. John and I are introduced to photographer Brooke Palmer, an energetic Canadian. On a bright white set, constructed solely for these pictures, we attempt to replicate the poster illustration of Jeeves and Bertie. Austin Shaw is there like a genial housemaster, helping to direct operations, very hands-on.

A catered lunch is provided – not enough to go round. As a producer myself I feel oddly guilty about this, and find I am suggesting that more food is sent for before discontent sets in.

Brooke tells me he's enjoying this shoot better than his previous engagement, which was publicity for a film starring three hundred rats. Fortunately there are none on our ship. We hope. And we still seem to be afloat, even if we haven't yet docked at New York.

I finish the session early and wander down the street to Chapters Bookshop where specially written Harry Potter *Comic Relief* volumes are on sale. I heard this morning from Libby Asher and Richard Curtis in London that my Michael Frayn *Comic Relief* reading did well last week. It was deemed the winner by the telephone voters and transmitted on Radio 4, thereby raising a few more thousand pounds. Shavings though, compared to the many millions raised already by the phenomenal J.K. Rowling sales.

Feel low this evening. Worried about Moni, Olly and the new baby – who is now late by three days. I go through the script, as we have a walk-through tomorrow for Nick Morris and his camera crew.

Wednesday

No news from Olly and Moni.

Working on the set with the cameras. Haunted at every turn by *The Making of By Jeeves* crew and their fly-on-the-wall technique.

Producer Heather Goldin asks me (very pleasantly) if I would care to sign my contract and I (equally pleasantly) decline, saying that I haven't yet had the all-clear from my agent. This reminds me of a similar situation when I was shooting my cameo role in *Titanic* in Mexico. One of the assistant producers used to appear every day with yet another incorrect version of the contract and, every day, I would send her politely away. She wasn't so phlegmatic as the charming Heather; she usually left my room muttering dark threats about replacing me with another actor, and I would smile back blithely and say, 'Bring him on by all means.'

Spoke on the phone to BBC Worldwide producer Mary Kalemkerian today about the 'Talkies' (the British Spoken Word Awards) and her invitation for me to host them in September. I tell her I can't yet commit, I may be on Broadway. Hmm.

An email arrives from Miriam Margolyes with a copy of Peter Hall's reply to hers, regarding the *Romeo and Juliet* shenanigans. Basically he applauds her concern and professionalism, but there's not much he can do about it. In any case he's completely involved in directing *Troilus and Cressida* off-Broadway. Let's hope those two lovers don't take it into their heads to take a hanky-panky night off in downtown Troy.

To a new film with Steve Wilson this evening, *Enemy at the Gates*. It's well-shot, though the 'estuary speak' of some of the actors doesn't remind me of Russian peasants – or Russian-educated folk. Two of the stars are Joseph Fiennes and Rachel Weisz. Doesn't seem long since Rachel was smoking nervously at the read-through of *Scarlet & Black*, the mini-series we shot in Eastern France. (Ewan McGregor was also there, playing the young tutor Julien Sorel. He was very engaging and shy.) Jo Fiennes came to see *The Doctor's Dilemma* in Oxford when we were on tour from the Almeida Theatre only three years ago. That was just before *Shakespeare In Love* was released and, when he came round to the dressing rooms afterwards, I had no idea who he was. Now they're all film stars.

One of the trailers shown before the main feature is for *The Score* with Marlon Brando, directed by Frank Oz. Appropriate choice of director perhaps, as Brando doesn't look quite real. I remark to Steve he resembles a great white muppet. Steve replies at once, 'I'd hate to be the guy who has to put a hand up his ass to operate him.'

Thursday

Olly's answer machine is on all the time. Where is he? Is something happening?

We work through the show, rehearsing with just a few cameras. Tomorrow there'll be eight. Sheila Carter has arrived to fine-tune the choreography. I seem to have remembered the details of my little dance.

Still hurts though.

I'm in my hotel room at around eleven p.m. when Ros rings from Los Angeles. She's just had the news from Olly that Amber Antonina Jarvis has arrived. I call Olly immediately. He's at home, it's four in the morning UK time. All is well. 8 lbs 3 oz. Moni is fine. She's in Macclesfield hospital and likely to come home tomorrow. She's exhausted. So is Olly.

We have a very emotional chat.

Friday

The Ayckbourns arrived last night.

A cast meeting this morning during which I make the announcement that they are now working with a grandfather. The fly-on-the-wall crew lap it up. Strange to accept people's congratulations when one hasn't done anything.

We run the play before lunch, after which Alan gives notes. He makes his usual 'take out the improvements' comments. Hopefully I've retained Jeeves' serious economy, as Alan only mentions my pronunciation of 'Not *at* all, sir,' as being 'rather American'. This provokes a lot of laughter – the one Brit in a cast of Americans getting a comment on his accent. Martin Harbury tells me that unfortunately they didn't have the camera running when I replied, in my best American, 'I'll try to work on my British.'

Some typically Ayckbournian tips to Steve Wilson (as Cyrus) 'not to enjoy'. Alan reminds him, 'This guy is deadly serious, he doesn't have fun.' A classic comedy caution.

Dress rehearsal in the afternoon with all eight cameras. I mime my patter number to playback for the first time, as I had got out of time performing with the pre-recorded music on its own this morning.

Austin Shaw provides several bottles of champagne after the rehearsal to toast Amber. Dinner at La Fenice with Alan and Heather, camera director Nick Morris and his wife Fiona, Roger Glossop, Sheila Carter and Austin.

The champagne's on me this time and I split the cost of the meal with affable Austin, my new best friend.

Back to the hotel bar where John joins us. Also Court and Tom. Later various others, but Grandpa Jarvis is starting to get decidedly woozy.

Saturday

Far too wearing, this grandfather business. Thank goodness it's a day off. Woke up in the early hours, slumped over the laptop, in the chair. Still dressed. Not sure I remember coming to the room.

Later on Heather tells me she heard I was 'very entertaining' in the bar last night. This is confirmed by John, who says I performed the butterfly dance from *Dr Who*. Several times. I do now have a vague memory of staggering about demonstrating how I attempted to land on the BBC rock in full Menoptera regalia. Court is amusing about my leaning towards him to say, intensely, 'You should do *Cats*!' Apparently, whilst swishing my glass around, I was suggesting to Sheila that Court and Tom should come to England and perform *Cats* in Scarborough. Intriguing idea.

After an unsteady morning I stagger down the corridor to the elevator. I'm going to the two o'clock matinee of *Mamma Mia* for which Austin has arranged complimentary tickets. In the lift I fail, for the third time, to recognise Molly Renfroe's mum. Molly's parents are staying in the hotel to help look after two-year-old Charlotte, and each time I encounter Mrs Renfroe I forget who she is. It happens again.

'Hello, Mart'n.'

I look at her blankly.

'I'm Bobby,' she laughs.

Of course. I remember now she told me her name in Pittsburgh. I have a slight problem with that as, with her American accent, I have assumed her name is 'Barbie', which I had thought surprising, not wholly appropriate for Charlotte's grandma.

Wade Russo is already in his seat in the theatre when I arrive. So are John and Steve. They look at me oddly and that's when I first get the inkling that there's a blank in my life. John asks if I remember saying we'll meet in the hotel lobby at 1.30 p.m. No recall.

Mamma Mia is bizarre – a musical based on the hits of the pop group Abba, loosely strung together to form an even looser story. Never mind, it's already a worldwide triumph for producer Judy Craymer, and is now on its way to New York. As it ends and the audience gets to its feet for a standing ovation, both John and Wade (sitting down) shrug, shake their heads and say, 'And we're still looking for a theatre.' That's showbiz.

Court Whisman says much the same thing at James Kall's apartment at seven o'clock, and does a brilliant parody of the final walk-down of the show. James lives here in Toronto and is giving a little soirée. Most of the cast attend. We have a few laughs about my state last night. I leave after an hour or two – as do some others who are going on to a gay club. I get a taxi back to the hotel and retire gracefully.

Earlier I 'spoke' to Amber – and Moni. They both sound fine.

Ros has now left Los Angeles. She's accepted a job in London, having been told she's too young for Jack Nicholson.

Sunday

A second day off.

Working on the text of *Wolf Winter*, the Clare Francis novel that I am going to record as an audiobook. I suppose I shall have to find voices for about thirty different Norwegian characters. Better, probably, to find just one – a reasonably authentic Nordic flavour and then rely on some (hopefully) subtle variations of tone and attitude.

I decide to go up the CN Tower. I stand on the famous glass floor, resolutely not looking down.

To a new movie, *Heartbreakers*. It's about a mother and daughter who are confidence tricksters. Not as compelling as *The Grifters* or *Dirty Rotten Scoundrels*.

It's Oscar night and Jeralyn Badgley's husband Dennis Doty (he of the practical deal advice) is producer of the television transmission. Ian Knauer invites us to watch the event in his room. It's all good fun and Steve Martin craftily mocks the pretensions of the evening, whilst simultaneously hosting it. Hollywood irony deficiency works in his favour. If the audience as a whole really perceived how far he is sending them all up, they might be less content. As it is, in an over-flowing cocktail of nerves and complacency, they adore him for his daring cuteness.

Gladiator slays most of the opposition and wins five Oscars. The great Albert Finney, nominated for a fifth time, is passed over once more. He's not there anyway.

And nothing for Judi Dench this time.

Monday March 26th

Because of the nature of *By Jeeves'* Parish Hall setting, Alan has decided the audience must be very much a part of the filmed version. In other words, they'll be rigged out in period costumes. So we now have two hundred wigged, permed and moustached extras, ready to react spontaneously (perhaps) to the action. They'll be with us for the next two and a half days.

Tuesday

We start our master recording of Act One. It feels very artificial. The togged-up audience does laugh from time to time, but we miss the immediacy of our real live audiences in Pittsburgh. This lot seem tired and uninterested. Court Whisman notices that some of them are rather demanding, summoning 'make-up' and 'wardrobe' whenever there's a pause for a re-set of cameras. 'Mart'n, it's all about them,' he says in open-mouthed astonishment, 'they think it's a movie about an audience watching a show.'

Kathy Campbell has driven seven hours from Pittsburgh to be a member of the Little Wittam audience. Stephen Klein is here too. They're in costume: she as a homely matron, he a bearded business-man. Typecasting for both. Stephen tells me how much he loves seeing the production taking shape again for the screen and wishes he was bringing firmer Broadway news.

The Toronto backstage crew are a well-meaning group, if slightly vague. One of them earnestly offers me a copy of tomorrow's shooting schedule just as I am walking on stage for my next scene. There's nowhere to sit when I come off the set, make-up and wardrobe staff having bagged all available seats. I suggest to the runner, Annique, that a chair I could actually sit on during some of the longer waits would be acceptable. She organises one to be brought in. Next time I make an exit I notice the seat bears my name, hastily scrawled. Oh dear. Did I go too far? I sit down. But soon I'm on stage again and, by the time I return, a fat wardrobe woman is heavily ensconced in it. Back to square one.

Later, I speak to Erin from the hotel. The contract has still not been finalised to her satisfaction.

Wednesday

Wake at four in the morning and can't go to sleep again properly.

A heavy day. Long takes. I was called three hours too early at eight o'clock. I don't get on the set till nearly eleven. Well, I'm used to that: in Mexico, shooting *Titanic*, I was once called three *weeks* early. I spend most of today's waiting time doing publicity for various cable television channels.

Small, jokey 'cod' interviews with each cast member have been taking place over these two days, filmed by Martin Harbury. I watch Court doing his. In close-up, he talks earnestly about the pleasure and privilege of working in detail with Alan Ayckbourn, delving into the text and exploring new depths of creativity. As he's expounding, the camera pulls back to show that he's dressed in his finale costume – a *Wizard of Oz* munchkin.

Heather Goldin asks me to sign a travel clause in my contract – same as yesterday. I tell her, once again, they need to pass it in front of Erin.

Rather in keeping with the plot of our play, it's all just a bit parochial here. At the end of shooting, Mary Young Leckie, one of the Tapestry producers, asks John and I to stay behind in costume for yet another photo. We wait on the set for ten minutes, only to find she is gathering up her entire family, plus one next-door neighbour, who have been extras for two days and all of whom want to have their picture taken with us. We oblige with fixed, knackered grins.

This evening I take Steve, John and Dan to dinner at the Milano. We discuss our undiminished enthusiasm for *By Jeeves*, the fact that it's moved to an even better level of performance here in Toronto and that, surely, it will go well in New York.

Won't it?

Thursday

We're lining up some close-ups for Act One when the cast are called to the meeting room. Everybody gathers round eagerly. Alan sits next to me. Austin has a sheet of paper in his hand. Ah. Is this the news we've all been waiting for?

In his Ham Peggotty voice, Austin announces, 'Well, I've received this letter. It's a fax from Andrew.' He clears his throat and reads it out:

> To the cast of By Jeeves:
> I am absolutely devastated to say that after unstinting efforts
> by Michael Price, backed up by several personal pleas and
> interventions, we have not been able to secure a theatre for
> our precious *By Jeeves* on Broadway. Both the Roundabout
> and Manhattan Theatre Club have basically chosen other things.
> The lukewarm *Variety* review did not help our case with the
> more conventional Broadway types and, as you know, the Martin
> Beck Theatre was not available for an immediate transfer. (*I think
> he means the Helen Hayes.*) I personally am distraught about all

of this. I know there is life for *By Jeeves* one day. I am only glad that we were able to get the finance to do a proper video so at least we all have a record of something that I believe to be very precious.

With all good wishes

Andrew.

Silence.

Austin folds up the sheet of paper. Stands there. Nobody moves. Everyone is stunned. I realise Alan, next to me, is in tears. Somebody thanks Austin for reading out the letter. Alan can't speak. I can feel his hot anger. Slowly we get up and troop out.

We are all remembering Andrew's warm message of intent, and the life-affirming 'it's not a question of *if* we go to Broadway but *when*...'

I talk to Alan and we share our furious disappointment. We wonder how long Austin has known about this himself. Of course he's in an invidious position. What a message to have to deliver.

We continue shooting. Throughout the day every break or pause is punctuated with members of the company exchanging thoughts as to what and why and how this could have happened. Has the *Variety* review persuaded Andrew that the Broadway critics might not be kind? It wasn't too bad a notice anyway.

We try to concentrate on other things. Alan has been asked to sign copies of his scripts on set, one of which is *Woman in Mind*. We talk about the successful run we had with it in the West End. He waxes lyrical about our Jarvis & Ayres BBC Radio production of the play last year, then breaks into a diatribe concerning the opening night of another of his plays. Staring morosely ahead he kicks at the chair in front of him and growls, 'Yes, poor Heather was reduced to tears at the disgraceful way they messed up the first act curtain. Disaster!'

Alan's anger at today's news seems to have provoked an emotional re-examination of good and bad stuff in the past.

Dinner tonight is a strange experience. Some of us have been invited by the Canadian producers to the Avalon restaurant. The food is excellent, the wine flows. But it's not easy. We're all depressed. Alan can hardly respond to a toast to *By Jeeves*, then mutters something about 'more like a wake' and 'appropriate, as we are, it seems, burying the production here.'

Mary Young Leckie reminds me of my friend Davina Belling – both are film producers and both, on and off the set, are always keen to bring people together, to make connections. An actress friend of Mary's called Fiona is one of the guests. Mary probably wants her to meet Alan Ayckbourn but Al's in no mood for small talk tonight. In desperation Fiona turns to me. Initially she thinks I am the camera director. I tell her I'm one of the actors. She turns away and chats elsewhere. Then she learns from John that I'm playing the title role (she turns back), then, that I live partly in Hollywood (she leans towards me, smiling), finally, that I sometimes produce things (she moves her chair closer, very chatty again.)

Don Stephenson, who knows I am considering writing another book and guesses what its subject matter might be, leans across and says, 'You haven't got an ending, have you?'

He's right.

Friday

Today, amidst shooting pick-ups from various scenes, the cast decides unanimously to send a response to Andrew's devastating fax. Half an hour later we have put together a reply. At their request I read it out to the group:

Dear Andrew,
Thank you for your letter which, as you can imagine, caused
quite a few tears, not least from Alan.

We are all shocked of course, especially in view of your exciting fax of 16 Feb. We were thrilled that you asked us to 'rest absolutely assured that we are going to Broadway' and that it was 'just a question of when'.

Naturally we are all disappointed that this extraordinary production, which has delighted audiences since it opened in Pittsburgh, will not, now, have the opportunity to find its audience in New York in the fall as you had suggested.

We are all so sorry to hear of this change of heart.

With continued good wishes,

The Cast of *By Jeeves*.

It's sent to Andrew in London. Austin, whose fax machine is utilised for the purpose, tells us he knew nothing of Andrew's February 16th fax of intent.

I'm sure our letter won't do anything to change the great man's mind. Who knows if it will ever reach him? But it makes us all feel better.

Journalist Robert Cushman is on the set today. I remember him in London in the early seventies when he was the *Observer's* drama critic. I think it was he who described my *Hamlet* as 'fast and funny'. As we shake hands I can't help but recall having lunch with him once in the BBC canteen. He mentioned at the time that *The Spoils of Poynton*, in which I had just opened at the Mayfair Theatre, wasn't very good. I remember asking him on what he based his opinion since I understood he hadn't attended the play. He replied that a friend whose views he respected had seen it and not liked it. Robert is now a top Toronto critic.

A crowd of us go to the Wedge restaurant for dinner. Austin – in effect Andrew Lloyd Webber – picks up the tab. After yesterday's news it's the least he can do, we all think. Molly Renfroe and her parents are there. (Producer Mary's daughter is babysitting for Charlotte.) This time I make a point of talking to Molly's mum, and make sure she knows I know who she is. And I call her Barbie. And Bobby. It sounds much the same in my all-purpose American accent.

Molly is a witty character who has kept us laughing during the last few days with the improvised fantasy that she is the hostess of a popular daytime television talk show called *Good Morning Poughkeepsie*. Her programme has many 'guests' – all of us – and she drops immediately into the character of the alluring, iconic host: 'Well, good morning Poughkeepsie, and my guest today, after some cooking hints and a new make-over segment, is the British star of *By Jeeves*, Mr Martin Jarvis. Tomorrow we'll have a real live knight in shining armour in the studio: Sir Adam Ackbern.'

She could do it for real.

Saturday

It's the last day of filming. The final day of *By Jeeves*. Broadway, we're not coming.

We shoot a variety of pick-ups and close-ups.

A photo taken by Brooke, the lively photographer, appears in the *Star* this morning, accompanied by an article written by a journalist who visited the set the other day. He had worn dark glasses the whole time. In his piece he describes me, curiously, as a 'well-known Canadian actor and scene-stealer'. Alan comments that the large number of inaccurate observations is presumably because he couldn't see through his shades.

My contract makes a positively final appearance in my room, delivered by the determined Heather Goldin. Hilariously, there is still a discrepancy. I insert (and sign) an emendation and later show it to Austin who acknowledges it's still not quite right. I ask him if he'd mind initialling my final corrections. Grinning, he does so.

There are speeches and gifts at the end of the day.

Back at the hotel I pack my case, ready for leaving early tomorrow. I'm flying directly on to London.

Then Steve Wilson and I take a taxi to Blues, the jazz club our producers have commandeered for the evening. It's the wrap party. In the cab I mention to Steve that it's probably wiser to settle any hotel bill 'extras' in Canadian dollars, rather than by credit card. This I'd got from Ros, Canadian dollars not being worth too much outside the country – bad exchange. Steve, as always, thanks me courteously but says, 'Great, Mart'n, but I don't have any extras.'

I have eight hundred dollars-worth. Mostly bar and restaurant.

At the party Martin Harbury, the director of *The Making of By Jeeves*, is screening all the personal pieces to camera recorded over the last few days by cast members. Many are deliciously surreal: Donna Lynne Champlin talking about the wonderful opportunities she has had since beginning in *By Jeeves* – camera finally pulling back to reveal she's serving behind the lunch counter as a location catering lady.

Wade Russo grins wickedly into the lens talking about Ozzie Nutledge, 'one of the great musical figures of the twentieth century, protégé of Judy Garland'. He'll soon be going to the Helen Hayes Theatre at the invitation of producer Marty Markinson, he says, to perform his one-man show, *Ozzie Nutledge Alone*.

Don Stephenson plugs himself into the mains electricity to demonstrate how he achieves Bingo Little's hair-on-end look. Emily Loesser is sweetly controlling, as the shot widens to reveal Don, her husband, groveling at her feet, cleaning her shoes.

Mine is merely Jeeves in the wings, discussing the various ways it's possible to inflect 'Yes sir', 'No sir', 'Certainly sir', 'Three bags full sir.'

The jazz band makes it difficult to talk. A tactical error, as this is the last time, unless a miracle occurs, that we'll all be together.

Most of the cast gravitate to the long tables furthest from the music, where Alan and Heather are sitting. We shout, nod and mime to each other. While Alan is talking, I take the opportunity to draw Heather aside and read her the fax we have sent to Andrew. I don't think it's appropriate to bother Alan with it, but the company feel it's right that she at least should know how they had reacted to Andrew's letter.

Alan, Heather and I take a cab back to the hotel. We sit in the Terrace bar for a last chat. We talk about new things, new plays, new ideas. Alan murmurs, 'It's all so effing sad.'

It is.

Sunday

The unit driver who missed me on the day of my arrival collects me at seven in the morning and we head to the airport. The clocks have gone forward an hour, hurrying us out of town.

As I move towards the check-in an airline official calls across, 'New York, sir?'

'No,' I reply, 'London.'

ENTR'ACTE 3

Cheshire

Saturday April 7th 2001

Ros and I are driving up the motorway in England. We're Macclesfield-bound, where Amber Antonina Jarvis, a new production, awaits.

London and Los Angeles

Summer 2001

Even two months after the dizzying disappointment kicked in, that *By Jeeves* was not after all Broadway-bound, the cast continued to write, individually and collectively, to Andrew Lloyd Webber and Michael Price. The reason: to see if there might be any chance of a further change of heart.

In May I received an intriguing email from Don Stephenson and Emily Loesser. They had heard that Andrew was talking once again to Alan on our favourite subject and – wait for it – possibly trying one more time to get a Broadway theatre. Could the bombardment of messages be having an effect?

Meantime life went on. Normal life. Visiting my parents at their Sidcup idyll. Bonding with Amber. A job in Chicago. Some radio recordings. Various Jarvis & Ayres projects. Audiobooks. A television film.

No further news from Andrew.

Ros and I made a quick trip to Los Angeles where I appeared as C. S. Lewis in *Shadowlands* for LA Theatre Works, with Harriet Harris as Joy Gresham. We caught up with John Scherer and Donna Lynne Champlin in *Three* at the Ahmanson Theatre. They were outstanding. At dinner afterwards we bemoaned the fate of *By Jeeves* and that it never finally made it to Broadway.

Ros and I flew back to England.

On June 5th Austin Shaw rang to ask if I could meet him at Andrew's offices in Covent Garden that evening, to approve the publicity photos taken in Toronto for the *By Jeeves* video.

After I had finished viewing the impressive pictures, Austin suggested we go to JL Sheeky's restaurant where he'd buy me dinner. I must say that as managing director of a company not known for its large pay-cheques he is an inordinately generous host. As we were walking down St Martin's Lane his mobile phone rang. He whipped it out of his pocket, nearly poking a pedestrian in the eye with his elbow. After listening for several seconds he muttered, 'Wow!' Then, 'Good, oh great. Great. That *is* good news!' He turned to me and mouthed 'Michael Price.'

Ah, the silver fox himself.

'Coincidentally,' said Austin into the phone, 'I'm with Martin now.'

Basically, Austin informed me moments later, Andrew had now secured the Helen Hayes Theatre and *By Jeeves* would be opening there in October.

'Good heavens,' I said. 'Definitely?'

'Definitely.'

I asked Austin was he sure that wasn't his wife on the phone, enquiring what time he'd be home?

He blinked earnestly. 'No, that was Michael all right. It's all happening. It's all on again.'

Well, good old Andrew.

As swiftly as the next day I received a follow-up email from Dan Rosokov, confirming news of the Helen Hayes and Broadway.

Then someone from the Charlotte Wilcox Company in New York, lined up to manage the production, rang Erin Connor in Los Angeles to check my availability.

So now it really is back on again, I told Ros.

It seemed to be, anyway.

After that flurry there followed a long summer of silence before, in August, most of the cast received formal offers.

Around this time I had a call from Don Stephenson to say that

Emily was expecting a baby in January. 'But,' affirmed Don, 'we've assured Alan that she'll be able to play Stiffy until at least December.' He went on, 'Mart'n, you know Emily, she's very small. It'll hardly show. And for God's sake, she's wearing her own pants.'

Whatever that meant I said encouragingly, 'Well, even if she does start to show by, say November, it might be quite funny for her to play it pregnant anyway. The whole thing's meant to be a parish concert, after all.'

Around this time Erin Connor put in a query to the management on my behalf, asking how the company proposed to house me in New York. The response that came after a couple of weeks did not, in fact, answer that question. All it said was that Michael Price had agreed that 'Martin can have a new tailcoat for Broadway.'

Heather Ayckbourn, when I told her, remarked sardonically, 'Perhaps they're hoping you'll sleep in that.'

At the Ivy restaurant my friend Gyles Brandreth bumped into Andrew who, in celebratory mood, assured him that *By Jeeves* was opening on Broadway in October. 'We've got the Helen Hayes. We need to cut ten minutes from the show, but otherwise it's all there.'

Ah. Oh.

A day or so later Alan told me he had indeed heard from Andrew about his intention to make cuts. Alan had then suggested to him they cut the first song. Andrew thought it best not to.

John Scherer and I had both discussed the possibility of small cuts, so that we could bring the first half safely to the intermission a little sooner. Trouble was, who would be the recipient of such trims? No one likes to lose their special moments. And neither John nor I felt we could suggest to Alan what those cuts could be. I said to Heather, who also mentioned Andrew wanted to jazz up the opening – whatever that meant – that only Alan could decide what, if any, excisions should be made.

Andrew then composed a beautiful new (shorter) opening number,

Alan penned a brilliant lyric to it: it involved Jeeves speaking but not quite singing, so we were all happy.

In September I flew to Los Angeles having completed shooting a feature-length episode of a television series, *The Inspector Lynley Mysteries*. I had even had a fitting (in London) for the spanking new tailcoat. No agreement had been reached yet regarding housing. Otherwise we were ready. It seemed that the first rehearsal would be in New York, on or about October 1st. Ros and I had arranged to fly there from Los Angeles for a few days to look for accommodation. There had been the usual negotiations and even though (like Toronto) a deal wasn't yet in place, I felt confident that everything would work out satisfactorily. Everyone was impressed that Andrew had decided after all, to re-establish *By Jeeves* on Broadway.

On September 11th two passenger planes, piloted by terrorists, embedded themselves in the Twin Towers of the World Trade Centre in New York.

Unimaginable horror, and yet we saw it, run and re-run across our television screens.

Attack on America.

Attack on the world.

Ros and I postponed our trip to New York to look for an apartment. No planes were flying anyway. It seemed sensible to wait until we went there for the beginning of rehearsals two weeks later.

Following September 11th the atmosphere in Los Angeles was weird, naturally. President Bush announced, 'We know who has done this,' but didn't identify who it was. Within a week of the attack, news items started to make it clear that the culprit was al-Qaeda, without mentioning Osama bin Laden specifically.

There was a frightening, very American and wholly understandable reaction to the terrorism. In essence it was, 'We're now going to bomb the bastards in retaliation. Look out, the Americans are coming. It's war, etc.'

Bomb whom? War on where? Afghan peasant farmers?

Terrorism has to be rooted out. But isn't it the so-called religious fanatics that have to be found and dealt with? The danger for us all, it seemed, was to be unaware of our own blinding fanaticism, religious and jingoistic. Unless America was very careful, the horrific situation would escalate into one big and final bang. I frequently heard one phrase during these numbing times:'Revenge is a dish best served cold.'

Then came a message from Michael Price. Following the tragic events that had occurred in New York, he and Andrew had decided to cancel the Broadway opening of *By Jeeves*. Apparently two of the major investors had backed out, due to the uncertain economic climate in the United States. Sadly, this necessitated 'an indefinite postponement'.

I phoned Erin Connor. She rang New York to find that the Charlotte Wilcox office knew nothing of this. They called her back half an hour later to confirm it was true.

A few minutes later I had a message from Alan. Andrew had phoned him to say that at least one major backer had withdrawn and that he was reluctantly pulling the plug on the project.

I discussed with Alan that I personally very much regretted the decision. It was true that although some Broadway shows were closing, others were surviving. And with even less competition mightn't the show have done wonderfully and been an antidote to gloom?

Ah well, we agreed, *By Jeeves* had been sidelined once again.

Within the hour I had calls from Don Stephenson, Donna Lynne and others. Only one thing for it: time for the cast to move into action once again. Especially as the message was coming loud and clear from New York's charismatic Mayor, Rudi Giuliani, that we should all do our darnedest to keep things going, to get back onto the streets, into the theatres, make every effort to show that an unholy war of this kind would not faze the people of America.

I know Andrew received messages from several cast members, all variations on the same theme: it was vitally important to keep the show going and, I certainly felt, to stand shoulder to shoulder with our American colleagues. Nevertheless, mine was a tricky letter to write. I began by sympathising with his position and saying how disappointing it must be for him to have suddenly lost his backing. A shame too, for the production, if no replacement funding could be found – especially, I nudged, as President Bush and the Mayor of New York were so keen for all shows to continue, for the City to resume as much of its normal life as possible. I mentioned that Ian McKellen was proceeding with the opening of *Dance of Death*, which seemed a much less attractive title at present than our own Jeevesian entertainment. I had in fact been getting calls from people who felt *By Jeeves* to be a perfect, now much needed, diversion. I finished my last-ditch stand by saying we all looked forward to hearing that the cancellation was merely a short postponement, and that New York might still have the chance to enjoy a well-deserved evening's entertainment and laughter.

My effort paled into insignificance when Michael Price received the following pile-driving, pulverising, passionate challenge and declaration of commitment from Donna Lynne Champlin:

Dear Michael,

You know I've been with this show since the beginning, and I've gotten THE phone call a few times saying 'We really tried, but it's not going to happen this time,' and I've been disappointed but I've accepted whatever circumstances were given to me.

But this time is different.

This time for me, personally, is much different.

With recent events in NYC.... we have all heard the battle cry of Mayor Giuliani and President Bush.

Go on with your lives…

GO to theatre…

GO to restaurants…

DON'T let them see that they've ruined daily life for you…

DON'T let the terrorists win.

I went to the Javitts Center to volunteer – they turned me away saying that they probably wouldn't need my help for weeks, maybe a month. But in the back of my mind I thought 'at least I have BY JEEVES in October – and I'll be able to help then… I'll be able to make people laugh for two hours and help them feel better…'

I have always been proud of this show.

I have always been proud of how we keep getting back up to give it one more shot.

I have always been proud to be a member of this company.

But when I got the news that we were postponing due to recent events.

When I found out that we were postponing because our backers were AFRAID.

When I found out that we were… falling right into the hands of whoever did this horrible act…

For the first time… I was not proud to be in this show.

I read online today some people were talking about our cancellation, saying, 'Looks like they have been looking for any reason not to bring this show in… how tacky of them to use this recent disaster as an excuse for a show that probably wasn't going to come in anyway.'

My heart just sank when I read that.

I wanted to retort - to tell them it wasn't true…

But I thought…no matter what I say, the only way to show these people…the city of NYC…the Broadway theater community… the nation – that we are NOT afraid is to DO this show ON SCHEDULE – AS PLANNED.

And it's not like we're planning on opening TOMORROW…

BY JEEVES is opening in October… a whole month away…

I have read countless stories about people – tourists who are cancelling their various trips to Italy, Paris…specifically to come to NYC. To make the statement that people are NOT going to be scared…people are NOT going to let these terrorists win. By the time we actually OPEN…the theater/tourist situation will have vastly improved, definitely.

I was in the UK when Tony Blair made his speech about how Britain will stand 'shoulder to shoulder' with the US.

Perhaps some people interpreted that as just militarily…but I didn't.

I assumed that that meant in all respects, which would include artistically as well.

If this show doesn't happen, we as Americans will have played right into the hands of whoever bombed our east coast a week ago. And the British involved in this show will have also gone back on the word of their Prime Minister and their country as well.

So, do with this what you will…copy it and hand it to our (ex?) backers if you want…read it and let it inspire you to do whatever you're trying to do over there to keep this show from falling prey to fear.

But–

know that…

at least for me…

this is more than just losing a Broadway gig…

this is more than just losing a job in general…

this is more than 5 years of blood sweat and tears…

This is about patriotism, this is about not letting fear get in the way of sending a positive message to NYC, to the Broadway community, that we AT LEAST will TRY to do this show…before giving up.

I mean we gave up before we even gave it a good shot.

Where is the honor in that?

Michael Price's response, no doubt after he had picked himself up from the floor and accepted a glass of water from his secretary, came zinging back. We learned he had been on the phone with Andrew and, he told Donna Lynne, 'I think we are going to be OK!'

This was followed a day later with confirmation that *By Jeeves* was indeed back on track yet again, and the first preview would be opening as planned on October 16th at the Helen Hayes. Lloyd Webber had moved with the speed of light and found new investors to replace those mysterious backers who had abandoned the production.

Andrew was quoted in a press statement as saying that *By Jeeves* wasn't in fact his production, 'But when I heard about this, the first thing I thought was whether there was anything we could do. Broadway is very important to me and there is no better time to be supportive of Broadway than right now.'

Andrew Lloyd Webber, the good lord in the white hat. The John Wayne of American musical theatre.

Alan was in dark wartime humour in Scarborough. He told me he felt it all seemed very weird and unreal, rather more like a forthcoming ENSA concert than a Broadway show. At least with an ENSA concert, he observed, the troops actually wanted you there. Whereas, judging from current attendance figures for both Broadway and the West End, he suspected we were more likely to get a moral welcome, rather than an all-out physical one, and we'd all be home for Christmas. He added that it would be nice to see everyone again, put in the new stuff and sing a few songs in the shelters. And concluded:

'It's a bloody odd world at the moment, isn't it? Still, at least you can get a table at the Ivy.'

ACT THREE

The Great White Way

Seven of the Provincetown Players are in the army or working
for it in France, and more are going. Not lightheartedly now,
when civilisation itself is threatened with destruction, we who
remain have determined to go on next season with the work
of our little theatre. It is often said that theatrical entertainment
in general is socially justified in this dark time as a means of
relaxing the strain of reality, and thus helping to keep us sane.
This may be true, but if more were not true – if we felt no deeper
value in dramatic art than entertainment – we would hardly have
the heart for it now. One faculty, we know, is going to be of vast
importance to the half-destroyed world – indispensable for its
rebuilding – the faculty of creative imagination. That spark of
it which has given this group of ours such life and meaning as
we have is not so insignificant that we should now let it die.
The social justification which we feel to be valid now for makers
and players of plays is that they shall help keep alive in the world
the light of imagination. Without it the wreck of the world that
was cannot be cleared away and the new world shaped.

George Cram Cook, 1918

★

Thursday September 26th 2001

Ros and I fly apprehensively to New York today. The woman on the check-in doesn't ask for any identification and as we're passing through says vaguely, 'Oh, did I ask you for your ID?'

We can't help eyeing askance any (even marginally) odd-looking person who might be boarding our flight. One man looks particularly edgy, with a mad gleam in his eye. Ros points him out, but I think he looks more like an ex-agent of mine. Exactly, says Ros.

It's a strange feeling to be flying in to the city – and as we approach JFK I'm certain many of us are recalling the horrific television pictures of those planes slamming into the Twin Towers.

Over the bridge by taxi into Manhattan. The skyline emerges, apparently unassailable, glowing bronze in the evening light. We can't see the space where the towers were. The Empire State building stands proudly, red, blue and silver, once again the tallest building in New York.

We've booked into the Wyndham Hotel on 58th Street, in midtown, until we can find an apartment. It's old fashioned, eccentrically furnished, with multi-layers of chipped paint carbon-dating the establishment back to the Thirties. Our suite includes a semi-kitchen known as a 'co-pantry', which boasts an ancient Acme fridge.

We're on the eleventh floor, which we reach courtesy of an old-style elevator. It's manned by a constantly rotating team of middle-aged Croatians – Caesar, Neville and Ralph, who lurk in the basement and have to be summoned by a bell. We are obliged to wait for them while they respond to our call and rattle up towards us each time we want to venture out. Not good when late for rehearsals. Let's hope we won't be here for long.

This evening we walk down Broadway towards Times Square. We stop at one of the fire stations. It's more like a shrine. There are flowers, bouquets and posies strewn on the sidewalk and on the fronts of the great red trucks themselves. Photographs of lost fire-fighters are pinned around the open doors. Crowds of New Yorkers and visitors from out of town gather to pay their respects to these heroes. Candles burn from the altar of one of the fire-truck fenders. Several of the surviving firemen are standing there talking to members of the public, who wring their hands and shed tears before moving on. I feel guilty that I am merely strolling down Broadway to look at the outside of our theatre.

Apparently our marquee has gone up. From Times Square we turn right on to 44th Street and locate the Helen Hayes, a compact jewel box playhouse tucked between the larger St James's – where the *The Producers* is pulling in packed houses again – and Sardi's restaurant. I find I'm a little excited at the prospect of seeing my name on the front of a Broadway theatre for the first time.

But no. Our theatre is blank and dark, with nothing to suggest that any form of entertainment is opening there in two weeks. The box office is closed. Ros spots a single sheet of A4 sized paper pinned into one of the otherwise empty display cabinets. It is, literally, a note from Bertie Wooster announcing we'll be here on the 16th. From the locked gates leading to the Helen Hayes' stage door alley we turn to look across the street at the Broadhurst Theatre, where *Dance of Death* has just opened for previews. A bright, colourful photograph of Ian McKellen beams cheekily down from on high.

We call in to Sardi's. I introduce myself to the barman and tell him, in a burst of Broadway bonhomie, that we're going to be neighbours.

He smiles and says his name is Joe.

'Set 'em up,' I say.

He smiles less expansively. He's heard it too many times.

★

Friday

Today we meet Natalie Mosco, actress, dancer, writer and currently – realtor. She's going to show us various apartments available to rent. We inspect a few, all in the theatre district. They're cramped, noisy and oppressive. It would be like living in the heart of Soho, in London. She then takes us to the Upper West Side – 66th Street, just above the Lincoln Center. That's better. More expensive, of course.

We visit an apartment on West 67th. It's charming, though small. The woman renting out the place has lit candles and is obviously keen that we will like it. She loves actors, she says. She's wearing a huge amount of make-up and her face has that giveaway 'windswept' look.

Natalie has a sharp sense of what people are like, as well as properties. As we are leaving the building she suggests that, similar to the owner of the flat, the place was very well prepared and put together. As far as the woman is concerned, Natalie thinks it's not all the force of nature. It has reminded her, she says, of an older actor she knows – something of a roué. She mentions his name and we realise he's appearing on Broadway at the moment and is quite well known. Natalie tells us he'd taken up with a much younger girl a few years ago and had been paying for her plastic surgery. Then she left him. Then they got back together. Some folk in the Broadway community expressed surprise. 'But,' says Natalie, 'I'm not surprised at all. He's buying her piece by piece.'

We look at a small but neat apartment in the fashionable Phillips Club. The rent would take up substantially more than the accommodation allowance the company has now agreed to pay me.

Can't seem to find anything suitable. Another realtor, Susan Barken, takes over and shows us a place on 66th Street. She's a dewy-eyed startled fawn with a Disney voice, who can't quite believe we aren't ecstatic over the tiny apartment. It might have suited Squirrel Nutkin. Susan herself lives in the building, she tells us. I'm not surprised. The cosy corridors, decorated with a russet-coloured furry substance, remind me of rabbit warrens. The walls are thin. I keep thinking it's a hotel. It's not, she reminds me, these are condos. She shows us the 'party room', where various children in fancy dress and with specially made-up animal faces are having tea. I wonder, are they from the families who have been put out of their homes because of the tragedy? No, they're children of residents. It's a surprise birthday party for one of them.

We put our heads round the door of the apartment once again. Would we fit in? Maybe, but in any case, it's pricey. And we'd have to cover everything, including brokers' fees, tax, the lot. Also we'll need to rent on a month-by-month basis. Who knows how long the play might run, or not run? Ros tells Susan the place is not really large enough for our requirements and explains, 'We really need somewhere we can swing a cat or two.' Susan's startled fawn demeanour moves up several notches to 'appalled female deer' and I can see she's relieved that we aren't going to take it. This British couple would never fit in, and such unnatural cruelty to animals would be abhorrent to the neighbours.

Tomorrow we're having coffee with British theatre journalist and director Ruth Leon, whom we know from England. She has an apartment on 68th Street, and is looking for a temporary flat-share. She's married to the critic Sheridan Morley and, she says, only spends an average of three days a month in New York. I can't quite imagine myself sharing with not one, but two critics. She's very nice though and, maybe, we'll have to bite this particular Broadway bullet.

Tonight we have dinner with our old friends, screenwriter Luther Davis and actress, soap opera star and ex-bunny girl, Jennifer Bassey, at their elegant penthouse on the Upper East Side. We see them often in London and Los Angeles but this is the first time we have visited them in New York. As we sit there enjoying a drink, Luther suddenly remarks, 'I bet you're wondering where we sleep.'

I'm about to reply, 'Well, in the—' when he gestures to a neat oblong shape on the wall, which I had taken to be the front of a cupboard.

'The Murphy bed,' he announces.

Jenny grins as she replenishes my Chardonnay. 'There is no other room. This is New York, Mart'n. No space!'

Saturday

We visit Ruth Leon in her surprisingly spacious two-bedroom 26th floor apartment overlooking Broadway. Cats can be swung freely and we decide to take it immediately, at a reasonable rent, despite the fact that occasional visits are scheduled by Ruth herself, husband Sherry, his son Hugo and, curiously, Mary Archer. We can move in next Wednesday.

I hurry back to the Wyndham. John Scherer has already arrived as arranged, walking up from his apartment in the theatre district. We're going to read through Alan's new scene and discuss the new opening number. We also rehearse all our shared dialogue, surprising ourselves at how much we remember, even though it's six months since Toronto.

We've both seen the big colour ad that has appeared in today's *New York Times*. It's quite impressive, though the billing is interesting. The company, especially the new understudies who don't actually appear in the show, will be delighted to be advertised equally with the Broadway cast, plus Alan and Andrew. As a wholehearted supporter of the Almeida and the Donmar, where everyone is billed identically, I suppose I shouldn't complain.

John and I link up with Ruth and Ros at lunchtime. Ruth tells

stories about her Gershwin musical – the one she devised and
directed. Not to be confused with the Hershey Felder vehicle that
kept us out of the Helen Hayes in April. Unlike *Gershwin Alone*,
her production received generally good reviews off-Broadway. She
mentions that Andrew had asked her, 'Can't you do anything?' –
which she took to mean 'review *Gershwin Alone* and thereby help
to get it taken off'. She felt she couldn't do that while her own production was still running. In fact Hershey Felder floundered anyway
at the Helen Hayes after poor notices, and it came off in the early
summer.

Ruth is a powerhouse of energy. She canters through many a
theatrical story. I explain to John, in her presence, that he's only seen
the half of it. When her husband's there too it's impossible to get even
one word in. She appreciates the joke. And agrees. She makes a very
jolly landlady.

Monday September 30th

Ros has started amassing various props for the apartment. We need a
printer and a phone fax. And chairs for our sparse bedroom.

I set off to my music rehearsal. The management company isn't
employing John and me until later in the week, so this is unpaid.
Only the new people are officially rehearsing today. But we've agreed
it's better that we get the updated material under our belts as soon as
possible.

I decide to travel by subway. I purchase a metro ticket, but having
got on at 57th Street and 6th I lose confidence that it's going to Times
Square and scramble off at 49th. I walk to the 42nd Street rehearsal
rooms via our theatre box office, where I meet youngish Michael and
older David. 'Hey, we're doing business,' they tell me cheerfully.

John and I arrive at the Duke's Rehearsal Studios at the same time.

The rooms are custom-built, spacious and light. The new 'swings', or understudies, are being put through their paces by Ian Knauer. 'Martin, welcome to New York,' he smiles, flashing the impossibly white teeth. It's nice to see them again.

Michael O'Flaherty and Wade Russo are by the piano. I've heard from John that Wade may no longer be 'Ozzie', and that Michael himself will be taking it over. He did it originally at the first American performance at the Goodspeed Opera House five years ago. It looks as if cheerful Wade will have to content himself with being a member of the orchestra, playing the keyboards.

Dan Rosokov is here too and introduces John and me to the swings. And to a tough-looking middle-aged actor, Sam Tsoutsou-vas, who is taking over the role of Sir Watkyn Bassett from Heath Lamberts. For some reason, drum major Heath is not joining us on Broadway. I'm sorry not to see him as I thought he was eccentric and funny as Sir Watkyn. Perhaps his mafia-style agent has secured him an offer from elsewhere that he simply can't refuse.

We also meet Dan's new assistant, a smiling girl in dungarees called Lisa.

John and I go through our new joint number with Michael and Wade. John sings; my part, happily, is spoken. We all agree it's amusing and gets the plot going even more effectively than before. We record the accompaniment on cassette to take home for practice and learning.

I ask which train I should get from Times Square to 57th.

'57th and what?' says John.

'Er – I'm not sure.'

'Near you?'

'Yes.'

He tells me to get the 'R' train. I walk along 42nd Street and plunge down below the sidewalk to the sweltering subway platform. It's like entering a public sauna. My metro ticket entitles me to ten trips. I

Above: 'Where's Court Whisman?' Two thirds of the ensemble trio – Tom Ford and Molly Renfroe.

Above right: Elfin Heather, gnomic Martin.

Right: Pittsburgh: Triumph (the show) and Disaster (the hat) side by side.

Broadway heroes.

John
Scherer

Martin
Jarvis

Donna Lynne
Champlin

David
Edwards

Tom
Ford

James
Kall

Ian
Keuer

Emily
Loesser

Cristin
Mortenson

Molly
Renfroe

Don
Stephenson

Jamison
Stern

Sam
Tsoutsouvas

Becky
Watson

Court
Whisman

Steve
Wilson

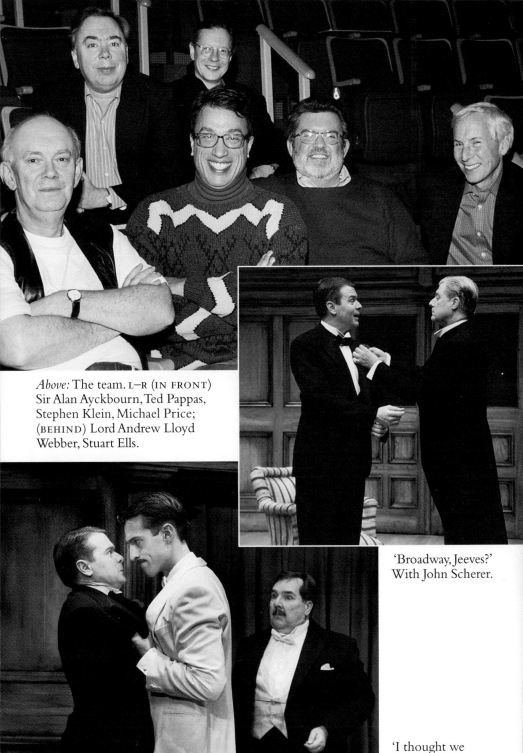

Above: The team. L—R (IN FRONT)
Sir Alan Ayckbourn, Ted Pappas,
Stephen Klein, Michael Price;
(BEHIND) Lord Andrew Lloyd
Webber, Stuart Ells.

'Broadway, Jeeves?'
With John Scherer.

'I thought we
were going to
Broadway!'

L—R: John Scherer,
Steve Wilson,
Heath Lamberts.

Top: 'Er – I think it goes like this...' The Wizard of Oz finale.

Centre: On a high. Balcony curtain call.

Right: Back-seat driver. With John Scherer and Donna Lynne Champlin.

'Was that a cell phone, Jeeves?'
With John Scherer.

The ancient art of downstaging.
With John Scherer.

'The little dance.'

Above: 'Don't make me laugh, of course there'll be pictures outside the theatre!' With John Scherer (L) and Michael Price.

Above: The boy done good. With John Scherer.

Left: Mr and Mrs Jeeves. With Rosalind Ayres.

Top: 'Broadway, my lord?'
'Naturally!' With John Scherer
(L) and Andrew Lloyd Webber.

Above: 'Which Madeleine
are you?' L–R John Scherer,
MJ, Andrew and Madeleine
Lloyd Webber.

Right: 'Every time a fairy
blows its nose, a baby's
born.' Becky Watson and
John Scherer.

The Master –
Sir Alan Ayckbourn.

Below: 'By George, by Jove,
by Jeeves.' L–R James Kall,
Don Stephenson, John Scherer.

'At your service, sir.'

wait. Plenty of 'W' trains. And 'Q' trains. I'm still waiting patiently. No 'R's. Looks like I'm not going to make even one trip. Eventually, after an hour, I get a 'Q' which takes me to 57th and – somewhere. Which leaves me with an interesting, if puzzling, walk home.

Tuesday

I'm trying to learn the new material. And revise the whole script. Ros takes me through it. Or, rather, puts me through it. Or is it me putting her through it, as I get irritable when I can't remember parts of the text that came so naturally to me six months ago? Later we pass the Jekyll and Hyde Club. I could be a Life Member, I suggest.

John and I have already discussed the lack of any kind of forward publicity for the show, and our concern at that bleak, empty theatre front, still staring blindly out on to 44th Street. I send Michael Price an email suggesting some promotional thoughts. I tell him that Ros and I were dining the other evening with our friend Sherry Bebitch Jeffe, political analyst on CNN and the *Los Angeles Times*. She and her lob-byist husband Douglas are avid theatre-goers and have suggested it might be helpful, possibly appropriate all round, if the following were to receive an invitation to the *By Jeeves* opening. I list the names for him. Rudi Giuliani, Mayor of New York. George Pataki, Governor of New York. Senator Hillary Clinton and her well-known spouse. Sen-ator Charles Schumer. And Laura Bush, reachable via her press secretary, Noelia Rodriguez. I reinforce the point that Sherry and Doug have offered to assist in making this happen. Worth a try, surely.

I have no idea if we could get these high profile people to our opening night. But it's clear it would provide focus on the image of Broadway 'coming back' and, in this particular case, an example of the British standing together with their allies. I mention that John Scherer is as eager as I am to help in publicising the show in any way we can. I invite Michael to be in touch if he or his PR team can think of anything we can usefully do. I include my cell phone number while in the city.

Michael calls almost immediately. He welcomes me to New York but says he hasn't received my message. How else did he know my number? The silver fox moves in mysterious ways.

We're moving into the apartment tomorrow. But next Sunday I think I'll be moving out again, to the Algonquin, to allow Mary Archer to have the room for two nights. This was agreed, as Ruth had already offered her use of the bedroom before we arrived on the scene. Ros will have gone to Los Angeles to direct a radio theatre production of Pinter's *Betrayal*. All my stuff will be temporarily stored in one part of the large closet. I have an image of my returning to the apartment having forgotten something vital, and groping around the darkened bedroom. Oops, sorry Mary. Very Jeffrey Archer.

Wednesday

We have moved to Ruth's from the oppressive Wyndham. Delighted to be shot of the old-fashioned elevator, and having to talk all the time to the hefty lift-men who fill the rattling cages morning noon and night with their Croatian farts.

Despite only having been in New York for a few days, we've got three suitcases instead of two.

No sooner have we arrived at the apartment on the Upper West Side, with its devastating views of the East river, Central Park and Broadway itself threading its way up and down Manhattan, than I have to leave again for another voluntary music rehearsal.

John has learnt the new material perfectly and hasn't even brought his script. After endless plodding, and with Ros's help, I know it fairly well.

When the short rehearsal is over, I walk to the Helen Hayes to see if I can have a quick look round. My new box office chums let me into the auditorium where I encounter a man up a ladder screwing in a light bulb. He seems to be an all-purpose janitor and electrician. He descends, tells me his name is Hector, and takes me downstairs to the dressing rooms, under the stage. The memory of Jeffrey Archer rises for a second time in twenty-four hours. Jeffrey once owned the Playhouse Theatre in London, where the spacious dressing rooms upstairs had been sold off as offices. Thereafter the actors had to survive by crouching in small windowless cells beneath the stage. Now poor old Jeffrey is crouching in a cell of his own.

There doesn't seem to be a lot of space here either. And not that many rooms. I wonder how I'll get my contractual dressing room on my own. Can't seem to locate it.

The auditorium seems fine, again like the Playhouse. Probably seats about six hundred. Standing centre stage, I can see that the stalls are well raked. Everyone gets a good view. There's one dress circle, known here as the mezzanine. Like many theatres, though elegant, it seems tired and threadbare under the glare of the working lights. It'll look more inviting when those individual art deco lamps and gold sconces are tactfully illuminated. I clamber over various crates and boxes and make my way through the wings, out of the stage door, into the alley and on to 44th street.

Bravely I try the subway once again. Lines 1 or 9 will take me to West 66th Street, two blocks from the apartment. I have to buy a ticket as, of course, I have mislaid my metro card.

I spend the rest of the afternoon attempting to set up the fax / phone. Ros tells me it doesn't have a remote way of checking messages. Off she goes to get various other things from the shops, including an answer phone. While she's gone I discover it does have that facility. Amazingly I get it going. I ring her on her cell phone. It's switched off. She returns having bought another answer machine.

We have a glass of wine later with warm-hearted Ruth, who will be here for another day or so.

Thursday

I'm gazing out of one of the apartment windows. The morning sun streams down on to the skyscrapers that stand between here and Central Park, like great canyons in some silent African landscape. Unless you look directly down to the street you can't see a single living thing. A little cricket pavilion-style house with a white picket fence sits, incongruously, on the flat roof of one of the high buildings across the other side of Broadway. Two flags billow in the wind. A plastic bag appears, floating on the thermals thirty storeys high like a coasting vulture, before whisking itself away towards the Dakota building up to our left, and eventually out of sight.

I'm supposed to be working on the new number, with the assistance of the tape. According to John this is a version of the song Andrew wanted us to use before we opened at Pittsburgh. I seem to remember Alan listened to it then and gave it the thumbs down. But now it's in. Not quite as hot off the presses as I had thought. It's good, though.

Michael O'Flaherty tells us today that when he first heard it hammered out on the piano by Andrew he wasn't sure he liked it. Now he does. He points out it's a sort of Twenties waltz and, we all agree, it sets up and clarifies the story line – introducing the improvised acting scenario that Jeeves hopes Bertie will attempt in preference to the planned banjo recital.

I visit the production office, ostensibly to sign my contract. But it's the usual thing: adjustments haven't been made, it's not ready. I chat to Charlotte Wilcox who is a pleasant, hard-working theatre company manager. Her other major production is the musical, *The Full*

Monty, still playing to full houses. I meet her ebullient assistant, Bruce, who tells me he was Jerry Lewis's touring manager for many years. He reminds me of a large shaggy dog. His voice comes out in sharp barks as he announces that he and other members of Charlotte's staff are now leaving for the Winter Garden Theatre to witness the public dress rehearsal of *Mamma Mia*.

Rather them than me.

Friday

Today the first proper rehearsal takes place. In other words, John and I are no longer unpaid volunteers. Initially it's just him and me and the three swings: Cristin Mortenson, fair-haired, sweet-voiced; David Edwards, bespectacled and earnest-looking with what looks suspiciously like an over-abundant rug atop his head; and Jamison Stern, a lithe young man who moves like a trained dancer and sings well. The rest of the cast, no doubt for budgetary reasons, are not called until Monday. We have heard the whole production is capitalised at just over one and a half million dollars. Even I know this is a frighteningly low figure for any show on Broadway, let alone a musical. John has also whispered to me that he hears there is very little money in the budget for advertising and publicity. Having seen the front of the theatre I'm not surprised.

Heath's replacement, Sam Tsoutsouvas, arrives, punchy, curly-haired and compact. He tells me virtually straight away that his background is Greek and Welsh. There's a sense of tremendous positive energy about him. He'd be well-cast as Fluellen in *Henry V*.

It becomes clear during one of the tea breaks that Sam is obsessed with things English. He rhapsodises on his favourite British actresses Dorothy Tutin and Gwen Watford and asks if I know either of them personally. I feel terrible having to give him the bad tidings that both are dead. He can hardly bear it. His energy seeps away. He recovers sufficiently to inform me he is basing his entire performance as Sir Watkyn Bassett on Donald Sinden. My hearts sinks. American imitations of fine British stylists never seem quite to hit the mark. But after watching him for only a short time I can see he's excellent. He already knows the part, though his delivery has more of quirky Ralph Richardson than flamboyant Donald.

After he has sung through 'It's a Pig' with the understudies, he walks across to me with a woebegone face and confides that he's apprehensive about meeting Alan. 'You see Sir Alan wasn't here when I came up for the role, Martin. He didn't cast me. I'm worried he'll feel he's bought a pig in a poke.'

I try to put his mind at rest. There's no question – Alan will approve when he arrives on Monday.

The work John and I have been doing, together and separately, is paying off. We have ideas about the new section, which we begin to put into practice and can't wait to work on it fully with Alan. Incredibly, we only have just over a week before the first preview. My heel, though still not completely recovered despite physiotherapy in England over the summer, stands up pretty well to the little dance. I had a phone conversation with Sheila about it a few weeks ago and she is happy to substitute a less bruising piece of choreography. But I'm loath to lose it unless I really have to. It's one of the high points of the show and, well, I like that.

Odd lapses of memory in the text as we run it through, but in general it has all come back. So here we are, rehearsing a Broadway musical on 42nd Street. Unbelievable really, with Times Square bustling below to the left, a monument to neon, visible through the huge windows. And down there on the right is the Amsterdam Theatre, where eighty years ago Fanny Brice came over from New York's East Side and became a star. Now, its glittering marquee proudly proclaims *The Lion King*. The Roundabout's new production of *The Women* is rehearsing next door, in a high, bright studio similar to ours. I help myself from a large jug of coffee in the shared lobby. Rue McClanahan (ex-Golden Girl) smiles graciously at me and shakes her head. I replace the cup sheepishly. Not for us? No, *Women* only. Our management isn't providing coffee.

Saturday

Ros returns to LA today to start work on Pinter's *Betrayal* for LA Theatre Works. Ruth Leon returned to London yesterday.

I take a taxi to the theatre. The subway, I have now decided, is too sweaty. The combination of hot and cold air makes me feel I have been washed, rinsed and spun-dried in a colossal laundromat.

I arrive at rehearsal from the steamy yellow cab, only marginally cooler. Michael O'Flaherty passes on a message to me from Andrew Lloyd Webber that says he has never understood why Jeeves doesn't sing. (I know why.) I could sing bits of it if I wanted, says Andrew. Ah.

'It's not an issue,' says Michael quickly. But of course, as we run the new number, I try it out on a couple of lines. More wobble than warble. Nothing is said. When I demonstrate it to Ros on the phone later she is more straightforward. 'Don't,' she says.

Ian Knauer is in charge of rehearsals until Alan arrives, putting in the understudies and playing everybody's part. He's an excellent theatre man – and organises it all with natural grace and tact.

We finish at four. John and I walk the two blocks to the Helen Hayes, where he introduces me to the stage door-keeper in his hutch. 'Rob, have you met Mart'n?'

Rob, lean and energetic, leaps up and yells, 'Mart'n! Everyone has met Mart'n except me! I'm the only one here who hasn't met Mart'n! Hi Mart'n!'

Inside, Dan is sitting halfway back in the stalls focusing the lights.

Since my last visit, the set has gone up. I walk on stage for a moment or two and meet Jennifer, Mick Hughes's assistant. Then, led by Dan, John and I dive below to the subterranean dressing rooms. I'm nervous about this and half-ready to relinquish my solo room. I certainly couldn't puzzle out the other day how we could all fit in. But somehow – rather like New York apartment sizes – it's been done. The rooms are really not much bigger than Rob's hutch. But there we are: John and I in our separate units, each just big enough for an upright chair and one armchair. Eat your heart out, Jeffrey. Others are more cramped. Apparently there's been some jockeying for position over the summer – Donna Lynne, Emily and Molly are all billeted in one room. Becky and new girl Cristin are together in another.

James Kall has arrived for a costume fitting. It's his birthday tomorrow. I take him and John to the upstairs bar at Sardi's next door for a glass of champagne. John is 'so excited' he says. He keeps exclaiming girlishly, 'We're going to Broadway!' and bursting into fits of giggles. And yes it does all seem, suddenly, exciting.

Bartender Joe has forgotten me from last week. After a second Chardonnay I tell him again, 'You're going to be seeing a lot of us!'

Maybe.

I've arranged to stay at the Algonquin for two nights so that Mary Archer can have my 'en suite' room in Ruth's apartment as arranged. Apparently she has been handed a set of keys in London. To complicate matters Hugo Morley, Sheridan's son, will be arriving to use the other bedroom (Ruth's) for a couple of nights. He doesn't have any keys, so I've been instructed to leave them for him at the front desk. That's strictly forbidden by the building's management so I have to disguise them as something else. I'll secrete them in a script: *Key Largo*? *Lock up Your Daughters*? In the end (and rather pleased with its aptness) I slip them into an envelope hidden in the centre of the video of *A Man For All Seasons*. By Robert Bolt.

Not only do I not quite know what time Mary is arriving, I'm not absolutely sure which day. According to Ruth Leon it could be tomorrow (Sunday) or maybe Monday. Probably not Tuesday. Ruth emails me from England that she had tried to get her to be more specific but thought it depended on the Archer son, Will, who lives in America. Anyway, says Ruth, Mary has keys and there's a note at the front desk so they know a 'house guest' is coming. Ruth advises me not to worry, and gives me Will Archer's cell phone number in case of emergencies.

She finishes by saying everybody in London keeps asking in patronising tones whether New York is back to normal yet, which she thinks suggests they perceive the entire US population to be composed of hysterics who don't know about stiff upper lips.

I'm still confused about Mary Archer's schedule. Since she may be arriving tomorrow, at any time, I've booked the Algonquin for tonight and Monday night, as advertised. But I have a second, disturbing, fantasy that I might arrive back at the apartment on Tuesday, late after rehearsal, only to find Mary slumbering there. Still, I suppose a touch of New York bedroom farce might work quite well in contrast with proper angst down on 44th Street. I strip the bed and remake it with fresh sheets for Mary. It's no easy feat as the mattress rests on a series of slatted planks that suddenly clatter to the parquet. If you turn over suddenly in the night you are woken by what, at first, you think may be machine-gun fire coming from the street below. I dive beneath the bed and rescue a few stray slats.

Just as I'm emerging, Ruth rings from London to say that Mary is currently in Washington with her son: she won't after all be here tomorrow. She'll arrive in New York on Monday, late morning, for one night only.

Right.

Having made up Mary's bed, I now move around the room like a dervish, stripping it again. A few planks clatter floorward but I'm getting better at balancing them. I know the line-up now. I replace them carefully, throw the Archer bedding into the closet, retrieve the Jarvis sheets and tuck them in. Not a slat out of place.

I think briefly of *News of the World* headlines: 'I was Mary Archer's bedmaker.'

I call the Algonquin. I will go there for Monday night.

I collapse on the communal bed.

Only one slat clatters to the floor.

Sunday

Day off.

I decide not to pay a specific visit to Ground Zero. Despite the many times during the last weeks we have seen footage of the grey expanse of desolation, I can't help feeling odd about making the journey down to the lowest tip of Manhattan to view the skeletal remains. More than once in the short time here when I have considered travelling those few miles, I have felt like a would-be voyeur, ready to crowd around the aftermath of the ultimate massacre, the most monstrous traffic accident ever.

Some others, I know, think differently.

Maybe, if I happen to be passing by, I'll just have to take a look at the decimation, to remember, in situ, the blood spilled.

So what does the actor do instead? He walks a few blocks to buy some make-up stuff at a theatrical supply store, Abracadabra. My purchases take for ever as the cadaverous young man behind the counter never stops talking. He is obsessed by British things (clearly an acquaintance of Sam Tsoutsouvas). He wants to tell me the plot of every episode of *Are You Being Served?* which he's seen on video here in New York. The many references in the series to a favourite pet, 'Mrs Slocombe's pussy', seem particularly to appeal to him, and appal him. 'Hey, I'd sit all my friends in front of the TV and play them the shows, and you know what, they just could not believe it! My God, what the British can get away with. And, by God, that was 1974!'

Dinner with Cindy Katz and Jon Shapiro. She and I played opposite each other in David Hare's *Skylight* three years ago. I go to their apartment on Lexington, next-door to the Armoury. Then they insist on taking me to a chi chi restaurant near Madison Square Park. When Jon is away from the table Cindy tells me how fabulous he is and that she thinks he's going to propose tomorrow. Jon tells me (when Cindy is away from the table) how wonderful Cindy is. I tell them (each in the absence of the other) how wonderful they both are. And they are.

Back at the flat, Hugo Morley arrives around midnight. He is a shaggy, enthusiastic, bear-like young man and has flown from Miami, arriving in time to see the second half of *The Producers*. We chat for over an hour covering, it seems, the history of theatre over the last ten years. I think to myself, 'Wow he's a chip off *both* the old blocks – grandfather Robert and father Sheridan.' Ruth does pretty well, too. They can all talk for England. He's hugely agreeable but after ninety minutes I have to make my apologies and retire.

Monday October 8th

I strip my bed once again and make up Mary Archer's. I'm going to the Algonquin tonight. I listen to the rough edit of *Our Brave Boys*, a Radio 4 series directed by Pete Atkin, which Ros and I are producing.

Then to the theatre. Alan and Heather Ayckbourn arrive, walking past me up the stage-door alley while I am on my cell phone to Pete in Bristol with comments on what I've heard. Most of the rest of the cast are arriving too – so it's a somewhat fragmented reunion.

Just as we are about to begin our meeting in the stalls, stage-door Rob comes in. There's a phone call for me. Urgent. I mouth apologies to Alan and creep out. It's Will Archer. His mother, Mary, is with him. The news is not good: one of the keys Ruth gave to Mary in London doesn't work. They can't get into the apartment. Oh lord. This is all I need. I suggest he collects my own key, which I'll leave here at the stage door, so they can get in. Then they can have a new one cut, before returning the original to me. I leave the key with Rob, and a note wishing them luck.

I pick up the threads of the meeting. We carry on with our work. Alan is making interesting changes. Most of the adjustments, while typically imaginative and clever, seem to put more time on Act One rather than reduce it. Rob nips in to tell me somebody has picked up the key and my note.

Alan blocks our new number. His ideas for its staging are brilliant, though I find myself reacting slowly, purely because we've been working on it in isolation. Surprisingly, John isn't fully on top of it either and we leave it unresolved.

Later on in the afternoon, as my key hasn't found its way back yet, I ring Will Archer. I'll be at the Algonquin tonight but I'd be lost without it tomorrow. Everything's fine he says – they've had a new key cut. He'll get mine back to me shortly. I suggest it's delivered to the Algonquin in case we finish early here. During our supper break I walk along the street and check into the hotel, which is just the other side of Times Square. The key hasn't appeared nor, when I get back, has it been left at the stage door.

We work through the evening. I return to the hotel. Still no key. The front desk knows nothing about it. I'd like to go to bed. I ring Will's cell phone again.

He answers with a crisp, 'Yes?' then says the key will be with me in about three minutes. He's quite terse. He tells me he's with his mother now in a restaurant, having a 'few last quiet moments'.

I hope Mary is all right. She hasn't, in the various calls during the day, spoken to me or sent any message. We know each other and even worked together when I helped her present a scientific lecture at the Royal Institution. But how can she be 'all right' after the outcome of her husband's recent trial, and the fact that he is even now languishing in a room the size of my dressing room. Though his bed may be more comfortable than Mary's and mine.

I go to my room. An hour or so later the phone rings. It's the night concierge. He has a package for me. That's a relief.

He brings it upstairs. I open it. There's the key and – ah – a note is wrapped round it, I can see the handwriting. Well that's nice. No doubt a message of grateful thanks for helping to rescue the situation. Probably from Mary. I unwrap it. Oh. It's my own. I mean, literally my own writing. Just the note I left with the keys at the stage door this morning.

Tuesday

Coffee in the diner next door to the Algonquin. Alan and Heather are here having the 'full breakfast'. I weaken and order poached eggs.

This morning we work through Act Two. I'm trying to revisit the character afresh, rather than just reproduce the same performance. Alan encourages everybody to play it very seriously for a couple of days.

John has a cold so I don't suggest we go over the blocking of the new number, which we haven't quite finalised. But he wants to anyway and after half an hour it begins to work out. I go upstairs to the theatre offices to record a telemessage in the character of Jeeves, to be heard when people ring the phone lines to purchase tickets. Assuming they do. Later I have supper with James Kall. After perusing the menu he orders his meal, and I am reminded of what a tight budget he and most of the others are on. Donna Lynne has told me that because of the seating capacity of the theatre, the management is able to employ many of the cast, absurdly, on a non-Broadway contract. James selects chicken soup and a toasted bagel. I have the same. Delicious.

More work in the evening. Then a final fitting for the famous new tailcoat.

I'm discovering that the backstage facilities are not great – there are no wash basins in the hutches. And the air-cooling isn't working. It's a hell-hole.

Back to the apartment tonight. Mary has gone. There's a sweet note of thanks on the bed.

Wednesday

Mum's birthday. I hope she got the flowers. I'll ring today to find out.

Yes, they arrived safely. We have the same conversation we have had several times over the years. Before they moved from South Croydon, Mum used to say, if I commented on the terrible weather the south of England might be enduring, 'Yes, but we don't seem to get it here.' Sometimes she would add, 'I think it's because we're in the lee of the hill. We live in a little pocket.'

Whether or not major weather patterns were giving St Mary's Road a miss, it always seemed a wonderfully optimistic attitude, and rather lovely to feel you are dwelling in a little Shangri-La just off the A23. They've now been in their comfortable retirement home in Sidcup for a year and it appears their kindly weather protection has travelled with them. I ask Mum what it's like there today, and mention I've read that London has been in the grip of high winds and driving rain. 'Yes, I believe so,' she says happily, 'but we really don't get it here. We haven't seen it at all.'

The water system for our entire building has been turned off today. I can see plumbers swarming over the roof.

It's a technical rehearsal day at the theatre, though the emphasis is still on trying to re-establish our performances. Some bits go all right, though I'm finding areas where I still can't make everything neat and tidy. The usual problem with the character of Jeeves: striving for economy. There are so many Wodehousian antics going on all around that Jeeves must maintain a still centre.

My dressing room phone is now installed. I call Erin Connor in Los Angeles who is anxious to know about my contractual fridge. I tell her that, as yet, there is no fridge. She says I must on no account 'get into any of that'; she'll ring the production office and find out what's happening.

Later Dan Rosokov lowers his penguin lashes, twitches his mouth humorously and says, 'Hey, I hear you and John are getting fridges in your rooms.'

Ah – has the parity fairy been at work again?

Alan is having more ideas. He now has Jeeves making a new entrance in the 'Love's Maze' morris-dancing number, apparently controlling events from the upper level and ringing a hand bell in time to the music. It's very funny. If I want to, suggests Michael O'Flaherty, I can shake the bell on the downbeat. Oh yeah? More musical responsibility.

Bobby Grayson is here. He hasn't had far to come; his salon is upstairs in the same building. It was probably once a palatial dressing room. He shimmies to and fro, restyling my hair rhythmically into the urbane short back and sides.

We've been assured the air will be turned on later, but it hasn't been yet. So, at work we have water but no cooling, and at home cooling but no water.

Ros's radio theatre production of *Betrayal* has opened to an air-cooled packed house.

Everything is cool in Sidcup.

★

Thursday

Approaching the theatre I pass three women on the sidewalk outside the stage-door alley, one of whom seems to be a tour guide of some sort. They are all talking loudly about how keen they are to see the show. 'I've seen the website,' says one, 'I've heard *By Jeeves* is great.'

I think she's referring to 'Ask Jeeves', one of the internet search engines. They are right in my path and, as I am about to open the iron gate, I assure them it's a great show.

'Really? Hey! Are you in the show?'

'Yes,' I confess. Their leader gives me an immediate hug and asks for the management's number. She says she wants to bring a party of eighty and could she come round after and interview me for her tourist magazine?

'You'd better,' I reply.

'Wow,' she whoops. 'An interview with a Broadway star!'

Of course the party of eighty could be her mother.

We have our first dress rehearsal tonight. Alan is continuing to put stuff in. It's all good, but how long is Act One going to be?

The new number goes smoothly. And the little dance is getting back into shape.

The loo situation in our under-stage dungeon is not so good. One men's lavatory, two corridors away, is shared by all the male cast, stage-management and crew. Frustratingly there is one girl's loo on our side of the bunker, as opposed to the distant always-in-use men's loo. It's going to be a nightmare on our first public performance, first night nerves being what they are.

★

Friday

Someone shows me a cartoon in the current *Private Eye*. It's a book-shop with two separate displays. One shows a huge pile of audio-cassettes and a notice that reads: 'Books on Tape read by Martin Jarvis.' The other display is a meagre pile of cassettes and a notice: 'Books on Tape read by someone else.'

A better joke, I say to Heather, who demands to see it, would be 'Plays by Alan Ayckbourn.' And 'Plays by somebody else.'

There's a slight panic today – John has a problem with his voice. He grinds to a halt during one number at this morning's rehearsal and later decides not to sing at all, only speak softly. Alan is concerned of course. John has had a cold for the last few days. Result, the evening dress rehearsal is cancelled. Pity, though I think it's the best thing in the circumstances.

This afternoon we have another scare. Various companies, including the NBC television studios and the *New York Times* newspaper offices (almost next-door to our theatre, just the other side of Sardi's) have apparently received mysterious packages. They could possibly contain anthrax. In Florida a woman is suffering the effects of the white powder. This one may well be a hoax, but we are told we can't go out in the street, and nobody is allowed back into the theatre. Luckily we are all here and perhaps our fetid bunker is the best place at present. Later, all is clear.

Company manager Bruce pads across, barking a request for next Monday week – will John and I consider appearing at Bloomingdales to perform a ten-minute excerpt from the show? This is a message from the enigmatic promotion people who seem to keep well away from us. Bloomingdales? The department store? I suppose so. Anything that will help to advertise the production.

Bruce then launches into a discussion about my contractual car: an arrangement whereby, once our performances begin, a hire car will collect me from home, deliver me to the theatre each day and take me back afterwards. I have already decided that, despite the pleasing idea of a 'limo', it could become restricting. I waive the car for the moment and go for the more spontaneous cab option. I'll just give Bruce receipts at the end of each week. Throughout this exchange I feel uneasy, as I know John can hear us through the paper-thin wall. I'm worried that the parity fairy may have missed a trick on his behalf. But then, I tell myself, he only lives a few streets away.

The stage-crew guys are very much chips off the old Pittsburgh block. But their New York accents remind me of any number of characters from *The Godfather*. Butch – smiling, giant-sized, paunchy, is their congenial boss. Mike – crop-haired, muscle-bound, punchy, is more worrying. He invariably seems to be asleep until just a second before his many cues to tug the upstage-right curtain and let me and others onto the stage.

Yesterday I requested a designated chair, as I spend a lot of time in the wings waiting for my next entrance. There's not quite enough time to go down to the bunker. Whenever I come off, somebody else (just like Toronto) seems to be sitting in it. Today, courtesy of Butch, a fold-up chair with my name on it has appeared.

Saturday

A 'wandelprobe' in the afternoon to introduce the new band, con-ducted with headmasterly efficiency by Michael O' Flaherty. It's a good opportunity for John and I to practise our new piece. We go through it twice and we're getting fluent.

John is feeling much better.

Wade Russo has told me, sadly, that he was not re-offered the Ozzie Nutledge role. 'I'm deeply downcast about it, Mart'n,' he says. I can see he is. Michael will be Ozzie for the first six weeks, before the musical associate from the Goodspeed Opera House takes over. Wade will be on keyboards.

Half an hour later he's laughing again. He has invented a new character, for his own and others' offstage entertainment, based on someone he and John know – a man who can't stop telling people of his sexual orientation. For example, 'You see this tie I'm wearing – I really love it – well, y'know, it's because I'm gay…' Or, 'Oh, I just *adore* that music – well of course, it's because I'm gay…' The permutations are endless and funny.

Tonight is our scheduled second dress rehearsal, now our first. I feel apprehensive. I would dearly like to have had a previous one.

Michael Price is here. John and I tackle him at once about the lack of photographs in the empty frames in front of the theatre. He affects a certain surprise, but whether at the temerity of our questions, or that there are no pictures, we're not sure.

Sunday

This morning I visit the delicatessen on the corner of 68th Street and Amsterdam Avenue, having bought a copy of the *New York Times* at the kiosk on 70th and Broadway. I bring my coffee and croissant, plus some brown bag purchases for tea this afternoon, out to the seating area on the street. So now I look like a real New Yorker – or perhaps just a homeless person taking up the whole bench with my belongings.

Back upstairs to the apartment and work through the play. I ring James – we arrange to see *Serendipity*, a new movie directed by Peter Chelsom, whom Ros and I have met in Los Angeles. I also invite Steve, who lives round the corner. *Serendipity* is a cute-meet romance set in New York (though shot in Montreal) and clearly appropriate for the atmosphere in the city now. Like *By Jeeves*, it's non-controversial and warm-hearted.

Steve is waiting for us outside the cinema afterwards, having been knee-deep in laundry all afternoon. We return to the apartment, where James has left his shopping, and drink pink lemonade out of the Morleys' cocktail glasses, then wander up Broadway to a diner. Finally home to read the *New York Times*, watch TV in bed and of course, check the script, compulsively, yet again.

Monday October 15th

Further refinements from Alan this afternoon. Andrew will be here tonight.

Then, in the evening, it seems like a first night. A real bubble of anticipation in the auditorium. It's only a final dress rehearsal but the house is full of what sounds like, listening to them over the tannoy, a predominantly young audience. I know there are many friends of the cast out there. Ros has made it just in time from LA.

Although I had, of course, wanted another dress rehearsal in the afternoon, it becomes increasingly clear that we needed to put it in front of an audience. They lap it up. New boy Sam Tsoutsouvas gives a clear and strong performance. John and I get cheers, both at the beginning and (increased) at the end. Andrew isn't here after all; his flight was cancelled minutes before take-off.

There are many compliments afterwards, and a large crowd of fans jostle at the stage-door. Ros is pleased with my progress.

Alan discusses with me the possibility that at the end of the play I might say something like 'The British are here...' to the audience. Hmm. I say, 'Well, as long as it doesn't sound arrogant.' I know what he means though: the British standing shoulder to shoulder with their American colleagues at this particular time.

★

Tuesday

It's the first preview tonight. Again just a few 'fixes' in the afternoon.

I ask Alan about the Brit bit at the end. Has he had any further thoughts?

'Yes,' he says, 'bad idea, the play is doing that already.'

Yup.

We have a Sheila Carter warm-up. She laughed the other day as I taught my new dancing partner, Sam, the rudiments of the Gay Gordons. Today I am partnered by six foot five Steve Wilson. He's the girl.

Ros has slipped into the theatre, enhancing my room with extra drawers and wooden furnishing. Folk put their heads round the door admiringly. They assume they're from the management, part of my Broadway contract. John spots them. He looks relieved when I tell him they're from Ros.

Tonight, my first paid performance on Broadway. Below stage the lavatories are working overtime. Everyone is tense. Steve Wilson, ready in his cricket whites and Clark Gable moustache says, 'My God Mart'n, I woke up this morning – I've haven't felt so excited since my wedding day. Real butterflies, but rarin' to go.'

I feel the audience is a more typical one, older, and appreciating more of the literary references. But they're not quite so demonstrative as last night. John and others think they're wonderful. Ros afterwards agrees with me. John Chardiet, an actor friend from Hollywood, is there. Surprisingly, Flo, John's agent, congratulates me in the alley afterwards, beaming fatly. But no sign of even a conspiratorial thank you for John's deal and all the trimmings.

Andrew has made it and puts his nose round the corner of the hellhole. He shakes me surprisingly warmly by the hand. 'Thank you, Martin. Thank you.' He appears to have enjoyed it. Tells me he's got one or two musical bits to tickle. Musical? Not me, I guess. Alan seems pleased. Heather is very complimentary.

Some of us go round the corner to Sam's Bar, where the waitresses serve beer and burgers at red-checked tables. They ask, 'Hey guys, how's the show going?' Ten minutes later they themselves are singing as sublimely as many a Broadway star, at the microphone at one end of the smoky room.

Wednesday

The matinee is full. Quite a large turnout of the fluffy-white and blue-rinse brigade, and the show is a riot. Ah, is this our audience then?

As I leave the theatre and start walking up 8th Avenue to find a taxi, I hear the tones of an unmistakable voice in the centre of a knot of people walking fifteen yards ahead of me. It seems to be asking about American breakfast food. 'Tell me, what are "grits"?' There's something about the querulous vibrato that lends the enquiry a dramatic, almost cosmic importance. It's Ian McKellen, just too far ahead for me to catch him. As always.

I get home to find Ros struggling with a basket chair she has bought from Gracious Home, trying to manoeuvre it down the passage and through the narrow doorway into our bedroom. I attempt assistance. We twist it around at every angle, but it's impossible. Time is up. I leave her sitting in the narrow corridor outside our room, for once defeated.

I'm back at the theatre by seven. Andrew is here to talk about some new underscoring. After he has subtly altered the tempo of part of the finale I hear, emerging from my mouth, one of the more unlikely remarks I have made in the course of a production: 'But I can't dance this slowly.'

Tonight the play doesn't go as well – or is it that we find this audience, after the easier one of this afternoon, harder to please?

Tony Ring, of the British P.G. Wodehouse Society, is here and has enormous praise for the production. He pronounces it the most authentically Wodehousian of the versions he's seen. Who are we to argue?

It's Molly Renfroe's birthday and we're invited to Café 123. Ros has decided to stay at the apartment, battling the furniture. Molly's husband, urologist Dan, foots the whole bill. We're all surprised at this generosity – there are about sixteen of us. Alan redresses the balance by writing something on the paper tablecloth for Molly, plus a personalised cartoon. I suggest she tears them off. Rather like an instant Picasso – an Ayckbourn original to treasure.

I get home to find that Ros has somehow managed to impel the basket chair through the narrow bedroom doorway. How? By taking the door off its hinges, using those extra few inches, then rehanging it.

Simple when you know how.

Thursday

Ruth Leon is arriving again today, so we retrench to our own self-contained room, leaving her desk in the living room clear of all our office stuff.

There's a three-thirty rehearsal call at the theatre. John and I chat beforehand and discuss once again the fact that Act One is no shorter. Several of John's visitors have mentioned to him that, while admiring the show very much, they would have liked the first half to finish sooner. Ros has felt the same. I know Michael Price wanted time taken off – he discussed that with me many months ago. Besides emailing Heather on the subject of new material and the possibility of 'getting to the interval that crucial five minutes earlier', John and I agree there's nothing more to do, short of confronting Alan with what John's friends have been saying. Tricky. And are they right? Not necessarily. Ten minutes later, as if our thoughts have been hovering in the air, Alan mentions in the note session that 'over his dead body' will he make cuts in any areas.

Emily Loesser is not appearing tonight. She has a chest infection and because of her pregnancy can't take any medication. Molly will play Stiffy and the new swing, Cristin, will cover all Molly's stuff and perform in the ensemble. Molly sings beautifully in the rehearsal. Husband Dan has two important operations to perform in New Jersey tomorrow but is staying here in New York to witness Molly's major Broadway debut, and says he will even postpone the ops if necessary. That's showbiz. Her brother Owen, director of the soap opera *General Hospital* arrives, having flown up from LA.

It's not an easy house. Seems to be made up of various groups, some enjoying it, or 'getting it', more than others. John is worried by the gaps in the seating – there are people, he thinks, who didn't return after the interval. It ends up well though, and there are cheers. I have felt there was something wrong tonight, some uneasiness in the audience, but can't quite put my finger on it.

My own groupies are out front. Luther Davis and Jennifer Bassey (they of the bedroomless apartment), Peter and Liz Levelle, British friends visiting the city on business, and Bill Bast and Paul Huson, screenwriters from Los Angeles.

They are all generally complimentary afterwards, but it turns out that they were freezing cold. Liz and Pete especially, who were sitting beneath an open vent, through which an icy blast was blowing. I will investigate tomorrow. There is a theory that 'comedy is cold': in other words, don't keep audiences too warm or they'll get somnolent. But this seems too chilly for anyone's comfort.

Alan spends five minutes in John's room, but does not come into mine. My paranoia fairy pops up – can he think of nothing to say? Was I that bad? I pass him at the stage-door as we troop off to Orso, and ask if all is OK. He nods non-committally, so I really don't know what he's thinking. Maybe it'll become clearer tomorrow.

I dream tonight that I have committed a murder, but have escaped detection.

What does that mean?

Friday

The box office returns for the last four performances suggest we are averaging about $20,000 a night. Mostly reduced prices for previews. And there are lots of complimentary tickets. The advance booking figure a few days ago stood at around $800,000, which sounds fairly healthy to me, especially as the Helen Hayes is not large. But compared to *Mamma Mia*'s three million advance it won't keep us going for very long without some great reviews.

I take flowers to the theatre for Molly and Cristin, to congratulate them on their understudy debuts last night. We have a note session. Alan is looking like an old, whipped dog. Oh dear. He tells us, as we settle in the stalls and he on the steps to the stage, that he has been getting requests to – he rolls his eyes as if he can hardly believe it – 'take five minutes out of the show'. Act One, he hears, is deemed too long. He goes on to say that this is from the Goodspeed people and no one else. Why, he wonders? Is it just that the New York attention span is short? He gazes around, then upwards, as if seeking an answer from the gods. No one says anything. Well, this is the moment, I tell myself. It has come up too many times, I suppose, for there not to be something in it.

I decide not to raise this in public but in private, afterwards, with Al. Given that he himself has brought it up, it would surely be wrong to keep quiet and kind of pretend we are as surprised as he seems to be about these comments. In a lull while Alan is talking to Dan, I murmur to John that this is what I'm going to do. John has fear in his eyes. 'Do you want me there?' he asks. I say it's up to him.

Half an hour later, at the end of the session, Alan and I go up to the back of the stalls. John bravely joins us. I put the points that John and I have been discussing. Alan seems thrown, an odd look in his eye. I tell him I think it's fair, since he has now raised the matter, to pass on the comments I know many folk have raised – in the context, I stress, of loving the show – that the first act is too long.

He folds his arms, nods a few times, flicks his shoulders rapidly up to his ears and down again, then discusses how things could be cut. 'Not easy,' he says. Then, with savage humour, 'Trouble is, it's all this bloody music. We keep adding stuff.'

We joke, 'If only it weren't for the music we could get on with the show…!'

He mentions cutting some of our car dialogue. Ouch. Or a lot of Cyrus Budge's first scene. And, he says, the act would need actual rewriting to accommodate losing, say, five minutes.

He's right. I feel that I must say I'm game to try anything, even if it means losing favourite moments of my own.

Afterwards John tells me that 'loving Alan so much' he found that conversation very difficult. I did too. But it would have felt like a small betrayal if I had just sat there and said nothing. John knows what I mean.

Some 'tickles' are made, but it's decided no cuts tonight.

The show gets off to a great start and when we reach the car scene, which goes particularly well – we don't hang about with it – I think, oh dear, I hope we don't have to lose this.

I consult with Dan at the interval and guess that we took a minute off the act.

'Yes,' he says, 'we did, but I'll tell Michael Price it was two minutes.'

That probably won't solve the problem.

Our friends Larry and Davina Belling are here, with Larry's

brother Eddie who is an old-time Broadway box office manager. I tell him our advance is probably around $800,000. He shakes his head and looks sorry for me.

Larry comments on my make-up. Too pale, he opines, and undefined because of the harsh lighting in Act One.

'But,' I bleat, sounding like Nigel Planer's monumentally thespy character Nicholas Craig, 'don't you realise, I'm *meant* to be pale!'

Saturday

Sheridan Morley has arrived in New York. A great grey-whiskered badger, sitting at the table in the living room, correcting proofs of the American version of his Gielgud biography. He splurges for twenty minutes about his problems with the magazine for which he currently writes, and his future plans. He can't stop talking. That's what makes him, among other things, a terrific broadcaster, and a master raconteur. I sometimes wonder if he is still competing with his late father, the revered Robert. I must introduce him to Becky Watson.

I'm very fond of Sherry, having first met him when I played Henry V at the age of nineteen for the National Youth Theatre. He was a student at Oxford at the time and friends with various members of the cast. I still remember him enthusing to Simon Ward and me, after an early performance, 'Yes, yes, it's going to be all right: creditable verse-speaking, good breech speech, broad comic playing in the wooing scene – hugged myself with glee.' Even at that age he sounded like a critic, one who actually loves the theatre.

The matinee goes like a dream. Because of yesterday's adjustments we take nearly two minutes off the running time. Groups of (mostly) ladies of uncertain years wait outside the theatre asking for autographs and say nice things. Are we wrong about the first half after all?

This evening I make a tiny but boring error in Act Two. Alan is there but I don't see him afterwards. I run into Michael Price by chance in the street, outside Sardis. I ask him whether he still feels, despite the couple of minutes we've taken off, that we should lose those crucial five.

'You bet, Marv.' He nods his head emphatically.

Sunday

This morning I watch writer/producer Steven Bochco being interviewed on a television arts programme concerning exactly the same point Alan has been talking about. Steven is discussing the frustrations encountered in creating various television series and not being able to extend scenes to the kind of length he would like. He puts it down to the 'zapper' syndrome.

This encourages me to send an email to Alan this morning, saying that purely the psychology of his general chat to the company concerning Act One, plus those two tiny tickles we have incorporated, has resulted in our shaving off at least a minute's playing time.

I tell him that, typically of course, John and I have found that the car section leading up to the 'Travel Hopefully' number has never gone better than in the last three performances! I reassure him though that we're brave boys and ready to take any excisions and refinements he decides upon. I mention the Bochco programme and say that it does seem (as Alan himself suggested) that the culprit is nothing more than the American attention span.

Everyone is very nervous about the cuts, which we are going to hear about after the performance. We'll rehearse them on Tuesday. Don Stephenson, who has always been an advocate for losing at least ten minutes, buttonholes me in the wings, quivering with comic apprehension. I start to mutter something about the greater good but he runs away like a stuck pig, just before the 'Pig' number. He does it to make me smile. But I can see he's worried.

I may have found a new laugh. It's quite a good moment – after Bertie's 'Do you think they're following it, this lot?' Intriguing how a tiny move can make all the difference: instead of having my eyes already fixed upon the house, I shifted my gaze crisply from John towards the audience, as if to evaluate their intelligence. Big laugh. Then a firmer second laugh, as Jeeves decides, 'Impossible to tell, sir.' Well, it keeps one on one's toes.

Dan distributes the sheets of script that hold the dreaded cuts. Everyone grabs them as if they are exam results, each hoping the moderator has been lenient. We study them anxiously. They are really only small trims, all useful, but I doubt if they will take more than another two minutes off the running time.

I walk down the street to the Algonquin to meet Ros, Bill Bast and Paul Huson. Bill seems more positive about his reaction to *By Jeeves*. He's clearly thawed out from last Thursday. Having been virtually silent on the subject then, he is now especially complimentary. He raves, though, about the off-Broadway musical, *Bat Boy*, and tells us they have enjoyed seeing Ian McKellen in *Dance of Death*. Bill takes us a few doors down the street to the Iroquois Hotel where he used to live with James Dean. He was Dean's lover at the time of the fatal car accident, and is writing what will surely be the definitive account, *Life and Death with James Dean*. He proudly shows us a small back room, rather grandly named the James Dean Lounge.

Bill and Paul then leave for a business meeting. They are writing a television mini-series, *Power and Beauty*, about Judith Exner, who was mistress to both John F. Kennedy and mob boss Sam Giancana.

Yet more arrivals at the apartment: Peter, Sheridan Morley's driver. And friend. They will be sleeping in the living room. It's getting like the ship's cabin scene from *A Night at the Opera*, starring the Marx Brothers. Peter seems to be a theatre buff. Well, he'd have to be, working for the Morleys. He's fairly loquacious too. Theatrical gossip is currently bouncing off every wall. Sherry announces he's going to direct Enid Bagnold's play *The Chalk Garden* in London and would Ros like to play a three-scene part? Later he describes it to her as a two-scene part.

Just before we go to bed I find an email from Alan in which he discusses the fact that the show did look much tighter last night. Although Michael Price had been muttering about them being a 'tough crowd', he found them altogether rather friendly. He goes on to say he feels we are always going to lose a handful of people at half-time. Even if we cut the first half down to twenty minutes, we would. If you don't get the show, then you just don't get it.

I'm relieved he agrees about the zapper generation having put paid to anything lasting more than about twenty-five seconds. The writing was on the wall when people actually grew to miss the commercial breaks on television, welcoming them as a chance to unwind and refocus. Bad enough in the UK every twenty minutes, but here it's after every ten or less!

He's going to be excising a few bits on Tuesday, but, he says, nothing like as sweepingly as he'd outlined. He's tried to cut fairly and evenly but is nonetheless aware the brunt will fall upon John, inevitably. Cosmetic rather than butchering. He asked Dan to distribute the list this afternoon so that people can prepare for Tuesday. If the cuts demonstrably damage the show then they can always be restored for Thursday and we can say, 'Well, we tried,' before the press arrive. He tells me he is already being petitioned by one company member not to cut anything of theirs, and finishes by suggesting that the proof will be in the overall show.

Of course.

★

Monday October 22nd

It's a day off and as usual it feels like a Sunday.

Ros and I wander in the sunshine to Central Park. I speak on the cell phone to my sister in England. She feels guilty that she can't pluck up the courage to come to New York. She wants to, but like many others is fearful of the atmosphere and the situation caused by September 11th. Greg, her architect husband, would like to come, as he's interested in the steel structure that fatally collapsed because of the heat engendered by the burning fuel.

The anthrax scare continues, with small amounts of the substance appearing in various offices, mail rooms, television stations etc. It doesn't seem clear whether this is really connected with the Taliban or just the mindless actions of bandwagon extremists/weirdos. US bombing also continues and there are reports of heavy attacks on Taliban strongholds in Afghanistan – Kabul and Kandahar.

I've hardly heard of Kandahar since it featured in a Sixties film, *The Brigand of Kandahar*. Welsh actor Ronald Lewis secretly took part in this modest epic when he was supposed to have been acting on stage every night in *Poor Bitos* at the Duke of York's Theatre. I had the small but showy part (my first play in the West End) of an escaped convict who has to shoot leading man Donald Pleasance in the head. Ronnie had taken time off owing to, he told producer Michael Codron, a large boil on his bottom. Donald wasn't best pleased at the sudden absence of his co-star but as he remarked to us all, cold eyes growing positively glacial, he could hardly demand to see proof. Ronnie's doctor (a fellow Welshman) had advised that he should not appear for at least ten days as his part required a great deal of sitting down. The understudy filled in until Ronnie showed up at the theatre two weeks later, sporting a wide grin and a heavy tan.

On its release, I went to see *The Brigand of Kandahar*. The title role was played with great panache by Lewis himself as a sort of Robin

Hood of the desert. I noticed he spent much of the movie in the saddle with no perceivable signs of discomfort.

My Jeeves promo outfit has arrived at the apartment. This is an off-the-peg version of the beautifully fitted tailcoat, impeccably striped trousers, neat waistcoat, collar and cuffs. The reason for a second 'reach-me-down' costume is that John and I have agreed to do those promotional appearances in the great stores of New York. This, say the elusive marketing people (whom we still haven't met) will attract attention to the show and help to sell tickets. Fair enough, that's what we want. I smarm my hair back and get togged up. Nothing quite fits. At half past four, feeling more like a busking toastmaster than the archetypical gentleman's personal gentleman, I creep out of the flat disguised in a bulky raincoat that has been hanging in the cupboard since before we arrived. I can hear Sherry and Ruth in the kitchen but slip away soundlessly. For some actorish reason I don't want them to see me as Jeeves before they attend the show on the opening night. And the raincoat is probably his.

Ros has slipped out with me and we travel by taxi to Blooming-dales, where John and I (with Wade Russo at the piano) are to perform 'Never Fear' on a small platform in the expensive 'designers' area. One subsidiary marketing man is actually there to greet us. Wade is clutching the frying pan that masquerades as a banjo in the opening dialogue. We were asked to arrive at five o'clock, so are not best pleased to find we have to wait for an hour before doing a sound-check. Other Broadway shows will be performing other items on other floors. Our appearance, we discover, will not be until half past seven. What? This is really foolish scheduling and John and I decide we'll have to be much stricter about time-wasting in future.

Like Vladimir and Estragon (with Ros as Lucky) we sit around in a windowless office, waiting. Naturally we discuss the proposed cuts we'll be rehearsing tomorrow. It turns out that John (like me) has timed them. We agree they will probably only take two minutes off.

Tonight's only bonus is that a television crew from the main New York news channel is here and we are called out to do an interview. We both mention the title and the name of the theatre as many times as we can.

Finally we are clambering on to our makeshift stage, more nervous than when we do the show for real. I introduce us and, just as we are getting going with the song, Wade's keyboard inexplicably becomes unplugged. John has to finish the number with no accompanying music. Annoying and unsatisfactory. We are neither of us best pleased with our marketing man.

He shrugs and fingers his kipper tie nervously.

We stride off into the night, hailing taxis – overdressed, tetchy and pissed off. Luckily, Ros is on hand to calm us down.

Tuesday

The afternoon of the short knives.

Everyone behaves very professionally about the cuts – though Don is a bit like a recalcitrant schoolboy, clearly not happy to lose anything. When we rehearse the sections, often joining two speeches together that originally had another sentence between them, he can't quite manage it. I feel sorry for him, though he's losing very few lines. Alan is gently implacable. The rest of us are stoic. We carry on. The cuts are implemented.

In the dressing room, Don tells me that each one of his laughs is very important to him. 'Mart'n, they're like my little babies. I nurture them and think about them all the time.' I offer him the Noël Coward quote – that sometimes we have to murder our darlings. He shakes his head. He cannot be comforted. He flings himself into the armchair then looks up at me in anguish. I feel like Magda Goebbels. A second later I'm hurrying away, as John and I have another promotion to do in our second-hand gear. On the way out Alan mutters to me, 'I cut two of his lines but they might as well have been his balls, I'm afraid.'

The appearance begins badly with the car arranged by the marketing company arriving twenty minutes late to pick us up from the front of the theatre. The venue is Grand Central Station. This time we really do feel like buskers. A shaky stage has been set up in the beautiful old ticket hall under high ceramic ceilings. The acoustics are atrocious. There are approximately a hundred and twenty people idly gathered about. We peep out from our hiding place – a scruffy store room. We've agreed we're not going to be kept waiting this time.

'Come on,' says John, 'let's get it over with,' and we stride out across the concourse with a kind of desperate flamboyance, and onto the podium. There's barely a smattering of applause. I introduce the three of us but could just as well be selling sausages. They can't hear a word and my voice goes scrambling up into the roof and stays there. It's irrelevant whether Wade Russo's keyboard plugs are firmly in place or not – most of the spectators drift away shaking their heads and looking at each other with a bewildered air, as if seeking some sort of explanation.

Ten minutes later we are waiting on the sidewalk in our period outfits. Wade is carrying the frying pan that is supposed to add authenticity to our guest appearance. If we didn't look like street entertainers before, we do now. Eventually the car turns up and we sit in fuming silence as we are driven back to the theatre. No more busking, we all agree. That's it, however much we want to promote the show. It's too demeaning.

But what an upsurge an hour later. Undoubtedly the best audience we've had. Lloyd Webber and his wife Madeleine are here. The cuts work like a dream. Don Stephenson valiantly zips things along and gets more laughs than ever. The first half runs only one hour and ten minutes. Hurray!

★

ACT THREE

Wednesday

A British tea-party in front of the theatre, hosted by Andrew and Alan. The entire company has been asked to appear in costume. We wait in the stalls for a signal to emerge onto the street. There's a flurry as the head public relations man, who has yet to introduce himself to John and me, hustles Alan into a special UK/NY T-shirt. I find myself overseeing this costume change in an uncalled-for Jeevesian manner and can't help leaning over to pull it down at the back. 'Hang on,' Alan snaps, 'I haven't finished yet.'

The event is actually very effective. At least two film crews are present, plenty of press people, and the whole thing engenders a large crowd and a good deal of interest up and down 44th Street. With any luck it should gain us some coverage. I had agreed only to appear for a few minutes but (of course) stayed half an hour. John wasn't coming at all – and stayed even longer. I attempt to detain the PR boss but he, I'm certain, sees me coming and ducks away into the crowd, unmet.

Plenty of those ladies and gentlemen of uncertain years give the matinee performance as much of a standing ovation as they comfortably can. An American friend, Suellen Nessler, comes dashing round afterwards and exclaims enthusiastically, 'Mart, you've got the best part!' I shush her at once, as this would not be good for John to hear – true or not.

Both Alan and Andrew have been spotted in the stalls afterwards, together with Michaels Price and O'Flaherty. These sightings are confirmed later by lookout Donna Lynne, who has overheard Andrew discussing the fact that there's too much 'sprecht singing'. Oh dear, that's me. 'Like in the Pig number,' reports Donna Lynne. Ah, that's not me. I wonder if it will be raised at the note session tomorrow.

The evening show. Not an easy audience. John is subdued, though

219

on stage he's as powerful as ever. I'm thinking about this speak-singing business and utter a wrong word in the patter.

Thursday

Our first press night.

Unlike the West End, where critics mostly attend the show on one specific evening, in New York they're likely to be here on any of three or four performances leading up to the opening, by which time they've all seen it.

Alan's session this afternoon is another of his masterclasses in theatre. He bemoans last night's audience. He thinks it's a Wednesday club: wives dragging unwilling husbands, ticket concessions, people who really don't know what they have come to see. Nevertheless, he reminds us, it's good to have a less responsive house. It shows us where our weaknesses lie. He makes all sorts of classic Ayckbourn points to the assembled company. 'Don't confuse speed with pace.' 'Go for the whole speech. Don't sacrifice the "whole" for seventeen sub-points.' 'It's a story.' He mentions the actor who once said to him, 'It's very difficult to *work* this material.' To which Alan replied, 'Work? It shouldn't seem like working.'

My only note is one I have had before: don't over-colour the patter song. 'The curse of creativity,' says Al with one of his quick, tight smirks in my direction.

I try it out during the rehearsal that follows and, of course, it's much improved. Michael O'Flaherty takes the ensemble through several of Andrew's musical requests.

Alan is in anecdotal mood. He had dinner with Stephen Sondheim last night and says Stephen agrees that Wednesdays are always bad nights in New York. He then tells the story of when Sondheim was writing *Company*: he went back to his townhouse on the East Side, and worked late into the night, loudly singing at the piano, composing madly. At two in the morning an irate woman in a turban tapped at the garden window. 'Please can you keep it down, you're disturbing the neighbourhood. Some of us have to start early tomorrow.' It was Katharine Hepburn.

Ten minutes before the show Molly Renfroe decides to call us all together for a company hug. Rather like a rugby team getting into a huddle before the big match. She asks for someone to say something. John turns and looks at me. I speak briefly about how amazing it is, after our roller-coaster ride, that we are all finally here – old friends, new friends, newest friends, and that there's no reason why we shouldn't remain where we are for some time to come. Seems to be appropriate.

We discover, throughout the evening, that Alan's last minute fine-tuning has worked, and sense that the story is being told as well as it's ever been.

Loyal Kathy Campbell is here from Pittsburgh with news of their latest production and dark hints concerning the temperament of its leading actor, F. Murray Abraham.

Erin Connor's friend Bill, a manager whom I have never met, does not appear afterwards. I had arranged with Bruce that there would be tickets for him to pick up at the box office. He's bringing 'an important casting director'. I go out to the front of house and ask various folk, 'Excuse me, are you Bill?' They aren't. But the box office has no uncollected tickets. So was he here?

I leave a message on Badgley Connor's machine telling Erin I never hooked up with Bill.

★

Friday

There's a message from Erin. Yesterday her friend Bill did come to the
theatre beforehand. He asked at the box office for his seats. There
were no tickets there for him. He and his guest left. I'm appalled at
this news and call Bruce at once. I even have the confirmation slip he
gave me. He examines it.

'Huh,' he barks, 'I screwed up.'

I ask him to call Erin immediately to explain.

This afternoon is probably our last meeting with Alan. He has virtually no notes for us. He suggests that all the major critics were in last
night. So that's a relief.

My old chum Martin Jenkins is here tonight, hot-foot from a
Manhattan studio where he has been directing John Turturro in a
BBC reading of *The Big Sleep*. I hope the title isn't a bad omen for us.

Everything goes wonderfully well until I miss out two lines in
the patter number. It's because Martin is here and we have a long-
standing joke about my embarrassing singing attempts in an obscure
Strindberg play he once directed. I come back into rhythm a
moment later, but dammit, I'm angry with myself.

Martin says afterwards he didn't notice. Hmm.

Saturday

Before the matinee I bump into Ted Pappas in Schubert Alley,
just round the corner from the Helen Hayes. He's looking svelte
in dark suit and tie and raincoat. Ebony-framed specs complete the
ensemble. We chat for a few minutes, and I tell him the company
feel we wouldn't be here at all if it weren't for him. I'm thinking of
his initial commitment to try out the play in Pittsburgh. It's true.
He's pleased.

The wretched patter starts going round and round in my head, turning into 'When you're lying awake/With a dismal headache' from *Iolanthe*. All goes well this afternoon but in the preceding scene I make a mini-error. Of course I'm thinking of the up-coming number.

Sunday

The critics have all been, we believe. So what is there to worry about now?

Well, it seems I might not get there in one piece for the official opening, from the way my taxi races down Broadway. An ambulance is right behind, in pole position to administer emergency first aid if we smash into something. Then it overtakes us. My driver leaps into its wake as if we are now part of its urgent quest. The ambulance cuts and weaves amongst the Broadway traffic. We duck and dive, sticking to it like white on rice, overtaking everything else in our path.

I unbuckle, and stagger out clutching my receipt.

I'm early at the theatre, which is full of flowers. I distribute my presents – glitzy stars – and cards. I have bouquets from Jean Diamond, ICM in Los Angeles and from the Badgley Connor agency. I'm immensely touched by the personal messages from my colleagues. And staggered by some who suggest that I have led them from the front, by example. Tom Ford describes me as 'the beating heart of the company'. If only they knew of the flutters.

Something called the Gypsy Robe ceremony takes place on stage. Almost incomprehensible, it seems to be a chorus line tradition dating from way back, in which musical theatre companies keep adding pieces of material over the years to an elaborate garment that looks like Liberace's nightshirt. Whatever it means, it brings us all together for ten minutes. Alan and Heather watch from the stalls.

They look bemused as David Edwards, our male swing, parades up and down like Wee Willie Winkie in the voluminous costume while we stand in a circle and applaud him. Then we go below to get ready.

It's a good performance, focused and tight despite all the oddities of a friends/backers/celebrity audience. An uneasy mix of nervous supporters and wellwishers, and possibly a few who don't wish much for it at all. But it feels like it's going well and I even find one or two new unforced laughs. The response to the patter is best-ever.

'Friends in the balcony, Jeeves?' improvises John as the applause continues.

'My guests only occupy the best seats, sir,' I hear myself reply. I'm thinking of Ros with Cindy Katz and Jon Shapiro in the fifth row.

The party is at Sardi's. Of course. There are various journalists making the rounds and two television crews. I'm interested to spot an actor of my acquaintance who, Alan tells me, makes a habit of appearing at first nights. A few years ago Joan Collins was asked what she thought the title of this gentleman's autobiography should be if he ever wrote one. She is said to have replied without hesitation, '*Brown Nose, Black Tie.*' He makes no attempt to join us. Whatever he thought of the show he clearly doesn't rate me as worth brown-nosing.

Actresses Rosemary Harris and Judy Campbell are here, as well as Sheridan and Ruth. Doyenne television anchor Barbara Walters inclines her head graciously as I catch her eye, and mimes delicate applause. Penny Fuller, an American actress we know from Los Angeles, is fulsome. Actor Jim Dale grins and smiles. Rue McClanahan raises her glass in my direction – no drinks embargo tonight. And no sign of the Clintons, Giuliani, Pataki and Co. Ros is the cynosure in a long Donna Karan dress.

Alan is cowering a little and wants to escape to eat. He doesn't like shepherd's pie, Heather explains. It's Andrew's choice.

Before he and Heather flee, Alan tells the story of their visit to

Lloyd Webber in his palatial New York apartment in the Trump Tower. Their coats having been taken by a Hispanic maid they spent an enjoyable evening. When the time came for them to leave, the maid was nowhere to be found. Andrew rang his wife Madeleine, who happened to be in Italy. 'Where's the cloakroom?' he asked.

'Next to the dining room,' she replied.

Off he went to look, but returned to the phone a minute or two later and called her again. 'Where's the dining room…?'

His lordship seems tired and understandably emotional this evening. Some of us are standing around near the upstairs bar. Moving along the line he suddenly beams at James Kall, thrusts out his hand and, in a voice that reminds me of Prince Charles at some interminable function, says, 'I'm Andrew Lloyd Webber. Who are you? What do you do?'

James, without a flicker, replies, 'I'm your Gussie.' At which Andrew hesitates, looks around for assistance, finds none, and moves on.

Michael Price weaves his way into the group and says the Associated Press is a rave. But what about the *New York Times*? I'm starting to get a funny feeling. Is that why Andrew and Alan look battered?

Have they seen an advance copy?

Monday October 29th

Alan and Heather leave town today.

Good reviews are coming through. Along with news of hundreds of bodies still unidentified in the World Trade Centre tragedy. And information from the FBI that another attack on America is expected from al-Qaeda. Tony Blair makes a similar announcement in England but suggests the target could be anywhere in the world.

Our instincts were right. *By Jeeves* doesn't get a good review in the *New York Times*. Unfortunately it wasn't their number one critic

Ben Brantley, who had loved the show out of town, but a second stringer. I'm disappointed that he gives no credit for what audiences are certainly recognising – that the Brits are braving Broadway at a difficult time. Better stuff comes through, and some excellent notices for John and me in *Variety* and the *New York Post*.

I'm feeling oddly buoyant until I discover a message on my cell phone. It's a voice of doom. 'Marvin, this is Michael Price. Would you give me a call?' He leaves three numbers, so it's urgent.

Oh God.

Well, this is it.

Various possibilities run through my head, all leading to the same conclusion: Andrew has pulled the show after reading what he considers insults to his musical score in the *New York Times*. His backers have surely withdrawn.

Has somebody got cold feet again?

ACT FOUR

Survival

Still – Monday October 29th

I feel angry. Is the show to be over before it's begun? Why? There are great quotes from all the papers, including the *New York Times*.

I can't reach Michael Price but leave messages for John in case he has any news. Ros and I go out to dinner. After all, it's a day off.

Later I check the machine. There's one. From Michael.

'*Marv*, I just wanted to tell you about our advertising and publicity campaign to turn this show into a great success on Broadway.'

Oh. Good heavens. He hasn't pulled it after all.

So that's all right then.

John rings later and we talk the notices through. We congratulate each other and look forward to recording the radio commercial we have been asked to do which – we hope – will contain many good quotes from the reviews.

Perhaps, now, we'll meet the publicity guy.

Maybe we'll survive.

Tuesday

We record the radio advertisement. Basically it's a double-act between Bertie and Jeeves, in which we jabber about all the fun and games going on down at the Helen Hayes. The quotes sound juicy.

Later Michael Price calls to say they can't find a single good phrase to use from the *New York Times*.

'Nonsense,' I reply, 'I can think of several.'

He asks me to fax them to him, saying he can only see 'slapstick farce'. I send him 'loony bravado', 'Wodehouse would have chuckled', 'irresistible' and about six others.

Tonight I decide to follow Molly Renfroe's example, and before the show I call the company together – via Molly – for a very short chat. It seems important that, just because the *Times* review was less than perfect, no one should get the idea we've failed. I mention Michael Price's phone call and how positive it all is, with the campaign to turn us into an out-and-out Broadway hit.

Wednesday

The *Wall Street Journal* and *Time Out* are both raves. This is excellent news and must, surely, help to convert the show into more of a perceived success. I trust they'll be reproducing the reviews and putting them outside the theatre. There's nothing there at present. And where are some of the hundreds of colour photographs taken in Pittsburgh and Toronto?

A familiar fluffy-white or blue-rinse audience is out front this afternoon. They're having a great time. The box office return, though, is down on last week. It's going to take time for the good reviews to kick in.

Ros meets me after the matinee. I discuss with her an idea Ian Knauer has mentioned to me – that at the end of the show every night, John and I should come out of character and make appeals from the stage on behalf of Broadway Cares – the organisation that raises money for Aids charities. Neither Ros nor I are sure about it, despite the obvious good intentions. I'm nervous that it may affect the final 'Wodehouse' image of the show. I decide, reluctantly, it's not in the interests of the production.

We have a small audience this evening. It's Halloween and many people don't want to go out. Also the fake horror of the night sits uneasily with the genuine horror that this city has undergone. And, it's Wednesday – we do seem to be learning that Wednesday is never a great audience night on Broadway. I rally the troops and remind them of Alan's thoughts about such unresponsive houses – they're useful to play against, allowing us to reassess the truth of what we're doing. Steve Wilson sees the force of this and says, 'In a way the show can be even more truthful without having to hold up for rolling laughs.' I look across at Don. He winks back.

After the performance, Ian, John and I have a meeting about the charity. I make my points and express my concerns. John tells me I am entirely wrong. Every show on Broadway does it, he says. Audiences love it. The company will stand at the back of the auditorium with buckets. We'll raise a lot of money and a portion of it should go to the Twin Towers fund. He's fiercely adamant and I stand totally corrected. We work out a way it can be done. We'll rehearse our joint speech tomorrow and start the appeals on Friday. It will be every night for a month.

Thursday

Alan, back in Scarborough, has sent an encouraging message to the cast, regretting that the reviews haven't been better overall, but pointing out that some were nice about individuals and many aspects of the show were praised. He then relates a story about British producer Michael Codron presenting the moderately camp mime artist Lindsay Kemp on Broadway.

Codron knew things weren't going right at the first preview, as row upon row of blue-rinsed matrons sat tight-lipped, silent in their disapproval at the onstage raunchiness. Finally came the scene where

Lindsay dances suggestively, eventually seducing a young sailor. The piece finishes with the two men walking hand in hand upstage into the sunset. As they did so, from the stalls a matronly voice was heard to utter, 'Well, South Pacific, this ain't!'

His point is that *By Jeeves* is 'itself' and God bless the many people who accept it as that. *South Pacific* it ain't, either. He ends by reiterating how extremely proud he is of the show and the whole company. On opening night everyone excelled. He knew we would.

In reply I let him know about the terrific reviews he probably won't have seen. The *Wall Street Journal* compares Alan's own ingenuity with that of Jeeves. It's 'a plum of a production'. Everyone is highly praised. Sheila's choreography is 'a hoot'. John and all received high praise and I, apparently, am 'wonderfully wry'. Roger Glossop's set is applauded. I've heard from Charlotte Wilcox and others that the excellent *Time Out* review was an important one to get.

Our accommodating landlady Ruth is still here. We had understood she was only going to be around for roughly three days a month. She's great company, though.

Pregnant Emily is still off and Molly plays Stiffy again. An attractive dark-haired actress, Ana Maria Andricain, who is to take over from Emily when she finally leaves, is brought round backstage to say hello. It's odd that Molly, so excellent as Emily's understudy, hasn't been awarded the role. John points out to me that she is too useful as a cover also for Donna Lynne and Becky.

Tonight the house is fuller, though numbers are still down because of the World Series: the Yankees are playing at their stadium in the Bronx. At one point during the performance, when I sit down for a moment offstage, I find I am surrounded by a circle of hefty crew members, grunting, muttering and cheering the game as it's transmitted on the colour TV set up in the gantry. They grab the binoculars from each other, raising them to their eyes like racegoers in some weird grandstand, dancing and whooping at every pitch and toss and home run. The show continues all the while onstage.

The crew is an amusing, almost universally obese group of New York teamsters. They remind me of amiable Mafiosi. I've heard they are all 'family' members of their union and guard their jobs with exemplary care. They're earning a great deal more than most of our actors, just for handing me the banjo, paging the doors or lining up a few props. The two hardest-working (well, sort of) are Mike and Tommy who have the responsibility of – magically, from the audience's point of view – opening and closing the upstage right and left curtains each time we make an entrance. But they don't let that task get in the way of their obsession with baseball and the Yankees, the New York team who seem at present to be playing almost every night. Mike has his own little television set on a shelf beside his chair in the wings and, even as he's listening on headphones for his cues from Dan, he is also watching and listening (on another set of cans) to the game. When things get particularly exciting he snarls and shouts at the screen in fannish frenzy. He's now in a world far removed from Jeeves and Wooster, and has to be shushed by Lisa, who runs the backstage efficiently, despite these complications. She reminds me, in her careful dealings with these characters, of Nurse Ratched from *One Flew Over the Cuckoo's Nest*.

There are two other fellows: moustachioed Roger, the quiet one in charge of props, who has the responsibility of handing me a folded copy of *The Times* twice in the evening; and sack-like Ron – baggy pants, matted grey hair and tinted specs. He smells of stale beer and stands around in the wings, often swaying slightly, nodding, smiling and not doing much else. He'll let out an occasional boozy yelp and then disappear down to a small grotto below stage, where he can be glimpsed lolling on a decrepit sofa that may have appeared above ground years ago in, say, *The Little Foxes* or *The Man Who Came to Dinner*.

As amusing as I find them, I can see they think me entertaining too. When I practise my dance in the wings just before I go on for the finale, the entire crew, having watched me over the last couple of weeks, all join in and do it with me. Ron is a little unsteady when it gets to the one-legged bit, but Butch and Tommy are frighteningly proficient. Mike is not interested, eyes glued to the screen.

Best of all, when there's a major home run or something equally crucial, Mike suddenly leaps up, and scuds across from his own stage-right territory to the opposite side, yelling and whooping. He engages in fierce argument with Tommy (not a Yankees supporter) who growls a godfatherly 'Forget about it', and shoves him, both men grinning, back to his own side of the stage.

If I try to shush them, Tommy in particular just titters and gestures to the others in imitation of my Jeevesian attempt to keep things calm backstage. There's nothing I can do. We all know where the power lies.

John isn't happy tonight and calls a meeting with Dan afterwards. Apart from the noise from behind, I think he's worried about some of the things going on in front. He has already mentioned to me he feels the pace is dropping again, and there's still some hanging about for extra laughs.

Screenwriter David Freeman and his wife Judy Gingold come round afterwards. David is interesting about the mystery of Jeeves' character, and talks about the knife-edge nature of the show. He feels that someone needs to write a press piece about the play's Wodehousian accuracy, which could help to find its correct audience. The *New York Times* didn't do that, so it would need to come from somewhere else. The *Wall Street Journal* did it, though he thinks that may not be the right place.

But at least we are beginning to settle into our run.

If it *is* a run.

★

Friday

There's no baseball game so the house is packed. We launch the appeal: Broadway Cares – Equity Fights Aids. Nine hundred dollars is collected. Ian and John are proved triumphantly right about the audience's appreciation of our fundraising efforts.

I find a note in my room from Ian McKellen, welcoming me to Broadway. His show has opened to mixed reviews. They're only doing the same kind of business we are. The audience must rattle around in that much larger theatre.

Saturday

There are some new backstage crew members this evening. All related to either Tommy, Mick or Butch, naturally. And a jacket smelling of a hundred cigarettes hangs over my backstage chair. I look around for the offender, like a world-weary housemaster. Nurse Ratched is not in sight and I daren't touch it. Later I see it disappearing on the back of Tommy's teenage son, when they all repair to the alley for a smoke during 'Half a Moment'.

Another Yankees game tonight. A crucial home run coincides with my final exit through the magic curtains and pudgy Mike, glued to his TV, leaves me stranded onstage. Loyalty to the team takes precedence – he can't desert them even for a second.

'Sorry Mart'n,' he mutters, not very shamefacedly, as he finally tugs on his cord and allows me to make a belated exit.

★

Sunday

A note from Michael Frayn. He's staying at the Mayflower Hotel on Central Park West. I leave a message that we'll be at the Algonquin for a drink after the matinee. I ask John to come along; I'd like him to meet Michael. But Michael hasn't picked up the message yet.

We decide to go to Joe Allen's for dinner, where John obsesses about the show.

I obsess alongside.

Monday November 5th

Ros and I catch up with Michael for coffee at the Café Luxembourg. His wife, Claire Tomalin, is here talking to her American publishers about her almost completed Pepys biography, *The Unequalled Self*. Michael is attending to the Broadway production of his farce, *Noises Off*, just opened. He's also dealing with the national tour of *Copenhagen*, plus the US publication of his latest novel *Spies*, which we are to produce for the BBC's *A Book at Bedtime*. Tonight he's bringing his two directors together – Michael Blakemore and Jeremy Sams. Chuckling, Michael says that Blakemore (who directed the original *Noises Off*) managed to behave very well at the first night of Jeremy's new production.

We talk about how much preparation is ideal for an actor when learning a large role. Frayn tells how Len Cariou is, understandably, having memory problems, trying to absorb his huge part in *Copenhagen*, and how Philip Bosco had difficulty too, in the Broadway production two years ago. At one rehearsal he took a prompt on virtually every line. He would close his eyes in a vain effort to remember the script, says Michael, and it became a play about this *blind* physicist.

The *New York Times* is running a large colour advertisement in the arts section, carrying all our favourable quotes. It looks enticing. I have heard we now have a proper marquee outside the Helen Hayes, displaying all the reviews, quotes, photos etc. Ros and I walk down to have a look.

There's nothing there.

Tuesday

Two more notices come out today. An excellent one in the *New York Magazine* from John Simon. A disappointing one from John Lahr, a theatre writer I much admire, in the *New Yorker*.

I record a voice-over for World of Fun in a studio on Lexington Street. I'm linked by satellite to a studio in Kansas City. 'Ah,' I comment amiably, 'where everything's up to date.'

'Pardon me?' says the producer, who sounds about twelve years old.

It turns out to be a typical commercial session: they hired me because, 'Hey, we love your British accent,' but end up asking me to do it American anyway.

Back at the theatre, John and I have something new to obsess about. Still nothing has appeared front of house. And what's happened to the campaign? I decide to ring one of the advertising men, Greg Cardetti. He has a voice that sounds like Robert de Niro in *Goodfellas* and assures me that everything will be up by the end of next week.

Next week? The end of? That's ten days away.

Michael Price is skulking backstage. I lure him into the dressing room, and enquire about the display. I tell him what Cardetti has told me. He shifts uneasily, like a fox with one leg in a trap, and says he thought it was going to be the end of *this* week. He thought? He's the producer. Something funny is going on. It must be to do with costs. Are they still debating whether the play will run at all?

The whole cast have now commented on what a pity it is that the theatre still looks utterly blank for passers-by, especially as the Thanksgiving holiday is coming up and with it the likelihood of an extra influx of tourists along 44th Street.

Ros has her own problems. She is preparing a production of James Goldman's play *The Lion in Winter* and the writer's widow, Bobby Goldman, who lives in splendour over on the Upper East Side, is making large demands with reference to casting.

Wednesday

British writer Valerie Grove and legendary William Deedes of the London *Daily Telegraph* have arrived in New York on Concorde, along with Tony Blair and entourage. It's the first trip since the Concorde disaster. No normal press junket this. It's part of a concerted governmental effort to demonstrate that it's possible to fly safely to the city, whether by Concorde or any other kind of plane. Valerie and Bill attend *By Jeeves* tonight. Tony is occupied elsewhere.

Afterwards we have dinner at Sardi's, or Shardi's, as Bill can't help calling it. He talks about being in government during Harold Macmillan's time. Though of a different political persuasion, he's a great friend and admirer of Tony Benn, who came to see them off at Heathrow this morning. Bill is in his late-eighties and announces he has had a most enjoyable time at the show. He loved the play. 'If I were sixty years younger,' he chortles, 'I would have invited the blonde, Madeline Basset, out to supper.' His exuberance and diction remind me of Sybil Thorndike. He is complimentary about 'the Jeevesh', as he puts it: 'Oh, the Jeevesh was shplendid. The way the Jeevesh held his handsh to his sides was marvelloush.'

Because of the way he couches his comments I'm not absolutely sure he has realised the Jeeves was me.

★

Thursday

Backstage magazine has published an interview I gave a couple of weeks ago. It mentions the show a lot. Which is, after all, the object of the exercise.

John Sessions rings from London. He's developing a radio script for us about a 'royal watcher'.

Ros and I join producer Susan Loewenberg and our friends Maja and Susan at the Doge restaurant. They've been to see *Noises Off* and, while admiring the play, found some of the acting perplexing. Patti LuPone's accent is apparently unrecognisable as anything even faintly British. Michael Frayn had privately confided to us much the same thing the other day.

Friday

We rehearse Ana Andricain as Stiffy Byng, ready for her takeover. Donna Lynne whispers to me that they have worked together before and didn't particularly get on. She adds, 'That was aeons ago when we were young. I guess we've both grown up a little.'

She's barely thirty now.

Saturday

Michael Price calls me regarding the Tony Awards. He has officially informed the awards committee that both John Scherer and I should be up for nominations as Leading Actors in a Musical. I ask him if that isn't pushing it, as I don't sing a note? Couldn't they put me up for Best Supporting? I certainly don't want to compete with John, and it might even give us two bites of the Tony cherry. He considers a moment, then, 'Sure, that's a sensible idea. I'll put it to them. Thank you Mart'n.'

Not at all. At least he's got my name right.

Sherry and Doug Jeffe, whose offer to help secure those high-profile politicos for the opening was never followed up, are in front tonight.

The crew boys saga continues. Now it's American football they are watching. Mike misses two cues and it's becoming a real problem. Beery Ron, whom I have recently discovered is the boss of the gang – not Butch – falls asleep waiting to open a crucial door for me. But then, I ask myself, who wouldn't? It's hardly man's work. Though many might feel that gliding around in a Twenties tailcoat, with gleaming hair and a lofty expression, is not exactly grown-up either.

I talk to stage manager Dan between shows. I tell him I like these guys, they are great characters, but it really is starting to affect our concentration. I know John can hear them from on stage too. Sooner or later something is going to go seriously wrong. I emphasise I don't want to be seen as a complainer – they are semi-mafiosi after all! Dan agrees. He's aware that Mike especially is a problem. He says he's already dealing with it.

Nevertheless I am surprised to see, when I go up into the wings ready for tonight's show, that Mike's television set has disappeared. Mike himself is slumping in his chair like a sulky kid who has just had his toys confiscated.

'Hi Mike,' I say, as usual. Instead of the cheery 'How ya doin', Mart'n,' all I get is a morose grunt. Oh dear. And instead of the TV, the shelf in front of him is piled high with sweets, potato chips, a tin of nuts and two lollipops. Comfort food. Throughout the show he wrenches the curtains with a vengeance. In between cues he leans his head on the edge of the shelf in an attitude of despair. Now that he has nothing to interest him, our next problem will be when he falls asleep.

My sister Angela has decided she and Greg are coming to New York next week.

Sunday

It's Emily's last show. At the end, John and I call her forward for a solo bow. She's thrilled and thanks us afterwards for 'bringing her out.'

I'm pondering this question. If the show is virtually selling out – and at full price, as barking Bruce insists – then why are we only making just over $200,000 on the week? Seating capacity is currently eighty-eight per cent. Shouldn't we be bringing in nearer to $300,000? Are they giving more ticket concessions than they are letting on? Or does Bruce not know what he's talking about?

Dinner with the Jeffes at the Luxembourg. Nick Hytner stops by the table. He's in New York to direct the musical *Sweet Smell of Success*, which stars John Lithgow. He introduces me to a member of his cast. I think he says 'Jack Noseworthy', an actor who appeared in a film I was once nearly in myself. So I say, '*Mighty Ducks – Three*.' The young man looks at me oddly and mutters something like, 'Quite Wrong – One,' and they move on.

I chat to Doug Jeffe about the terrorism situation and the unsettling atmosphere. He thinks people are now recovering. Broadway certainly is. He is sure that there could be no repeat of September 11th, and feels air travel has now never been safer.

Monday November 12th

I set off to do a voice-over at a studio on 46th Street. The producer I am working for is someone called Jennifer.

As I ride up in the elevator at ten minutes to ten, a large Jewish gentleman seems to be receiving bad news on his cell phone. He suddenly announces he's hearing information that a plane may have come down and hit the Queensboro Bridge, three miles from JFK airport. He's not sure. I step out at my floor and go into the lobby outside the studio. Everyone is looking concerned. Clearly something odd is going on, but nobody quite knows what has actually happened. The receptionist is talking in low tones on the phone: 'Oh God, oh no, Jennifer is on that plane.' She's white with horror, and covering her mouth with her hand.

One guy emerges from the studio with an ashen-faced young woman whom I take to be the director. She says, 'Shall we tell them? It was a computer glitch.' Is she referring to the possible plane crash? Or merely saying that the recording equipment has broken down?

I go in. She seems dazed and introduces herself as 'Liz'. Her hands are shaking. She informs me that Jennifer couldn't make it.

Still nobody seems to know what's occurred, least of all me. I leave the building twenty minutes later having recorded my one line, and see a crowd of people standing round a television set in a local diner. I join them, and watch. A plane has come down in the Rockwells, an area of Queens. One of the engines fell away and eye-witnesses saw the plane hurtle to the ground. It is already becoming clear that all two hundred and forty passengers have been killed, as well as six people on the ground. Several houses have been set on fire and destroyed.

I go home.

We follow the horror on television. Donna Lynne Champlin lives in Queens. I call her. She's OK, she lives nearer to La Guardia airport, some way away.

So is this another act of terrorism? Or a mechanical failure? The question is already being debated on every channel. Weirdly, we hope it's the latter. It's deeply worrying on all sorts of levels.

Angela has booked to come next week. Now she emails saying

she's stunned and confused. She may not come after all. I fully understand and can't encourage her either way.

The Jeffes don't leave New York for San Francisco as they had planned – all flights out are temporarily cancelled. So they come with us and Eddie Belling to see the new David Mamet movie, *Heist*.

None of us can concentrate.

Tuesday

Despite current horrors, the struggle to survive within our own business is what finally exercises so many of us. Steve Wilson and Court Whisman attended an Equity deputies meeting today. They were quizzed by a fellow deputy who has seen me at a voice-over studio and now suggests to them I may be working illegally. Apparently he was enraged. 'Are his papers in order?' he demanded. I ask Steve to get the guy to call me. Perhaps he'd like to pop round to the theatre and I'll show him my Green Card.

John seems anxious this evening. It's Ana's opening performance and she has twelve friends in front who cheer her at every turn. John doesn't care for this particular house and says afterwards to Ana, 'I'm sorry you had the worst audience possible to play to.'

She answers, a touch smugly, 'Well, they were great for me.' Though she has the grace to add, 'With all my friends there.'

In my Broadway Cares speech I compliment the house on being warm-hearted. I actually believe the muted response is due, in some measure, to yesterday's tragedy and its continuing mystery.

★

Wednesday

The matinee is full. But, again, they're holding back a little.

I'm certain now that, somewhere in the back of their minds, audiences are feeling that perhaps they shouldn't be having such a good time while the question hangs in the air: did New York suffer a second terrorist attack on Monday morning?

The answer seems to be emerging that, possibly, probably, it didn't. It was just a mechanical accident. Weird times when we *hope* it was an accident, in preference to the further horror of terrorism.

Musical director Michael O'Flaherty is watching from the mezzanine tonight, not playing. Wade Russo is cheerfully at the piano, back in his old role of Ozzie for the evening. When I bump into him outside the theatre he immediately throws out his arms to encompass the whole of 44th Street and exclaims, 'Oh, you know what, I just *adore* being Ozzie Nutledge on Broadway.' And we both complete the mantra of our favourite offstage character: 'Well of course – it's because I'm gay…!'

Erin Connor has arrived in New York to see the show. It's Wednesday unfortunately and there's always that feeling it won't be a responsive house.

Sod's law – a party of a hundred and seventy people has not arrived by five minutes past eight. We hold the curtain for another six or seven minutes. Eventually some of them trickle in and we start the performance. It's hard enough to capture the audience's attention when we begin at several minutes after eight, but this is very difficult. Latecomers continue to drift into the auditorium over the next half an hour, and it's our worst evening yet as far as response is concerned. The party, Dan informs us, is a corporate group from Colgate Palmolive. It seems they have come straight from a reception. Many are carrying bouquets of cellophane-wrapped flowers, which make more noise than ten boxes of chocolates. Most of them, once arrived, talk throughout the act.

Never mind. We screw our concentration to the sticking place and the show goes well – if with minimal reaction. I wonder what Erin is thinking. I make the usual announcement at the end, and trot out the 'wonderfully warm-hearted' quote. (We learn later that the collection was much less generous than usual.)

John is angry. About the late start. About the varying audiences. About the pace being dropped in certain places. And generally enraged about the management's dilatoriness in promoting the production. I have attempted now to talk to him about the danger, in his role, of losing his 'joy'. Bertie Wooster must always be blithe, carefree. I finally tell him about a similar problem of my own when I was doing that much less good play in London twenty years ago. How, because of my frustration sometimes with certain members of the cast and their performances (as well as my own) my genuine anger started to seep into the fictional character. My playing started to turn a little sour. I assure him this is not happening to him – he is still an amazingly cheery Bertie – but he takes the point.

Erin comes round. She has registered our difficulties tonight but is complimentary.

To Joe Allen's where, with Ros, we map out the points Erin will raise tomorrow at her meeting with company manager Charlotte Wilcox, especially the fact that the front of our theatre still looks as if there's nothing going on inside.

Thursday

I meet Erin for coffee in Times Square and then she goes into the meeting.

She emerges half an hour later to report there's a further puzzle: Charlotte thought the theatre marquee was completed. What's going on?

I walk up Broadway with Erin, who goes off to Yale this afternoon to see Cindy Katz in Tennessee Williams' *Kingdom of Earth*.

Michael Price bravely slithers into my room before the performance, so I ask at once what's happening about the front of house.

He says he hasn't looked.

Eh?

He promises to investigate and call me tomorrow.

'And the advertising campaign—?' I begin, but just then Michael O'Flaherty puts his head round the door to say how encouraged he was by the standard of the show last night. It was particularly good, he thought, despite the subdued house.

I'm pleased about that and turn to continue my grilling of Michael Price. He's vanished.

The phone goes and another Michael, at the box office, tells me the show is 'sold out'. But it patently isn't.

Very mysterious.

On the way up to the stage, John confides he was so wound up about everything last night that he pulled a muscle during the performance.

Tonight, crew member Mike is not here to operate his curtain when we begin but suddenly appears, running like hell, panting, gasping, wheezing as he flops down in the wings at seven minutes past eight. For the next ten minutes he coughs explosively between cues. I fetch him a cup of water for which, I think, he is grateful. I'm happy to do this in between my own cues, since there may still be resentment in the air on account of the vanishing television set.

★

Friday

Before the performance I call in at the BBC's New York studio to record a parody of *Harry Potter* for Radio 4: John Simpson ('Johnny') liberating Kabul on his own.

Saturday.

I've broken the facing of one of my front teeth. I call Bruce, our increasingly defensive company manager. After the missing tickets incident I'm not sure how much help he is likely to be. I'm right; he has no suggestion to offer and doesn't know of an emergency dentist. I ring Becky Watson and she immediately recommends hers. Within an hour I am reclining in the chair of white-coated Elliot Packman who does a temporary rescue. Three hundred and fifty dollars. It seems a similar job, with bonding material, laser light and so on, to the more lasting one my London dentist does. Packman can do a permanent operation next week for a great deal more money. I tell him I'll think about it.

I flash my extra white smile tonight, especially at Ian Knauer. He flashes back. The winner.

Sunday

Mike's television set is back in the wings this afternoon. I wonder if this is anything to do with the fact that Ron, his immediate boss, has gone on vacation.

After the matinee Tom Ford, whose birthday it is, leads a party to see the Harry Potter movie. I've only dipped into the books but it seems very good to me. An instant classic: *Tom Brown's Schooldays* out of *Oliver Twist* by way of *Alice in Wonderland* via *Narnia*.

Ros and I and go for coffee at Barrymore's. John comes with us and talks more about his onstage worries. I tell him I have arranged a meeting with Dan Rosokov.

Monday November 19th

No day off today. That's on Thursday this week, because of Thanksgiving.

This evening Court Whisman is playing the Rev Stinker Pinker, as Ian is appearing in a concert, arranged before we knew we were coming to Broadway. Court is excellent – and his opening speech as the clumsy, well-meaning vicar is beautifully timed.

I leave the stage door tonight wearing a newly acquired Eddie Bauer leather jacket. James Kall is chatting in the alley to various friends. As I call goodnight I hear one of the girls say, 'Hey, was he Jeeves?'

James grins, 'Yes.'

'My God,' she says, 'I hardly recognise him, he's so hip an happenin'.'

Groovy.

Tuesday

The front of house display is still unfinished. The only slight improvement is that a blow-up of the rave review from the *Wall Street Journal* has now been pasted on the wall. The huge blank spot that we have been hoping will be filled with reviews and photos remains a black hole.

I catch Dan Rosokov on the move between noticeboard and office.

'Suppose we put up some pictures outside ourselves,' I suggest.

He pauses in mid-bustle, lips twitching in mock – or real – horror. 'Well, if you want to end up in the Hudson River, go ahead.'

'What do you mean?'

He regards me quizzically through the big specs before taking a quick look around. There's nobody else in the corridor. He lowers his voice. 'Broadway marquees and everything front of house are all sewn up by – ' he stops again, then makes two swift movements of his mouth like a flustered goldfish. I decipher, 'Mafia.'

He giggles, 'Don't do it, Mart'n. We need you.'

Even more depressing, when Court Whisman arrives he tells me that last night his agent hated the show and walked out. 'Mart'n, he didn't even wait to hear 'Half a Moment'. I'm so angry, I've never sung a big number like that on Broadway before.'

I suggest Court might want to seek new representation.

He agrees.

The theatre isn't full this evening but the tiny audience is terrific, and there are cheers at the end. Austin Shaw is there. Also Nick Morris, camera director of the video in Toronto, and his wife Fiona. We go to dinner at Joe Allen's where, once again, Austin picks up the tab for about twelve people. Couldn't he put the cash into an advertising budget, and we all pay for our own meal?

We're sitting round one large table. Austin finds himself on the receiving end of a battery of questions, the first being, 'Why is *By Jeeves* the only show on the street with no production photos on display?'

We follow up with, 'Since there are no pictures, no one could possibly have any idea, from viewing the front of the theatre, what the look of the show might be.'

Ian asks, 'Why is the large advertising board still empty?'

Molly and Tom tell Austin they have heard people on 44th Street inquiring whether the show has opened yet. Others have heard more frightening comments: 'Seems like it's coming off.'

249

Donna Lynne piles in with, 'Where are the leading actors' personal quotes? It looks as though John and Martin didn't receive any good reviews, otherwise the theatre would have displayed them.'

Austin has no answers and says he'll try to find out.

Later, James, who has been very quiet, leans across the table and tells me he's leaving the production. He's going to tour for a year with *Mamma Mia*.

What? Can he do that?

'Yes,' he says. The only advantage of the low-paying contract he's on is that actors can leave at any time, with two weeks' notice.

Wednesday

This morning, after sending a message to Alan about James's bomb-shell, I call Michael Price.

Fired up, I leave a volley of questions on his machine, ending up with something like, 'You certainly don't need me to tell you that no one purchases a ticket if they don't know there's a show to go to.' I continue, 'I imagine this is all to do with money and I presume under-capitalisation. It seems vital to return to the *well*' (I suppose I mean Andrew) 'to ensure that the show is at last properly funded. For God's sake Michael, put our minds at rest that it's still the inten-tion of the management to promote *By Jeeves*.' I finish up somewhat illogically, 'I'm sure we agree it would be tragic if the finger were pointed at the production, that it failed only because it couldn't afford to succeed.'

A few hours later, when I get to the theatre I find that the black hole has now been filled with a wrinkled photograph of John and me, and bearing a few quotes.

Inside, John is waiting for me. He is tight-lipped and his face is almost as red as his hair. 'Mart'n, how dare they? It's an *awful* picture.

It is not inviting, I have a scowl on my face, it's black-and-white, it tells nothing about what the show is, it's out of focus and looks like it was copied at Kinko's.'

He's right.

This afternoon we rehearse with Rob, the new music director, who will permanently replace Michael O'Flaherty, starting on Tuesday. Poor old Wade, whom I still think of as the 'real' Ozzie Nutledge, has been passed over again.

We then practise the piece some of us are going to perform for a charity gala called *Gypsy of the Year*, in which we'll be taking part at the Palace Theatre, on Times Square, in a couple of weeks. Ian Knauer tells me that a 'gypsy' is a Broadway term for a member of the chorus. Casts from nearly all the current musicals will be appearing; the event is to raise a great dollop of cash for Broadway Cares – Equity Fights Aids. Our contribution is a parody of 'All That Jazz' from *Chicago* – 'All That Jeeves'. The new lyrics, written by Donna Lynne, tell the on-off, off-on story our production has endured – and is still enduring. At five o'clock we sing and dance, even me, with special feeling.

Thursday

Thanksgiving. Perhaps not a great deal to give thanks for today.

There's a message from Alan. He tells me he's in the middle of dreaming up his sixty-first play. He had no idea that James Kall is leaving. These contracts are most peculiar, he muses, it seems that people can leave if they have athlete's foot. He's sad about the news, especially as he spent a long time trying to ensure that Michael Price hired him – James lives in Toronto and Price was initially unwilling to pay for his New York accommodation.

Alan goes on to say he recognises a real problem, in that the management has not been in touch with him or any of the creative team (wardrobe, choreography etc) regarding a replacement for James. This is exactly what John and I have been discussing today: if Michael Price regarded the show as in any way ongoing, he would surely have communicated. It does look as if the intention is to take the production off before James is due to be replaced. Alan feels this is the likely answer, if only from his long experience of trying to interpret management's body language.

What is interesting is that the response from those seeing the show is obviously good. Sadly, it seems all that matters is the figures at the end of the week. But then, it has to be said, this is show*business*. I know that Alan has waived everything he can in terms of his own royalties. That gesture was on the understanding that the money would be used to help sell the play. But if there is no publicity going out, then why the hell is he contributing to the cause?

There seems little doubt: someone, somewhere is pulling a plug.

Friday

My sister and Greg arrived yesterday. They're here for three days.

Ros and I met them at their hotel on 57th Street, just round the corner from the Wyndham. We strolled down to Times Square. Bumped into Sian Phillips outside Sardi's; she is rehearsing a play that she'll be taking to L.A. After Joe has set 'em up and we've knocked 'em back, we taxi to the most American restaurant we can think of: the Brooklyn Diner. It's great to see Angela and Greg here, especially as it's not an easy decision to make at the moment – for anyone – to fly in to New York.

Tonight is the biggest evening house we've had. The box office return shows that we have taken forty thousand dollars. But everyone backstage is restless about the management's intentions. As the overture plays, one of the actors shimmers into the wings and breathes into the ears of two of his colleagues, 'Maybe it's like *Murder on the Orient Express.*'

John Scherer and Court Whisman glance round uncertainly but before either can reply the whisperer continues, 'You know what I mean, all in it equally, advertising, publicity, price. Snuffing it out. All in it together, Inspector.'

'Except for Alan,' they both counter simultaneously.

The overture finishes and the whisperer moves across to his position behind the curtain, ready to make his first entrance of the night. As Jeeves.

Angela and Greg are in the fifth row. Afterwards I can tell that she was a little startled to see her tone-deaf brother almost singing. Her actress daughter Sophie Langham, my niece, is the singer of the family. Angela is sweetly generous and says she thinks I could now appear in Gilbert and Sullivan if I wanted to.

I'm not so sure.

Saturday

Tom Ford plays Bingo at the evening performance as Don has gone home to be with Emily. The baby's head is pressing against something and she's in a lot of pain.

It's all about birth and death today. In the theatre alley I meet Roger, the prop man. I've noticed that he often misses performances. I ask him, jokily, if he has another more fulfilling job that takes him away. He replies quietly, 'Yes Mart'n, I do. I have to take care of my wife. It's very fulfilling.'

Does that mean she has to be looked after in some specific way?

'Sure,' he says, 'she's home at the moment from the Hospice.'

Butch tells me later she is dying of cancer.

Tom gives a touching and truthful performance as Bingo.

Muscleman Mike is now training a new 'curtain guy', a brawny youth whose eyes squint myopically from behind blue-tinted lenses. The bound leading the blind. Interestingly, the recruit gets every-thing right first time. Righter than mafia Mike on a good day.

Sunday

Angela and Greg come up to the apartment. Then we go to the Saloon, opposite the Lincoln Center, for lunch. While we're sitting there, I look at my watch. It's two o'clock. I'll have to dash. The contrast between New York now, and Wodehouse then, sometimes strikes me as absurd. I say, 'I can hardly believe that in less than an hour I'll be walking onto the stage of the Helen Hayes dressed as a butler.' I suppose I'm thinking of the prep, checking the script – which I do before every performance – greased hair, make-up, microphone. But Angela says pragmatically, and quite right too, 'Well, it's only like putting on some overalls and getting under the car.'

I'm sure Alan would like that one too.

During the intermission the cast decide to meet up on Tuesday at six o'clock, to discuss whether we ourselves could help to raise money for advertising. Even to find a way of getting on to the enormously popular – if glutinous – daytime Rosie O'Donnell show. Apparently it costs $18,000 for a Broadway production to obtain a slot. Everyone says it's worth its weight in golden publicity.

Monday November 26th

Angela and Greg return to England, having had a great whistle-stop time in the city. Greg has seen the remains of the Towers, down at Ground Zero. I still haven't been. They have shopped and toured, visited museums and ridden horses in Central Park. They now know Manhattan better than we do.

I speak to Jeremy, a whey-faced assistant who is the only representative of the publicity firm we ever see. He tells me we are booked to appear on the Rosie O'Donnell show on December 19th. Really? Who's paying? He doesn't know.

Does this mean we are wrong and *By Jeeves* is going to survive?

Ros, John and I go to a movie. As we emerge from Loewe's cinema on 68th and Broadway I ring the apartment on my cell phone to check our messages. There's one from Steve Wilson.

On the way to the Café Luxembourg I call him back. He's had some alarming news from friends of his parents. A group of fifty has been trying to book to see *By Jeeves* in January, via Tele-Charge, and was told today that no bookings are being made from December 31st. The inference being that the show will not be running beyond that date. Steve immediately rang company manager Bruce, who told him sharply 'not to tell anybody, but we're coming off on December 30th.' Steve replied that he 'can't not share that information with the cast', hence his call to me.

'Should we still we have our six o'clock meeting tomorrow?' he wonders.

I suggest we do, in order to share what we know.

There's a message from Donna Lynne. Her mother has been told the same thing, with firm information that the show is coming off on the last day of the year.

We continue our meal in a sort of manic anger that this is how we, the cast, should hear about the show's demise.

As soon as we're home I email Michael Price asking for an explanation. I copy it to Alan.

★

Tuesday

Miriam Margolyes rings from London this morning, with one of her life-affirming monologues.

'Darling, I saw Andrew Lloyd Webber at the Savoy today for the *Evening Standard* Drama awards. I told him categorically he must keep the show running on Broadway as you were so marvellous. He said it just depended on word of mouth but he *loved* the show. So I'm sure you're wowing the audiences – I'm desperate to get there, can't before Feb, doing *Vagina* till then. The standard of speeches at the awards was poor. A young girl called Frances something made a total balls-up of hers. Johnny Mortimer redressed the balance though. I was mentioned twice for eating everyone's lunch – how embarrassing! Bye.'

Alan emails to say that last night's news had not been conveyed to him or his agent, or to anyone on the British team.

Finally Michael Price returns my call. He admits that *By Jeeves* will finish on December 30th.

So whodunnit? Is this Andrew's decision?

Price's explanation is that 'somebody' has advised that the show would not survive what may be a bloodbath of cut-price tickets in January, with the big musicals offering seats at vastly reduced prices. He says it's unlikely that *By Jeeves* could afford to compete with tickets going for only $40. I ask immediately if he has investigated any of the avenues that are usual in this kind of situation: a reduced theatre rental, additional backers, even temporary salary cuts for the actors while the show is nursed. He has no answer.

I then tell him the cast had arranged a meeting, before any of this hit the fan, at six tonight. Its purpose, I inform him, was to discuss how *we* could perhaps raise money to help with advertising and promotion.

'Mart'n, I'm speechless,' he says.

Speechless or not, when I enquire how he intends to impart the sad news to the company, he says he is sending Charlotte Wilcox along. 'I can't get in this evening,' he mutters.

I suddenly feel rather sorry for him.

We gather in the green room at six. Most already know the news. The meeting was initially to see if we could help the management. This doesn't seem an option any more. Inevitably we discuss how upsetting it was for Donna Lynne to be called by her mother to be told in effect, 'Your show's coming off!' Steve Wilson the same. We debate and come to the conclusion we should at least find out if we are still to appear on the Rosie O'Donnell Show on December 19th.

Charlotte Wilcox arrives at half past seven and gives the official news that *By Jeeves* closes on December 30th. The management can't afford to nurse it. The situation in January, even if September 11th hadn't changed everything, will make it impossible for many firmly established productions to continue.

And we won't be appearing on the daytime programme either. Our scheduled appearance is cancelled.

Another sadness: Tom Ford's father died yesterday.

Wednesday

A remarkable 'manifesto' came from Alan this morning, addressed to the entire cast.

> Like you, I am very shocked with the way all this has been handled and most especially by the way that you, the company, have been treated. This, despite the fact that you have all shown such extraordinary loyalty and faith in the show over the months and very often years. It displays, managerially, a total insensitivity and ingratitude as well as a complete lack of CARE.

I have (and maybe I didn't hide this too well when I was there) always hated Broadway for this very reason. Namely, that it personifies the type of theatre where the wrong people have all the real power and make the life or death decisions – with total disregard for any artistic or creative consideration.

These people generally have no scrap of artistic or creative ability of their own. Their start and finish point is the profit and loss column. In my experience – quite a long experience now – they are, as a result, almost invariably wrong because they base their judgements on the wrong criteria.

But then, ask this question. What kind of person goes into the theatre business with the object purely of seeing how much they can make from it, take from it? The answer is an exploitative shit.

Because what they are hoping to make money on is, of course, someone else's creative endeavours – namely our own. Personally, I have developed a deep mistrust of most producers, academics and critics whose so-called 'creative' existence is based solely on exploiting the talent of others. I reserve especial loathing for those of them who appear to do better from these talents than the original creators did.

Occasionally, art can produce a profit. We, the artists hope it does – partly because we want to survive to make another play, paint another picture, but also because we tend to use it as some yardstick of our own popularity in the market place. A full house warms all our hearts – though I suspect that the figures we are respectively counting on such an occasion are very different ones. What you, the company, have been experiencing has been one set of 'figures'. People in an auditorium, in general, having the time of their lives. What the management is staring at is a set of numbers not remotely connected to that human experience. Well, if truth be told, not even actual figures but projected figures. It was all summed up for me by Arnold Saint Suber, one of the legendary Broadway producers of his time, who once told me he never set foot in auditoria, because for him the only real music in the theatre was the jingle of the box office. Well, fuck him.

258

Later, at the theatre, I show Alan's letter to Donna Lynne, who grabs it out of my hand, scuttles away and a few minutes later posts it on the noticeboard. I'm not sure this is a good idea. My plan was to get it copied for each cast member.

Dan takes it down an hour or two later, but not before Bruce has spotted it.

'Huh,' he says, panting aggressively, 'That's his opinion.'

Fair enough. He's an odd character. His reaction to most questions is as though they're a personal challenge to him, his efficiency or integrity. As the weeks have gone on, they are, in a way. But of course he's not the villain of the piece. Maybe just a red-faced herring.

On stage, things are not getting any better. Don Stephenson is not with us as Emily's waters have broken. Since Tom Ford, now in Texas with his family, is Don's understudy, Jamison Stern, one of the swings, plays Bingo. Ten out of ten for effort. Less for appropriateness. Watching him capering about in Don's braided blazer, I am reminded of some nightmare where Julian Clary or Graham Norton might have wandered on from an episode of *Hi de Hi on Ice*. John takes it all in his increasingly lengthening stride.

Company morale is astonishingly good. I know we are determined to turn these five weeks into a joyous final celebration.

We rehearse the *All That Jeeves* parody. Donna Lynne's witty lyric, recounting the ups and downs of the production, presents Andrew as the hero of the hour:

> Come on babe, why don't we paint the town?
> Lord Andrew wrote the cheque, we're really Broadway-bound.

The sting in the tail comes with my final line: 'Closing December 30th…'

Tomorrow, reminiscent of a scene from *Chorus Line*, we'll be showing it to the Gypsy of the Year organisers, and next Monday, like Judy Garland before us, we'll be hoofing on the stage of the Palace Theatre.

★

259

Thursday

Last night I was attacked and fiercely savaged by a chocolate crois-sant. I heated it in the microwave, bit into it, and the lump of chocolate peeking out from the end was ten times hotter than the dough. It branded me on the chin, just below my mouth. Now I have a scab. I don't feel very chorus-boy as I enter the portals of the Dance Academy on 47th Street, next door to *Noises Off*. (I wonder if they'll be coming off in January too.) Their attendance figure was ninety per cent last week. Ours was less than the eighty something percent we achieved the week before that.

We gather together in the lobby and mutter through the words of our number, before being led into the large studio where we are greeted by the 'Gypsy' production team. Steadfast Wade Russo seats himself at the piano and strikes up. We strut our stuff. We're rather impressive. Even I get the dance steps vaguely correct. That's mainly because there's a long mirror down the length of the room so I can see everybody's reflection and keep in time. As we finish, the chief producer springs from his chair, holds out his arms in a generalised embrace and cries 'Fabulous!'

We'll be number five in the running order for the show next week.

Later, at the theatre, Bruce is glowering and resentful as he hands out pay-cheques.

We hear that Emily has produced a 4 lb 10 oz girl called Hallie. Mother and baby are doing well. The baby is small, but of course Emily is only tiny herself.

Don is not going to be here again tonight. I must confess I'm a little surprised. The hospital is only ten minutes away. I suppose I imagined that even if he had been there all day, he might have been able to come in to do the show. In Scarborough, or anywhere else in England for that matter, it would surely be the case. I can remember when my younger son Oliver was born, having witnessed his arrival

I raced to the set of *The Forsyte Saga* and was filming a scene, clasped in Susan Hampshire's arms, less than two hours later.

John shrugs. It means that Jamison is on again. Not a bad house though, and the reaction is very strong: lots of young people, whom I acknowledge in my speech (we're still doing the Broadway Cares appeal). I say I'm thrilled they have had the opportunity to experience this wacky entertainment created by two theatre geniuses – Andrew Lloyd Webber and Alan Ayckbourn.

I mean it.

Friday

Ros and I take a yellow cab to West 22nd Street to record a voice-over. Then all the way down to Greenwich Street to collect a film script that will be George Clooney's directorial debut. There might be a part for me as a British undercover man. Well, if they don't turn the character into an American.

At last we are passing Ground Zero.

We stop at the barrier and watch as the work of sifting and shifting and levelling and uncovering goes on.

There's a smell of burning.

Everyone is very quiet.

We stand there for a long time.

The steel skeleton reminds me of photographs of Coventry cathedral at the end of World War II.

There's nothing else to see.

Later, at the theatre, Dan announces that Don Stephenson won't be back until next Tuesday. Jamison will continue playing Bingo, as Tom is still away.

It's Tom's father's funeral today. He may return in time for Sunday's matinee performance.

Jamison does much better tonight. His British accent has improved and he's less outrageous. Julian Clary and Graham Norton have been replaced by, say, Les Dennis.

James Kall invites Ros, John and me to Langan's restaurant after the show, along with his partner, Randy. I had previously suggested to Michael Price that he might persuade James to continue longer as Gussie, even for the rest of the run. James now confesses that he is having a problem with Michael. He explains that he gave his notice a couple of weeks ago, and had expected to leave on December 17th. This was before anyone knew the show would be taken off at the end of the year. James says he'd be willing to stay on, but that Michael is making difficulties: 'After all that we did to try and get you to do the role, and paying for your housing, why should we keep you on now?'

Saturday

Roger the prop man's wife died yesterday.

Backstage and onstage the configurations are intriguing. Different people pulling the curtains. Different people playing the parts.

In the interval there's a knock on my door.

The silver fox slinks into the room. He stands quite still for a moment, as if listening for something. Why is he here?

He folds himself into my armchair, then tilts his head on one side, before murmuring, 'It's definitely not Andrew who's pulled the show, you know.' He leans in towards me, speaking just below the level of normal hearing. I think he says, 'It's those around him.'

'But surely,' I reply, 'if Andrew hadn't wanted it pulled, it wouldn't have been.'

He whispers, 'Not as simple as that. This is Broadway. Publicity and promotion call the shots.'

It's hard to tell as he's speaking so quietly, but I'm almost sure he mouths the name of the shadowy head of the PR firm who has never introduced himself to me. So is *he* our villain? We kind of need to identify him. It would be good to have someone to blame.

I'm reading his lips now. 'They were never much in favour of the show anyway.'

They? Do I hear a last blast on the whistle as that fearsome express hurtles further away along the track, carrying all the suspects, disappearing round the bend, dwindling out of sight?

I catch his eye in the mirror. I say, 'So, a joint decision? They're all sort of in it together?' Absurdly, I can detect 'Inspector' turning back, unuttered, inside my mouth.

He leans forward and suddenly raises both arms. For a moment I think he's going to place his head in his hands in a desolate motion of despair. But no. He merely smooths back his already sleek hair, then gets up slowly. He looks at me directly for a second, lowers his gaze and leaves, tail between his legs.

Sunday

Tom Ford is back. Very quiet. He's our third Bingo of the week as Don is still away.

Ken Danziger is here this afternoon from Los Angeles and witnesses one of the most unresponsive houses ever, though he laughs a great deal. I can hear his solo efforts echoing round the auditorium. When, at half-time, I tell the company about the owner of that guffaw he is immediately dubbed 'the laughing Englishman'. He appreciates all the jokes. Especially a brace of classical allusions, which often fall on unreceptive ears. He comes round afterwards and is practically mobbed by a grateful company.

I take him back to the apartment where we catch up with Los Angeles news.

Unfortunately he can't have dinner with Ros and me. He recommends we go to Vince and Eddie's, which he describes as 'northern Italian with a touch of mafia'.

Monday December 3rd

At 10.15 a.m., while the sun spotlights the lines of folk waiting at the half-price ticket booth in Times Square, I report to the Palace Theatre where we are dress rehearsing our appearance in the Gypsy of the Year Gala.

Strange to be lurking in the wings of this legendary American playhouse. I feel very much the new boy, as if I'm back at RADA. This time it's my Jeeves chums who are my classmates, all cowed together. Ready to trip our way onto the very stage from which Judy wowed them in the aisles. There'll be two performances – one later this afternoon and one tomorrow.

We are led by Donna Lynne Champlin and our doughty dance captain Ian Knauer, who has choreographed *All That Jeeves*. It's a mad scramble – we have to grab our microphones from the *Mamma Mia* cast in the five seconds between their exit and our lot going on. I'm ready, as the 'deus ex machina', to announce the good news followed by the bad.

Sam Tsoutsouvas tells me he has seen a dressing-room door with Ian McKellen's name on it. I didn't know he was taking part. Perhaps the committee have assumed Strindberg's *Dance of Death* to be a musical. I look around, but there's no sign of him.

After the rehearsal I take a taxi to Greenwich Street to film a 'screen test' for George Clooney's *Confessions of a Dangerous Mind* – a movie about Chuck Barris, the celebrated Gong Show television host. He was also, according to the script I have been sent, an undercover killer for the CIA. Clooney will view my attempt after his latest film, *Ocean's Eleven*, has opened. The casting director is helpful and asks me how *By Jeeves* is going. I tell her fine and enquire how she knows I'm in it. I'm thinking of the distinct lack of publicity. She replies coolly, 'I'm in casting, it's my business to know these things.'

To the Helen Hayes for a sit-down, before returning to the Palace for the show. Donna Lynne is there. We talk about her hopes of playing the young woman in Carol Burnett's new play, *Hollywood Arms*, to be directed by Hal Prince. She says Hal more or less gave her the part a year ago. Then he introduced her to Carol, whereupon Donna Lynne became hopelessly tongue-tied in the presence of an American icon and didn't impress. Now she's back to square one and has to audition all over again this afternoon.

Back to the Palace Theatre. We all pace around anxiously and go through the number in a room beneath the stage. We know our place. We watch the first items on the TV monitor. Then up the stairs to the wings, a moment's pause, wrestling mikes in the darkness from the *Mamma Mia* girls who have forgotten all about us, and now we're being introduced by Gary Beach from *The Producers*: 'Ladies and gentlemen, here are The Little Wittam Players with their "By Jeeves Bossa Nova".'

The lights blaze, two thousand people applaud and we're on, moving like mechanical dolls and doing well, though I don't get my feet quite right. No mirrors.

Ros is observing from the circle. I creep round after our segment is over and watch the rest of the show with her. Some of the items are brilliantly done – very showbiz, very Broadway, very gay. Many of them are critical of managements and deals and actors being sold down the river.

Afterwards we attend the launch of the Drama Bookshop's new premises. Thanks to my persistence, and a few phone calls to England, they have thirty copies of *Acting Strangely* on display. I am suitably surprised and graciously thankful.

★

Tuesday

We do the Gypsy show again. Our group meets below stage at the Palace at half past two. This time Sam has met Ian McKellen in the loo. I start off to find him but Sam, in his Donald Sinden voice, prevents me. 'Martin, you can't seek him out in the lavatory.'

We're all more nervous than yesterday. It goes even better and we get our laughs. My 'kicker' line, 'Closing December 30th', gets an ironic cheer and the audience applauds unreservedly. I zoom straight off afterwards.

Later, at the Helen Hayes, Sam tells me that he stayed until the end and Sir Ian was there. Or 'Sirina' as he is affectionately known by the New York acting fraternity. It turns out he was presenting the award to the company who were nominated 'Gypsy of the Year' – basically the best act in the gala. Not us. Sam says, 'Sirina came bouncing on at the end dressed as a gypsy woman. She took the place by storm. Kissed 'em all and made off with the most attractive chorus boy. A riot, dear!'

Chris Conrad is at the show tonight. She has just published an excellent biography of the late Jerome Robbins, *That Broadway Man, That Ballet Man*. As a young woman she had been his fiancée. Curiously, she is accompanied by a woman called Amanda, also a Robbins biographer.

We go to Orso, where we encounter Nick Hytner again, this time with John Lithgow. I don't ask him if he appeared in *Mighty Ducks Three*.

Wednesday

Audiences are becoming a little less responsive again. Is this, I wonder, because they've heard the show is coming off and therefore assume it's not so great? Audience psychology is intriguing. They can be very suggestible. It works in reverse too sometimes, if they haven't yet been told what to think. That's why, before the notices came out, we felt there might have been a holding back of some of the preview audiences' reaction. Later we began to discover, once the more positive reviews began to appear, people gave themselves permission to love it.

Luckily, or unluckily, depending on how you view it, the show speaks for itself.

James Kall has been prevailed upon to stay until the natural end of the run on December 30th. In return, Michael Price has agreed to give him several performances off so that he can spend time with his sick father. James feels this may be his father's last Christmas.

Thursday

The reaction from tonight's audience is as though English may not be their first language. Never have we had such an unsympathetic house. Not even the night Erin Connor was here. Or Ken Danziger. It's fairly full, too. The 'marker' laughs go by almost without reaction.

The cast are suicidal, and we move about backstage as though we've been bludgeoned by heavy instruments. Which is how the audience seems, too. When we reel back to the dressing rooms I make a point of saying that we all did our best, it's the same show that on other occasions goes so well, and we shouldn't be despondent. Usual Ayckbourn stuff.

Singer KT Sullivan (an acquaintance of John Scherer) was out front. She's appearing in late-night cabaret upstairs at Sardi's next door, and has invited some of us to join.

At Sardi's we are welcomed by Mark Nadler, a singing, tap-dancing, hectoring pianist who seems to be the star of the show. Others, KT included, are contributing just a number or two. As we take our places, John and I are introduced to the audience as special guests, but it seems that Mark doesn't recognise me as the Jeeves he saw when he came to the show last week. Well, I look different – no smarmed down hair, no tailcoat. Clearly hip and happening. He stands at the piano and looks across at our group. As he calls out my name and invites the audience to put their hands together, I can see he's gesturing towards the well-groomed James Kall. James acknowledges the applause with dignified aplomb.

Later, Mark invites John Scherer to get up and do something. John wittily obliges by rising to sing one note only. Similarly I bawl out three lines from my patter song. That shuts him up.

And, biting on a turkey sandwich, my temporary tooth crumbles.

Friday

Eliott Packman rescues me once again.

This time I elect to start the whole thing properly. So as Ros makes preparations to fly back to Los Angeles to direct *The Lion in Winter*, I am sent by Dr Packman to Ghi-Ghi Dental Services to have my teeth matched for colour.

Then back to the surgery for novocaine and drilling, and a sturdier temporary tooth. In a week or so he'll have the permanent crown ready.

The house is nearly full this evening but we're in some trepidation that it's going to be another bumpy night. Happily, all is well, and backstage we nod and smile in relief. The reaction and cheers at the end make up for last night's bleakness.

Fun and games in the dressing rooms regarding who, John or me, will be last up onstage and ready to start.

Last night I pretended, with great cunning, to be way behind schedule, calling to my dresser, Jill, that I wasn't ready, then seconds later walking past John's room and remarking casually, 'See you later John!' Tonight the saga builds with John screaming like Joan Crawford, 'Aaargh! My hair isn't done yet.'

'You're lying,' I call back. Fully dressed I shout to Jill, 'Where are my trousers?' then immediately stand outside John's door two minutes before time. He comes racing out for his visit to the loo, and collapses in horror as he sees me coolly ready as Jeeves.

'That is so not funny,' he roars, collapsing in hysterics.

Are we all mad? Probably. But it lightens the atmosphere.

Saturday

Two full houses. Wonderful reactions. Extraordinary, when you think of the coldness of a few days ago. It's the same show.

Don Stephenson, having returned for a few performances as Bingo, is absent yet again. The baby is coming home from hospital today. Tom Ford fills in excellently. John especially is happy about this, though puzzled that Don can so easily take time off.

We have a 'Secret Santa' draw. I have picked Cristin, the understudy. So now I have to buy her up to twenty dollars-worth of Christmas presents – anonymously – leaving poetic hints as to my identity.

The latest development backstage is that the crew now know most of the dialogue of the show, plus the songs. In the absence of any baseball games to shout at or argue over, they recite chunks of our words along with us. This is extremely disconcerting. I venture this evening to shush one of them (Tommy) but he and Joe (somebody's cousin) simply fall about with laughter. They're like well-fed mafia footsoldiers: they bear no personal ill-will, but find it hilarious that I should even attempt to give them orders.

★

Sunday

Author Simon Brett and wife Lucy appear suddenly in my bunker dressing room after the matinee. They're in New York for a few days. They have an hour before they meet Simon's literary agent for dinner so, naturally, I take them to Sardi's. I fill them in about the *By Jeeves* history – they know some of it.

Monday December 10th

To the cinema near the Lincoln Center where some of us see *The Affair of the Necklace*, directed by Charles Shyer. Fairly typical costume drama all about hair and wiggery, plus Parisian pokery. It was actually shot in Prague with what seems like all-American sensibilities. I wouldn't have minded being in it; there are a couple of parts I'd have accepted like a shot. Oh really? Yes, being a critical member of an audience is quite different (I tell myself) from being a well-paid feature film player in an interesting location.

Tuesday

Prop man Roger is back, following his wife's funeral. It's almost unbearable to watch him as he sits slumped in the wings on the phoney tree trunk, waiting to supply me with my newspaper.

Don has also returned.

John starts the new week with a freak-out. It's understandable. Not so the latest notice to appear on the board. It reads like one of those impenetrable mental arithmetic questions, 'If Jim is taller than Fred and Jack is shorter than Harry, then what is the weight of Colin…?' The notice states that when James is away for several performances

Tom will play Gussie. And when Ana is absent for four shows (her father will be undergoing major surgery) Molly will play two performances and Cristin will play the other two. Jamison will replace Tom in the ensemble. There will be a rehearsal for all this on Friday.

Incensed, John races to Dan's room. I scoot behind him in case murder is about to be committed. His question isn't in fact, 'Why are so many people allowed to have time off?' It's, 'Why do we have to rehearse?' He goes on to say he's incredibly tired. And that, anyway, Tom has played Gussie already.

'Well yes, months ago, in Pittsburgh,' counters Dan.

'And why the hell is Cristin going to play Stiffy for two performances?' John goes on. 'Molly is the chief understudy.'

Dan answers levelly, 'The management want her to.'

'Oh yeah, who on the management?'

'Charlotte Wilcox,' replies Dan.

'What!'

'And me,' he continues. 'And – um – Bruce.'

John is virtually puce with rage. 'Bruce!' he yelps, and storms out.

It's certainly odd that Molly isn't going to cover all four performances. Dan explains to me, after John has left the room, that really it's to give talented Cristin a chance to play the role. Good old theatre sentiment, that's all.

And why not?

Of course there should be a rehearsal. It'll only be a couple of hours.

I try and smooth things over. It's important that we don't finish up with bad feelings. And this is the start of a new week. Not good to kick off with a row.

John later comes into my room and apologises for his outburst. I know he has already apologised to Dan.

There'll be a rehearsal on Friday.

John is a splendid character. His motives are always for the good of the show. He believes it's our responsibility to ensure that audiences, who pay up to a hundred dollars a seat, see the very best possible version of *By Jeeves*. He's absolutely right.

And if there were a little more Broadway justice, by now he'd be an authentic star.

Wednesday

More Morleys.

Sheridan's sister Abby and her husband Charlie arrived around midnight last night. They live in Australia and, having been holidaying in Europe, are now on their way home. They've not been to the apartment before. I gave them a glass of wine and showed them around. They'll be staying in Ruth's room.

Tonight the audience is rapt. The bizarre ladder scene, usually greeted with amazed hilarity, is viewed in a reverent silence as if it's a great scene from Ibsen.

Maja Thomas, audiobook producer from Time Warner, is here. We go to Barrymore's afterwards.

Ros's production of *The Lion in Winter*, with Kathleen Chalfant and Alfred Molina heading the cast, will just be starting in LA.

Thursday

At a voice-over studio this morning I meet Tristan Layton, son of actor George Layton whom I have known since RADA days. I remember Tristan when he was seventeen and doing work experience as tea boy in one of the London recording studios. We chat about those times.

I tell him the story of his chirpy dad coming to my house many years ago – a tale of actors' sensitivity. George and I were drinking coffee and after I had placed a cup on the table directly on top of the current *TV Times*, the conversation suddenly faltered. George couldn't relax. He kept looking anxiously down at the magazine. Eventually, unable to bear it any longer, he leant forward and removed the coffee cup – from his face. His photo, as one of the stars of *Doctor in the House*, was thankfully revealed once more, grinning out from that week's cover.

There are plenty of Brits on the streets of Manhattan today. At the junction of Broadway and 57th I encounter Edward Hibbert. He's appearing in *Noises Off*. Edward says, 'I don't like to gossip on the street,' (we are, of course) 'but is it true what I've heard about *Dance of Death*, that Ian McKellen and Helen Mirren aren't speaking at all?'

I have no idea. He hasn't spoken to me.

Thursday Dec 13th

Television is showing taped footage of Osama bin Laden crowing over the Sept 11th attacks. It now seems clear beyond doubt that he was responsible for the attack on America.

I spend the rest of day writing trailers for our BBC radio production of *Colonel Clay – Master of Disguise*, which transmits over Christmas.

I send my first 'Secret Santa' gift to Cristin.

The show doesn't get so many laughs in Act One tonight. Various members of Becky Watson's family were out there – they tell us afterwards they loved it, and had no idea they were part of what we felt was an unresponsive crowd. Another lesson worth remembering.

★

Friday

This diary of our Wodehouse world of words and music, of make-believe, inevitably suggests we lead a somewhat hermetically sealed existence, here in the heart of New York. Apartment, paperwork, rehearsal, matinee, evening show, guests, dinner, bed. It's true, though it hasn't been my intention to record the day-to-day reports of the conflict that we read about and follow on television all the time. Nor to write about the intense, dedicated work of clearing and making safe that continues just a few miles south of 44th Street, at Ground Zero. Still, our own small battles for survival at the Helen Hayes seem trivial and frivolous in the shadow of the gigantic issues that are also part of our lives at present. But that's what we do. And perhaps our efforts to keep this streamlined theatre vehicle in tip-top condition, engine running smoothly, bodywork gleaming, is as important a contribution to the resurrected life of the city as anything else Mayor Giuliani requires of those who work here.

Today, television news programmes are telling us that US troops and air forces are closing in on the caves near Tora Bora in the north of Afghanistan where Osama bin Laden is reputedly in hiding. Shades of Hitler's last days in the bunker. Most Taliban forces have surrendered, though apparently there are pockets of resistance in Kandahar.

While I'm at the theatre, Abby and Charlie leave the apartment, returning to Australia. Their keys are left for me at the front desk, in disguise of course, buried deep in a box of Earl Grey tea. Very John le Carré.

We're rehearsing with Tom Ford as Gussie, preparing for James's absence. And with Cristin, for her two performances as Stiffy. John is here, on humorous form, and all is done within two hours.

At last a top-notch audience again. Relief all round. Steve and I discuss (together with Sam and John) that today's rehearsal was useful for all of us in refocusing various moments – without performance pressure. That probably helped.

★

Saturday

Both the afternoon and evening shows are full. And audience reaction is stupendous. Everybody comments on the fact that the show feels like a thumping great success, not one that is limping towards closure.

Sunday

Another lively matinee. An elderly man, Tim Torrance, waits for me afterwards, richly cocooned against the cold in an exotic fur coat. I don't know him personally but we have a mutual friend in actress Andrea King, ex-Warner Brothers star. I join him for a quick drink at (where else?) Sardi's. Turns out he knows just about everybody in the business, especially the stars, and is a particular fan of Jennifer Bassey on *All My Children*. Tim is eager to provide me with gossip of the current soap operas, on screen and off. Coincidentally, I'm meeting Jennifer and Luther at Café Luxembourg tonight. At half past six I hurry away.

After a jolly dinner I see them into a taxi and go on to a late screening of *Iris* at the local Loewe's on Broadway. Superbly done. Kate Winslet is excellent. Jim Broadbent and Judi equally so. Also Hugh Bonneville.

Every Broadway show, including those soon to close, has a block advertisement in today's *New York Times*, to help scoop up the Christmas trade. I open the paper. Except *By Jeeves*. We have nothing at all.

The Orient Express having long departed, the Marie Celeste springs to mind.

★

Monday December 17th

More resentment today, in a recording studio, from a fearful New York actor. Wonders what I am doing, working here. Am I legal? Seems some of them think I'm here to take work away from them.

Ros returns, knackered, from Los Angeles. Her radio theatre production was a success, with full houses for all five performances.

We taxi down Lexington Avenue to Cindy and Jon's. They tell us they are now officially engaged and take us step by step through Jon's romantic (on his knees) proposal.

Tuesday

An article appeared in *The Times* yesterday, full of misinformation, stating that the very Britishness of *By Jeeves* is a 'turn-off' to American audiences. The same piece mentions how successful *Dance of Death* is at the Broadhurst. In fact the Strindberg play has far emptier houses than ours. On Friday, Saturday and Sunday we had full houses, laughter and standing ovations at the end. The comments we are hearing daily are, 'This doesn't seem like a show that's finishing at the end of the year.' And, 'Why on earth is it closing?' So for whom is *By Jeeves* a turn-off, I wonder? And what were our weekend audiences cheering about? Is it a turn-off to these faceless promo people, perhaps? Was shadowy Mr X, the PR boss himself, turned off by those critics who didn't care for the show and therefore, on Andrew's behalf, pulled all advertising? Was the vessel scuppered as soon as it was afloat? Or even before?

It's all a question of perception.

Versatile Tom is on tonight, this time in place of James as Gussie.

Athlete's foot syndrome kicks in again: Don Stephenson's grandmother has died so he's off from tomorrow for three performances, having just returned after attending to the new baby. So we'll have

276

Jamison as Bingo. Ana (Stiffy) will be off next week, to be with her father. As we know, Molly and Cristin will be sharing performances. But James will be back. Jigsaw productions. As we walk up the stairs together ready to begin the show, John opens his mouth, rolls his eyes and emits a Munch-like silent scream.

Wednesday

Ros and I have decided to give a cast and crew party tomorrow after the show at Robert Emmett's restaurant, on the corner of 44th Street.

Tristan Layton comes this evening. Afterwards we go to Sam's Bar. He requests more stories about his dad. Told him of the time, twenty years ago, when I bumped into George during the opening night interval of *Dracula* at the Shaftesbury Theatre. Ros was playing Lucy, opposite Terence Stamp. Keen to get a sense of what other people thought of the show so far, I asked, 'Well George, how do you feel it's going?'

His reply: 'Oh, pretty good. I've just finished a telly, I'm starting a film next week and I'm writing a sitcom for Thames television.'

'Yes,' cackles Tristan, 'that's Dad all right.'

I've been trying to hunt down Michael Price, who has promised to provide seats for British actor Jon Glover and his wife on December 27th. I haven't smoked him out yet.

Thursday

Everyone comes to our Mr and Mrs Jeeves party. Ros has arranged for Christmas crackers. John Robelin, wardrobe supervisor, smiles in delight. 'Oh I know what these are. They're British. They're called poppers.'

Alan has sent a letter to the cast. It's passed round and there's not a dry eye. He begins by stating that he had wanted to write something funny and heartwarming that would fill everyone with happiness and goodwill to most men: 'But it's Christmas, for Christ's sake, and hardly the time for any of that.'

He goes on to say how much he'll miss everybody, mentioning that his admiration for American actors and technicians (with whom, admittedly, till he worked with the *By Jeeves* company, he'd had a somewhat eccentric experience) has rocketed. And he wishes us all a wonderful finale to this remarkable series of chapters in all our lives. 'God Bless America, God Save the Queen, and fuck 'em.'

He adds that he has just completed his sixty-first play, called *Snake in the Grass*. 'Though I deny,' he concludes, 'that the choice of title is in any way related to our recent experiences together…'

Friday

The party seems to have been a triumph.

The downside of things is that the absence of the promised advertising campaign is now being keenly felt. And for some incomprehensible reason, known only to the promotional company perhaps, there is no listing for our show in *Time Out*. It jumps from *Aida* and *Beauty and the Beast* to *Cabaret*. No *By Jeeves*.

David Weston and Dora Reisser are here tonight.

It's good to sit and talk afterwards about old times. David is a gifted actor who was a major figure in the National Youth Theatre and at RADA when I was just beginning. As a young man he starred in a number of feature films, playing the hero in *Young Dick Turpin*. He's currently on a break from the National Theatre. He has appeared in several of Jeffrey Archer's plays in London. He tells me he visits him in jail once a month and that Jeffrey sometimes fills the long hours

278

by listening to my audiotapes. Terry Waite did that too, though the incarceration wasn't quite the same.

Saturday

The matinee is one of the best houses ever. Naturally I'm happy about that as Kelly Ritter, one of our agents at Badgley Connor, is here with her husband and family.

James Kall is still away, as agreed, for one week, and Tom Ford continues as Gussie.

Sunday

The House Full boards are up.

This afternoon the revealing of the Secret Santas takes place. Cristin fails to identify me despite my rather odd gifts (toffees, a bell, a purse made of beads). My turn to guess and I'm fairly certain that my own Santa, who has been leaving seasonal goodies in my dressing room, is Steve Wilson. Keeping the tension going as long as possible, I pretend to the group that I think it's Sam Tsoutsouvas and, apparently just about to unmask him, switch to Steve at the last minute. Sam, whom I could see was getting ready to shout 'Wrong!' is fooled and booms instead, 'That's the best bit of acting you've done all week.'

Monday December 24th

Christmas Eve. Two whole days off.

Courtesy of the amazing techno-magic of the internet, we listen to the transmission of the first episode in our *Colonel Clay* series on Radio 4.

We've invited John and Donna Lynne for dinner. They arrive at the apartment at about seven o'clock. We have a glass of champagne, then walk to Café Luxembourg round the corner where, outside the confines of the Helen Hayes, we gossip about our fellow cast members. No reputations are sullied. I have rarely been part of such a generous-spirited company. And somewhere perhaps, not far away, someone is gossiping about us.

Christmas Day

Christmas in New York.

My brother-in-law Greg sends us, on the computer, photos of the parents and Angela having lunch an hour before, in Sidcup.

It's bright and cold, temperature about thirty-six degrees. Ros and I go down to the Rockefeller Center and take pictures of the huge tree and the skaters. Then to the old Ziegfeld cinema on 54th Street to see the remake of *Ocean's Eleven*. Finally to Vince and Eddie's for mafia beef.

Boxing Day

Back to more full houses. Molly is on as Stiffy. She is excellent and at the evening performance in front of her family, including my old friend Barbie, she sings her heart out.

★

Thursday

Sheridan Morley is here in New York once again, ready by the look of him to perform a scene from *The Wind in the Willows*, padding about the apartment in his vast dressing gown.

Jon and Caroline Glover attend the matinee. Michael Price has kindly offered to arrange their seats but at the crucial moment I can't find him. I stump up. Ros comes down to the theatre to meet them and we have tea at Sardi's.

Cristin is now playing Stiffy, though really there is no need. But it's been decreed she should have her chance. She does well, though she's not yet as experienced an actress as Molly.

Stewart Wilson Turner, a Los Angeles friend, is at the evening show. It's another great house. He brings Daniel Sackler, son of the late Howard who wrote *The Great White Hope*. I take them to Sardi's, where Mark Nadler is abusing his current audience. Before we are inveigled into a guest appearance we duck away and encounter Cristin in the downstairs bar. She is carrying a large bouquet of flowers but looking mournful on her night of triumph. Her boyfriend hasn't returned from Florida, as promised, to witness her Broadway debut. Stewart and Howard cheer her up no end.

Friday

We have been parcelling all the stuff we have accumulated since early October, ready for Ben Hur, the shippers, to collect today.

No one shows up. Finally, after many phone calls, two young men from the Dominican Republic arrive and get working on packing and loading.

★

Saturday

A real feeling of everything coming to an end – offset by these incredibly receptive full houses. This looks like being our biggest financial week yet. $172,000 by the end of this afternoon, with two more shows still to go – tonight and the final matinee tomorrow.

Autograph hunters are out in force in front of the theatre.

The evening performance is remarkable for its focus. The audience is probably the most vociferous in its reaction to the comedy.

Afterwards Steve Wilson invites Ros and me to Café 123, where we are joined by his dancer wife Roxane, who is currently filming the movie of *Chicago*.

Sunday December 30th

This lyric came for the company this morning, from Alan. It encapsulates many of the nooks and niches and private jokes that have been part of the show since it began. He calls it 'Curtain Call', to be sung to the tune of 'By Jeeves', the theme song so memorably performed each night by Messrs Scherer, Stephenson and Kall.

It is tragic but true,
That this show we've been through,
That we've grown to respect and admire,
Is now reaching its end
Like some venerable friend,
Who's lamentably forced to retire;
As it takes its last standing ovation,
It is time to look back and retrace…

By Goodspeed Start
By LA Sleaze,

By DC Joy
By Pittsburgh Freeze
By all the love this show receives,
Good grief! It's goodbye Jeeves!

As our life turns to norm
And we're forced to perform
In some shoddy sub-standard affair,
Nonetheless, still be glad
For those moments we've had,
For the mem'ries that only we share…

What we lacked was a bolder producer….
Where on earth does one find one of those?

By Scherer's feet,
By Martin's head,
By Don's small box
By DL's bed,
By all the spells
It make-believes
Good grief! It's goodbye Jeeves!

By Molly's bell
By Ian's chair,
By Becky's frocks,
By Sam's mad glare
By petals showering down like leaves,
Good grief! It's goodbye Jeeves!

In the years far ahead,
When we take to our bed,
If they question the things that we've done,

Should they constantly pry
For the what and the why
Tell them, this one we all did for FUN.

Notwithstanding your Hamlets or Heddas
This was madder than them by a mile...

By Steve's moustache,
By James's specs,
By statues, threats
Of broken necks,
By fisticuffs with rolled up sleeves
Good grief! It's goodbye Jeeves!

By Em'ly's rose
(And Ana's too)
By Court's full moon
By Danno's cue
By every prop that Tom retrieves,
Good grief! It's goodbye Jeeves!

Will all our lives be quite the same?
Won't future shows seem somewhat tame?
I know I'm frightfully glad I came –
Though I won't miss those terrible verg–es

By Cristin, David
Jamison, too –
If I've missed one
Then God bless you!
I'm older than the world perceives,
Oh, no! It's goodbye Jeeves!

By fond farewell,
But not goodbye,

By long last wave
But don't dare cry!
It's not a thing for which one grieves,
Look back on all the show achieves,
Good luck! Good health! Good times! Good life!
Good-bye! Good-bye! Good-bye–
Bye Jeeves!

A last full house. The crew boys are on wicked form, enjoying the final knockings. They empty half a ton of rose petals on Donna Lynne's head as she exits after her Act One song. I have prepared a little extra surprise myself, for John, during the bowing moments that follow my patter number. As the applause increases I draw from my inside pocket a cunningly secreted single rose which, in a dramatic gesture, I throw out into the audience. With typically spontaneous brio John then tears his own rose from his lapel and does likewise. The audience loves it, and for a moment it's a sparring match between Bertie Pavarotti and Placido Jeeves.

Tears afterwards and John and I clutch each other. We've had the most wonderful theatrical partnership. It's the end of a peculiar, exhilarating, extraordinary year.

The gathering in Emmett's bar is something of an anti-climax. A lot of us can't take it, and slide away as soon as we decently can.

In the taxi I find the box office return for the final week in my coat pocket. It's the best ever. Almost a quarter of a million dollars.

Back in the flat, Sheridan Morley regales Ros and me with an hour of theatrical tales. He doesn't ask how the last show went.

We don't tell him.

★

Monday December 31st

I'm up early. The pink dawn is inching across Central Park. We're leaving for the airport in an hour.

The little cricket pavilion house that sits on a roof the other side of Broadway is bathed in the warm morning light. An American flag in the neat twenty-sixth floor garden flaps its stars and stripes in the breeze.

A few feet away a Union Jack waves back, equally bravely.

EPILOGUE

London

June 2002

One morning last month I received a message from Donna Lynne Champlin. She was in Chicago where she had just opened in Hal Prince's pre-Broadway run of *Hollywood Arms*. (Yes, she got the part.) She seemed to be congratulating me on something. A few minutes later there was a phone call from Steve Wilson, then from Don and Emily. Apparently I had won a Theatre World Award for my efforts as Jeeves. It's presented every year, they told me, for an 'Outstanding Broadway Debut'.

Later I read in the paper that I was indeed a recipient and that winners would be attending the ceremony at Studio 54 in New York on June 3rd.

A generous note of congratulation arrived from Alan, and from Ted Pappas in Pittsburgh. No word from Michael Price. Gone to earth. Ros suggested he might be fearful I'd ask for my fare to New York.

In the ensuing days I heard nothing from any of our producers. Nor from that same keep-it-dark publicity company who, I learned, were organising the event. No invitation.

I did go to New York, under my own steam.

Ros, John, Donna Lynne, Steve, Sam, Court and Becky all came along. Cindy Katz and John Shapiro were there. So were Ruth and Sheridan. We had a good time at the ceremony. I accepted the award and made a speech, flying the flag one last time for the heroes of *By Jeeves*.

After I returned to London clutching my marble statuette – the two masks of Comedy and Tragedy – Heather Ayckbourn rang. She and Alan had just heard from the silver fox.

His message: 'Marvin has won an award.'

The butler did it.

ACKNOWLEDGEMENTS

Many friends and colleagues were extremely helpful to me during the writing of this diary and afterwards when I was assembling it for publication.

In particular, my grateful thanks go to Denise M. Bontoft, Michèle Brown, Donna Lynne Champlin, Sophie Hutton-Squire, Sherry Bebitch Jeffe, Stephen Klein, Fiona Mackenzie-Williams, Ted Pappas, Nigel Rees, Tony Ring, John Scherer, Antony Topping and Matt Wolf.

Also to Heather and Alan Ayckbourn for their encouragement and kind permission to quote from *By Jeeves*.

To Andrew Lloyd Webber, Austin Shaw, and photographers Brooke Palmer and Suellen Fitzsimmons.

I am much indebted to my editor Max Eilenberg for his enthusiasm and guidance.

Finally, as always, my gratitude and love go to Rosalind Ayres who not only heard me through the play many times, but saw me through it, too.

M.J.

INDEX